DEMOCRACY UNDER GOD

State recognition of Islam in Muslim countries invites fierce debate from scholars and politicians alike, some of whom assume an inherent conflict between Islam and liberal democracy. Analyzing case studies and empirical data from several Muslim-majority countries, Dawood Ahmed and Muhammad Zubair Abbasi find, counterintuitively, that in many Muslim countries, constitutional recognition of Islam often occurs during moments of democratization. Indeed, the insertion of Islam in a constitution is frequently accompanied by an expansion, not a reduction, in constitutional human rights, with case law from higher courts in Egypt and Pakistan demonstrating that potential tensions between the constitutional pursuit of human rights, liberal democracy and Islam are capable of judicial resolution. The authors also argue that colonial history was pivotal in determining whether a country adopted the constitutional path of Islam or secularism: British colonizers were relatively tolerant and accommodating of Islam, partly explaining why Islam in constitutional politics survived and became more prevalent in Muslim countries that were colonized by the British, and not those colonized by the French or Soviets. The authors conclude that it is important for policymakers to recognize that, considering the enduring political popularity of Islam in many Muslim countries, it may be inevitable that the pursuit of democratization in the Muslim world follows its own unique and distinct, non-secular trajectory that accommodates Islam.

DAWOOD AHMED is a research fellow at the Comparative Constitutions Project and has worked with the United Nations and the Max Planck Foundation for International Peace and the Rule of Law on constitutional design projects. He has published several journal articles and opinion pieces on public international law and Islam and democracy.

MUHAMMAD ZUBAIR ABBASI is a lecturer at Bradford University. His research focuses on the relationship between shari'a and state law, Islamic law and jurisprudence (usul al-fiqh) in the contemporary world, and comparative law, family law, and constitutional law. He is an editor for Harvard Law School's SHARIAsource and associate editor of the *Yearbook of Islamic and Middle Eastern Law*.

COMPARATIVE CONSTITUTIONAL LAW AND POLICY

Series Editors

Tom Ginsburg *University of Chicago*
Zachary Elkins *University of Texas at Austin*
Ran Hirschl *University of Texas at Austin*

Comparative constitutional law is an intellectually vibrant field that encompasses an increasingly broad array of approaches and methodologies. This series collects analytically innovative and empirically grounded work from scholars of comparative constitutionalism across academic disciplines. Books in the series include theoretically informed studies of single constitutional jurisdictions, comparative studies of constitutional law and institutions, and edited collections of original essays that respond to challenging theoretical and empirical questions in the field.

Books in the Series

Democracy Under God: Constitutions, Islam, and Human Rights in the Muslim World Dawood Ahmed and Muhammad Zubair Abbasi

Buddhism and Comparative Constitutional Law Edited by Tom Ginsburg and Ben Schonthal

Amending America's Unwritten Constitution Edited by Richard Albert, Ryan C. Williams and Yaniv Roznai

Constitutionalism and a Right to Effective Government? Edited by Vicki C. Jackson and Yasmin Dawood

The Fall of the Arab Spring: Democracy's Challenges and Efforts to Reconstitute the Middle East Tofigh Maboudi

Filtering Populist Claims to Fight Populism: The Italian Case in a Comparative Perspective Giuseppe Martinico

Constitutionalism in Context David S. Law

The New Fourth Branch: Institutions for Protecting Constitutional Democracy Mark Tushnet

The Veil of Participation: Citizens and Political Parties in Constitution-Making Processes Alexander Hudson

Towering Judges: A Comparative Study of Constitutional Judges Edited by Rehan Abeyratne and Iddo Porat

The Constitution of Arbitration Victor Ferreres Comella

Redrafting Constitutions in Democratic Orders: Theoretical and Comparative Perspectives Edited by Gabriel L. Negretto

From Parchment to Practice: Implementing New Constitutions Edited by Tom Ginsburg and Aziz Z. Huq

Democracy Under God

CONSTITUTIONS, ISLAM, AND HUMAN RIGHTS IN THE MUSLIM WORLD

DAWOOD AHMED

Comparative Constitutions Project

MUHAMMAD ZUBAIR ABBASI

Bradford University

CAMBRIDGE
UNIVERSITY PRESS

CAMBRIDGE
UNIVERSITY PRESS

Shaftesbury Road, Cambridge CB2 8EA, United Kingdom

One Liberty Plaza, 20th Floor, New York, NY 10006, USA

477 Williamstown Road, Port Melbourne, VIC 3207, Australia

314–321, 3rd Floor, Plot 3, Splendor Forum, Jasola District Centre, New Delhi – 110025, India

103 Penang Road, #05-06/07, Visioncrest Commercial, Singapore 238467

Cambridge University Press is part of Cambridge University Press & Assessment, a department of the University of Cambridge.

We share the University's mission to contribute to society through the pursuit of education, learning and research at the highest international levels of excellence.

www.cambridge.org
Information on this title: www.cambridge.org/9781107158054

DOI: 10.1017/9781316662618

© Dawood Ahmed and Muhammad Zubair Abbasi 2023

First published 2023

A catalogue record for this publication is available from the British Library.

Library of Congress Cataloging-in-Publication Data
NAMES: Ahmed, Dawood I., author. | Abbasi, Muhammad Zubair, 1982– author.
TITLE: Democracy under God : constitutions, Islam and human rights in the Muslim world / Dawood Ahmed, Comparative Constitutions Project; Muhammad Zubair Abbasi, Lahore University of Management Sciences, Pakistan.
DESCRIPTION: Cambridge, United Kingdom ; New York, NY : Cambridge University Press, [2022?] | SERIES: Comparative constitutional law and policy | Includes bibliographical references and index.
IDENTIFIERS: LCCN 2022035606 (print) | LCCN 2022035607 (ebook) | ISBN 9781107158054 (hardback) | ISBN 9781316610572 (paperback) | ISBN 9781316662618 (epub)
SUBJECTS: LCSH: Constitutional law–Islamic countries. | Human rights–Islamic countries. | Constitutional law (Islamic law) | Law–Islamic countries–Islamic influences.
CLASSIFICATION: LCC KBP2101 .A474 2022 (print) | LCC KBP2101 (ebook) | DDC 340.5/9–dc23/eng/20221101
LC record available at https://lccn.loc.gov/2022035606
LC ebook record available at https://lccn.loc.gov/2022035607

ISBN 978-1-107-15805-4 Hardback
ISBN 978-1-316-61057-2 Paperback

Brief Contents

Detailed Contents

Figures

Tables

Preface

This book adopts an interdisciplinary and empirical approach to the topic of Islamic constitutionalism, which gained much currency in the past three decades. Scholarly interest in this topic increased after the tragic incidence of 9/11 and was further enhanced after the Arab Spring about a decade later. The Taliban's takeover of the government of Afghanistan on August 15, 2021, and their reintroduction of stringent polices toward women's rights show that debates about Islam in politics are far from over. During the past few years, new books have been published that explore the relationship between Islam and human rights in constitutions.[1] The distinctive feature of our book is its interdisciplinary approach, which builds on scholarship in such diverse fields as law, history and political science. This approach is informed by and built on the collaborative research published in the form of two research papers: Dawood Ahmed and Tom Ginsburg, "Constitutional Islamization and Human Rights: The Surprising Origin and Spread of Islamic Supremacy Clauses" (2014) 54(3) Virginia Journal of International Law 615; Dawood Ahmed and Moamen Gouda, "Measuring Constitutional Islamization: The Islamic Constitutions Index" (2014) 38 Hastings International and Comparative Law Review 1.

Both papers have been very well received by the scholarly community and are widely cited. This book complements, updates, and builds on these papers. The primary data remains almost the same with a few minor exceptions. We have also compiled the constitutional texts of Muslim-majority countries on a portal that can be accessed online at https://beta.shariasource.com/projects/

---

[1] See Tommaso Virgili, *Islam, Constitutional Law and Human Rights: Sexual Minorities and Freethinkers in Egypt and Tunisia* (Routledge 2022); Rachel M. Scott, *Recasting Islamic Law: Religion and the Nation State in Egyptian Constitution Making* (Cornell University Press 2021); Pietro Longo, *Theory and Practice in Islamic Constitutionalism: From Classical Fiqh to Modern Systems* (Gorgias Press 2019).

islamic-constitutionalism. This is a collaborative project with Harvard Law School's SHARIAsource portal.

Despite our divergent disciplinary backgrounds, we and our collaborators share similarities, but our views also differ, albeit on sub-issues. One such issue and indeed the subject of much contemporary debate is the relationship between Islam and human rights. Scholarly views present a wide spectrum of opinions, from outright conflict to complementarity with a few exceptions. We utilize both quantitative and qualitative methods to contribute to this ongoing debate, which has attracted the attention of several scholars, researchers, and legal commentators. We hope that this book will enrich this debate both methodologically and substantively.

Acknowledgments

We would be remiss in not mentioning a great number of people who were instrumental in providing assistance and guidance in bringing the project to completion. During our academic life, we have been constantly impressed by the generosity of so many individuals who have taken time out to help with various aspects of this project.

DAWOOD AHMED

First and foremost, many thanks go to Tom Ginsburg, who not only introduced me to a method of analyzing constitutions from an interdisciplinary and empirical perspective but has always been a bulwark of support and encouragement for all of my endeavors. This book draws heavily on the paper I coauthored with him.[1] I consider him not only a fantastic scholar but also a friend and mentor. I would also like to offer particular thanks to Moamen Gouda for constructing much of the quantitative analysis in this book. The paper I coauthored with him is also substantially referred to in this book.[2]

Similarly, several people provided either comments or input on various sections of the book at different junctures, so I am grateful as well to numerous other individuals for their contributions and feedback, which have greatly improved this work: Intisar Rabb, Nathan Brown, Osama Siddique, Ayesha Malik, colleagues at the Max Plank Foundation for International Peace and

---

[1] Dawood Ahmed and Tom Ginsburg, "Constitutional Islamization and Human Rights: The Surprising Origin and Spread of Islamic Supremacy Clauses" (2014) 54(3) Virginia Journal of International Law 615.

[2] Dawood Ahmed and Moamen Gouda, "Measuring Constitutional Islamization: The Islamic Constitutions Index" (2014) 38 Hastings International and Comparative Law Review 1.

the Rule of Law, colleagues at workshops at the University of Chicago, the Harvard University's Institute for Global Law and Policy, participants at the ICTT Workshop at the Hamad Bin Khalifa University at Doha, and participants at the Harvard Law School Comparative and International Law Workshop. I would also like to gratefully acknowledge research funding from Harvard University's Institute for Global Law and Policy, the University of Chicago, and George Mason University.

Last but not least, I could never adequately thank my wife, Sarah; my children, Zackaria and Salahdin; my parents; my in-laws; and friends who encouraged me to complete this book (in particular, Salman, Kaz, Sohail, and Zeeshan), whose encouragement made all the difference during this journey.

ZUBAIR ABBASI

Dr. Zubair Abbasi would like to thank Sara Raza and Usman Mumtaz for their excellent research assistance. He is also grateful to his wife, Ayesha Ahmed; daughter, Aiza Amelle; son, Mikail Hani; parents; and close friends for their support.

Note on Translation, Transliteration, and Citations

We have used a simple system of transliteration and have avoided diacritical marks for the Arabic letters *'ayn* (') and *hamza* (') as much as possible. These marks are used in direct quotations and wherever it is necessary to convey the exact meanings of certain expressions. We have not transliterated commonly used expressions, such as ulama and shari'a.

As we have relied upon several primary and secondary sources available in English, Arabic, and Urdu, readers may find some inconsistencies in transliteration and capitalization. We have tried to avoid such inconsistencies as much as possible. Unless otherwise mentioned, translations from Arabic and Urdu into English are ours.

We have followed the Oxford Standard for the Citation of Legal Authorities (OSCOLA) for references.

Introduction

On July 3, 2013, General Abdel Fattah el-Sisi, Egyptian Army Chief, ousted President Mohamed Morsi from power. Morsi, elected in 2013, had been Egypt's first ever democratically elected president. Following the coup, the Chief Justice of the Supreme Constitutional Court of Egypt, Adly Mansour, was installed as interim president; Morsi was put under house arrest and several members of the Muslim Brotherhood – the political party to which Morsi belonged - were either arrested or killed. General el-Sisi also suspended the 2012 constitution, which was promulgated only a few months earlier, and issued a constitutional decree to make amendments to the constitution.[1] The amendments were to be proposed by a constitutional committee composed of fifty members.[2] The committee had hardly begun its work when foreign observers began to refocus most of their attention on speculating just *how* "Islamic" the amended constitution might be.[3] And indeed, the committee was soon in a gridlock over the role of Islam in the new constitution.[4] Egypt's 1971 and 2012 constitutions had contained clauses entrenching the principles

---

[1] Shadia Nasralla, "Rows Over Egypt's Constitutional Decree Signal Hurdles Ahead" *Reuters* (July 10, 2013) <www.reuters.com/article/us-egypt-protests-constitution/rows-over-egypts-constitutional-decree-signal-hurdles-ahead-idUSBRE96815R20130709> accessed July 1, 2020.

[2] Nathan J Brown, "Egypt's Daring Constitutional Gang of 50" *Foreign Policy* (September 20, 2013) <https://carnegieendowment.org/2013/09/20/egypt-s-daring-constitutional-gang-of-50-pub-53079> accessed July 1, 2020.

[3] Omar El Akkad, "Egypt's Draft Constitution Limits Role of Islam" *The Globe and Mail* (August 30, 2013) <www.theglobeandmail.com/news/world/egypts-draft-constitution-limits-role-of-islam/article14060190/> accessed July 1, 2020.

[4] Gamal Essam El-Din, "Fierce Debates Over Preamble of Egypt's New Constitution" *AhramOnline* (November 26, 2013) <http://english.ahram.org.eg/NewsContent/1/64/87562/Egypt/Politics-/Fierce-debates-over-preamble-of-Egypts-new-constit.aspx> accessed July 1, 2020.

1

of Islamic law as the primary source of legislation; accordingly, some had called the 2012 constitution an "Islamic" Constitution, while others had alleged that it leaned toward "conservative" Islam.

Would the amended constitution be more "Islamic" than its predecessor? As speculation over the "Islamicity" of Egypt's constitution intensified, one of the members of the constitutional committee was quick to dismiss any suggestion that the amended constitution would be any less Islamic than the previous one and claimed that the committee does not intend to "distort Egypt's Islamic identity whatsoever," adding, "What is being said in this regard is nothing more than unfounded speculation."[5] It was as if Egypt was experiencing déjà vu; with regard to the suspended Egyptian constitution too, much ink had been spilt within and outside the country about the risks of incorporating an Islamic supremacy clause in the new constitution.[6] Much of the commentary regarding the new constitution again narrowly focused on the treatment of Islam, to the detriment of other substantive issues.[7] Yet the constitution drafted by the largely secular military regime retains exactly the same clause as did the Muslim Brotherhood constitution.[8] One commentator argued that "Egypt's constitutional declaration issued late on July 8 contains more concessions to radical Islam than the constitution drawn up by the deposed President Hosni Mubarak."[9]

In writing the new Egyptian constitution, drafters confronted now familiar questions about the role of Islam during a constitutional design in the Muslim world: What role will it be given in this newly drafted constitution? How will lawmaking be affected by the adoption of Islam? Are constitutions in the Muslim world establishing theocracies or ostensibly liberal democracies? How does the incorporation of Islam in a constitution affect the adoption of constitutional rights? Will new popularly elected governments be constrained by Islamic law? Will courts be able to set aside laws for incompatibility with the shari'a?

---

[5] Safaa Azaab, "In Conversation with Kamal El-Helbawy" *Asharq Al Awsat* (October 12, 2013) <www.aawsat.net/2013/10/article55318241> accessed July 1, 2020.

[6] Robert Satloff and Eric Trager, "Egypt's Theocratic Future: The Constitutional Crisis and U.S. Policy" The Washington Institute (December 3, 2012) <www.washingtoninstitute.org/policy-analysis/view/egypts-theocratic-future-the-constitutional-crisis-and-u.s.-policy> accessed July 1, 2020.

[7] "An Endless Debate Over Religion's Role" *The Economist* (Cairo, October 6, 2012) <www.economist.com/middle-east-and-africa/2012/10/06/an-endless-debate-over-religions-role> accessed July 1, 2020.

[8] Draft Constitution of the Arab Republic of Egypt 2013, art. 2.

[9] Richard Palmer, "Egypt's New Constitution More Islamic Than the Last" *The Trumpet* (July 13, 2013) <www.thetrumpet.com/10805-egypts-new-constitution-more-islamic-than-the-last> accessed July 1, 2020.

These questions are not only of great importance in the Middle East but have remained an issue during constitution-making processes in the Muslim world. In 2014, the question gained particular prominence in a different international context, when peace talks were being contemplated between the governments of Pakistan and Afghanistan, and the Taliban. In the case of Pakistan, the militant group even refused to accept the offer of peace talks under the framework of a constitution that, in their view, was not sufficiently Islamic.[10] In 2014, as ISIS set about establishing an "Islamic State" in Iraq, attention once again turned to the question of constitutional democracy and Islam. Hence, war and peace can sometimes partly hinge on the question of how Islamic a country's constitution is.

The question of Islam in political life was propelled to a central position again due to the events of the Arab Spring. In the Middle East, as the zeal of the Arab Spring traveled, talk of writing new constitutions became pervasive; discussions about the future constitutional design of Syria commenced soon after the rebellion began; Jordan amended its constitution in ways designed to preserve its monarchy; Tunisia eventually passed a new constitution that has been hailed as a successful charter in contrast to the chaos that has gripped some of the other Arab Spring countries that also strove to rewrite constitutions – such as Libya and Yemen. Each situation turned out to be very different, but the question of Islam remained of primary salience in each of these constitutional design situations. Even in Tunisia – one of the most secular countries in the Muslim world, this question stood out. Each of these constitution-making situations is very different, involving local politics and various international actors, but Islam entered into these discussions. In fact, more than two years after the commencement of the Arab Spring, the coup in Egypt once again reminded us that the political stakes of resolving the issue of Islam in the constitution remain very high.

And this debate is not new. The status of Islam had also been a major issue for United States foreign policy in the process of producing the Iraqi and Afghan constitutions. Noah Feldman stated while discussing the Bush administration's involvement in the Iraqi constitution that "[a]ny democratically elected Iraqi government is unlikely to be secular, and unlikely to be pro-Israel. And frankly, moderately unlikely to be pro-American."[11] With regards to

---

[10] Dawood Ahmed and Tom Ginsburg, "Constitutional Islamization and Human Rights: The Surprising Origin and Spread of Islamic Supremacy Clauses" (2014) (54(3) Virginia Journal of International Law 615.

[11] As quoted in Larry Diamond, *Squandered Victory: The American Occupation and the Bungled Effort to Bring Democracy to Iraq* (Holt Paperbacks 2005) 49.

Iraq, Senator Richard Lugar went so far as to publicly state that the United States could not accept "a popularly elected theocracy," while John Voll dismissingly referred to the newly written constitutions of Iraq and Afghanistan – due to their incorporation of Islamic clauses – as impositions of "theocracy."[12] As Voll notes, "implicit in these concerns is an assumption that an 'Islamic' state, even if democratically established, would be transformed into an illiberal and undemocratic 'theocracy.'"[13] Anxiety about constitutional Islam seems to stem from the prevalent – and now, rather old – assumption that a constitution that incorporates Islam cannot provide for democracy and human rights. Indeed, some Western constitutionalist thought has historically tended to view the Islamic world as the "antithesis of constitutional government." As Ran Hirschl reminds us, "like early writings about the postcolonial world that tended to view postcolonial countries as a homogeneous bloc, populist academic and media accounts in the West tend to portray the spread of religious fundamentalism in the developing world as a near monolithic, ever accelerating, and all-encompassing phenomenon. The frequent formulation of this supposed dichotomy is that the West is largely secular and modernist, whereas the non-West is largely religious and traditionalist." Scholars including Samuel Huntington claimed that not only is "Islam" a violent religion, but that "Islamic civilization" was destined to "clash" with "Western civilization" in the name of authoritarian politics.[14] This narrative has penetrated not only academic but also policy thinking in the United States and Europe. The House of Lords in the United Kingdom stated that shari'a was "wholly incompatible" with human rights legislation.[15] A number of states in the US have attempted to enact laws that forbid state courts from considering Islamic law when deciding cases. For instance, Oklahoma has attempted to ban state courts from considering Islamic law when deciding cases[16] and thirteen states in the United States have introduced bills to circumvent the application of shari'a.[17] For these critics, the choice between the constitutional

---

[12] John O Voll, "Islam and Democracy: Is Modernization a Barrier" (2007) 1(1) Religion Compass 170, 171.

[13] Voll, "Islam and Democracy."

[14] Samuel Huntington, "The Clash of Civilizations" (1993) 72(3) Foreign Affairs 22, 22.

[15] Afua Hirsch, "Sharia Law Incompatible with Human Rights Legislation, Lords say" *The Guardian* (October 23, 2008).

[16] "Oklahoma Sharia Law Blocked by Federal Judge" HuffPost (May 25, 2011) <www.huffpost .com/entry/oklahoma-sharia-law-struck-down-_n_780632> accessed July 1, 2020.

[17] Zaid Jilani, "Report: At Least 13 States Have Introduced Bills Guarding Against Non-Existent Threat of Sharia Law" *ThinkProgress* (February 8, 2011) <https://archive.thinkprogress.org/ report-at-least-13-states-have-introduced-bills-guarding-against-non-existent-threat-of-sharia-law-49c0ab42be1f/> accessed July 1, 2020.

inclusion of Islam and democracy or rights was a zero-sum game: a constitution then, would have to make a choice between the two. To be sure, the concern is not completely misplaced. Self-proclaimed Islamic governments do have the potential to be undemocratic and oppressive, as the experiences of Iran since 1979 and Afghanistan under the Taliban show.

If these critics and their depictions of the "Islamic" regimes are accurate, then the question of including Islam in constitutions should be a forgone conclusion: it should be met with deep unpopularity in Muslim countries. However, in contrast, rather than downplaying the Islamicity of their constitutions, leaders in the Muslim world seem to be boasting about *how* Islamic their constitution will be. Sudan's leader, Omar al-Bashir, promised his constituents a "100% Islamic" constitution;[18] the Syrian opposition wants a constitution based on Islam;[19] Libyan leaders have suggested that the constitution will be "Islamic" and "half of the debates" in the Tunisian National Constituent Assembly have been about the status of Islam in Tunisia's constitution.[20] Indeed, one of the promises of the Islamic parties is the full implementation of shari'a in their respective societies. And the constitution, as arguably the most important legal document in most states, becomes the primary focal point of exercising this promise.

So rather than religion being marginalized, it is clear that religion seems to have witnessed a marked resurgence in law and government.[21] This revival has been witnessed across the globe, in regions spreading "from central and southeast Asia to north and sub-Saharan Africa and the Middle East."[22] In the case of Muslim countries, beginning in the 1970s, widespread calls for the

---

[18] "Sudan Constitution to be '100 Percent Islamic': Bashir" Reuters (July 8, 2012) <https://uk .reuters.com/article/uk-sudan-constitution/sudan-constitution-to-be-100-percent-islamic-bashir- idUKBRE8660IB20120707> accessed July 1, 2020.

[19] Oren Dorell, "Syrian Rebels Said to Seek Islamic Democracy" USA Today (September 24, 2012) <http://usatoday30.usatoday.com/news/world/story/2012/09/24/syrian-rebels-said-to-seek- islamic-democracy/57826584/1> accessed July 1, 2020.

[20] Robert Joyce, "Tunisia's Neglected Constitution" Cairo Review of Global Affairs (October 14, 2013) <www.aucegypt.edu/GAPP/CairoReview /Pages/articleDetails.aspx?aid=439> accessed July 1, 2020.

[21] Ran Hirschl, *Towards Juristocracy: The Origins and Consequences of the New Constitutionalism* (Harvard University Press 2007); Peter Berger, *The Desecularization of the World: Resurgent Religion and World Politics* (Eerdmans 1999); Gilles Kepel, *The Revenge of God: The Resurgence of Islam, Christianity, and Judaism in the Modern World* (Penn State University Press 1993).

[22] Ran Hirschl, "The Theocratic Challenge to Constitution Drafting in Post-Conflict States" (2008) 49 William and Mary Law Review 1,179.

implementation of Islamic law were observed.[23] Yet the issue is particularly important for Muslim countries because while a number of constitutions globally contain a state religion clause, constitutions in some Muslim-majority countries privileged religion most robustly.[24]

With this in mind, and as the idea of an "Islamic constitution" where state and religion are fused gains even more popular traction and can in some countries divide entire polities, it becomes immensely important to understand "constitutional Islamization" from an empirical and historical perspective and alongside its relationship to human rights in constitutional design and judicial decision making. But, there had been little empirically grounded comparative scholarship on constitutional Islamization.[25] In particular, there was no account as to why we observe variations throughout the Islamic world regarding whether or not the constitution is Islamized or which constitutions are most Islamized and how that relates to human rights. This gap exists despite the fact that the "Muslim world's desire for enacting these clauses shows no sign of abating."[26] And this is precisely where this book comes in: It seeks to elaborate how the incidence of Islam in a constitution correlates with the inclusion of human rights provisions, the link with colonialism and the effects of these clauses.

This is not to say that there has been no literature on the topic prior to this. Certainly, there is already a large body of literature discussing whether Islamic

---

[23] Sami Zubaida, *Law and Power in the Islamic World* (I. B. Tauris 2003) 1; Said Amir Arjomand (ed), *Constitutional Politics in the Middle East: With Special Reference to Turkey, Iraq, Iran and Afghanistan* (Hart Publishing 2008) 3.

[24] Danmarks Riges Grundlov 1953 (The Constitutional Act of the Kingdom of Denmark 1953), s. 4.; Stjórnarskrá lýðveldisins Íslands 1944 (The Constitution of the Republic of Iceland 1944), art. 62.

[25] Some exceptions include: Nathan J Brown, *Constitutions in a Nonconstitutional World: Arab Basic Laws and the Prospects for Accountable Government* (State University of New York Press 2001) 107–10, 161–93 (tracing the historiography of the idea that the origin of Western constitutionalism lies in Christianity and the history of the role of shari'a in Middle Eastern governance); Noah Feldman, *The Fall and Rise of the Islamic State* (Princeton University Press 2008) 103–40 (exploring the emergence of modern Islamism and its constitutional proposals); Jan-Michel van Otto, "Sharia and Law in a Birds Eye View: Reform, Moderation and Ambiguity. In Jan Michiel Otto and Hannah Mason (eds), *Delicate Debates on Islam: Policymakers and Academics Speaking with Each Other* (Leiden University Press 2011) (examining the changing role of shari'a over time in twelve Muslim countries); Ahmed and Ginsburg, "Constitutional Islamization and Human Rights" 615.

[26] Clark B Lombardi and Nathan J Brown, "Do Constitutions Requiring Adherence to Shari'a Threaten Human Rights? How Egypt's Constitution Reconciles Islamic Law with the Liberal Rule of Law" (2006) 21(1) American University of International Law Review 379.

law is in tension with human rights and democracy.[27] Similarly, in comparative constitutional law scholarship, scholars have described how courts have moderated this potential tension, specifically focusing on the "benign" judicial interpretation of Islamic supremacy clauses. For example, Nathan Brown and Clark Lombardi, citing the example of Egypt, suggest that constitutions that incorporate Islam may not in fact threaten human rights since a modern judiciary and strong courts can interpret laws in a progressively compatible way.[28] Ran Hirschl has written extensively about the means by which judges across the Muslim world have mitigated the potential illiberal effects of incorporating religion within constitutions or "constitutional theocracy."[29] On the other hand, Intisar Rabb has critiqued some of these positions.[30]

Yet, even as the concept of an "Islamic" constitution is bandied about with increasing frequency today by policy makers, commentators, and scholars alike, only a handful of studies have to date surveyed the constitutional landscape to exhaustively identify the prevalence of Islamic features in constitutions. Few scholars have raised some important questions, such as *how* Islamic are the constitutions of Muslim countries, does colonial history impact the variance of Islam in constitutions of Muslim countries, were some colonisers more tolerant of Islam than others or which Muslim country has the most Islamic constitution? That is, there is little empirical and historical analysis of Islamicity in constitutions, despite the immense political importance of the question. Most importantly, there is limited analysis of the relationship between constitutional Islam and rights from an empirical perspective.

This book begins with a different assumption about constitutional Islam and rights than is often assumed in the popular imagination, or rather it intends to question and verify some assumptions about how Islamic constitutions are and whether the incorporation of Islam in a constitution is necessarily antithetical to the pursuit of human rights. This book is careful not to assume there is only one paradigm of "constitutional democracy" or that simply because many of the Arab states were dictatorships, there is any

---

[27] Ann Elizabeth Mayer, *Islam and Human Rights: Tradition and Politics* (Routledge 1991); Abdulaziz Sachedina, *Islam and the Challenge of Human Rights* (Oxford University Press 2014); Syed Khatab and Gary D Bouma, *Democracy in Islam* (Routledge 2007); John L Esposito and John O Voll, *Islam and Democracy* (Oxford University Press 1996).

[28] Lombardi and Brown, "Do Constitutions Requiring Adherence to Shari'a Threaten Human Rights?" 379; Clark B Lombardi, "Designing Islamic Constitutions: Past Trends and Options for a Democratic Future" (2013) 11(3) International Journal of Constitutional Law 615, 627.

[29] Ran Hirschl, *Constitutional Theocracy* (Harvard University Press 2010).

[30] Intisar Rabb, "The Least Religious Branch: Judicial Review and the New Islamic Constitutionalism" (2013) 17 UCLA Journal of International Law and Foreign Affairs 75.

essentialist connection between Islam and rights. Indeed, it calls for a more nuanced approach to understanding democratization in Muslim countries and as it explores deeper connections between politics, colonial history, and constitutional Islam, it argues that the incorporation of Islamic law in constitutions and in fact, its application in law, is not necessarily antithetical to human rights and democracy. Alternatively, read in a different way, the arguments advanced in this book could be interpreted to mean that when Muslim countries democratize, it may not be the paradigm of Western democracy that should be viewed as the benchmark they strive for; rather they may chart their own trajectory of democracy. It is this question of constitutional democracy and Islam; and understanding modernity from a constitutional Islam perspective that has motivated the research that forms the core of this book. To be clear, it should not be read as making broad causal claims about constitutional Islam and constitutional democracy; rather, it should be read as proposing a different, modest lens through which to view the question of Islam and constitutional democracy and its relationship to colonialism. Further, its approach is in line with scholarship that views constitutions empirically, and its theoretical framework is by design narrow and simple: in analyzing the world of constitutional Islam, this book defines "constitutions" as the formal, de jure, large-C constitution of various countries and not the wider, de facto, small-c definition that would include the structural corpus of rules, decisions, understandings, traditions, and practices that make up the informal or small-c constitutions. This choice is not only consistent with the methodology deployed in the empirical literature on constitutions but also appropriate to the conceptual research questions tackled in this book and its ambitions.

Accordingly, relying on unique data sets based on the coding of constitutions of countries that are members of the Organisation of Islamic Cooperation (OIC), the book constructs its arguments through an empirical analysis of constitutions: it surveys the global landscape of constitutions of Muslim-majority countries – from Uzbekistan to Saudi Arabia, from Iran to Somalia – and charts out the universe of "constitutional Islamization." In doing so, it also develops a novel index – the Islamic Constitutions Index (ICI) – that measures and ranks the constitutions of all Muslim-majority countries according to "Islamicity."[31] It seeks to measure not only how well countries' constitutions live up to the popular ideal of being an Islamic

---

[31] Dawood Ahmed, Moamen Gouda, and Tom Ginsburg, "Islamic Constitutionalism Project" (SHARIAsource, Harvard Law School, 2018) <https://beta.shariasource.com/projects/islamic-constitutionalism> accessed May 1, 2021.

constitution but also verifies the popular assumption that the incorporation of Islamic law in constitutions is antithetical to human rights and democracy. It also specifically focuses on the question of how the incorporation of Islam or shari'a as a source of law impacts the human rights content of the constitution and judicial practice. In doing all of this, it also seeks to explain Islamic doctrine regarding constitutionalism, the origins of and reasons for the continuing popularity of constitutional Islam. Other questions this books tackles include the following: *How* Islamic are the constitutions of Muslim-majority countries today? Does the adoption of Islam in constitutions depend on the identity of the dominant colonizer? What types of Islamic clauses exist in those constitutions? How do constitutions incorporate Islam? Which country has the most Islamic constitution and which constitutions are secular? What types of constitutional clauses relating to Islam are most popular in the Muslim world? What regions have the most Islamic constitutions and most importantly, how do constitutional rights correlate with constitutional Islamization in design?

In a nutshell, the goal of this book is to illuminate the world of constitutional Islamization for academics and policy makers alike, so as to resolve a major tension during constitution making in the Muslim world and further, to lay, in some small way, the foundations for a research agenda that illuminates the broader relationship between Islam, colonialism and rights in constitutional design. Further, we hope, perhaps rather optimistically, that providing empirical evidence on the Islamicity of constitutions will assist fragile democracies during peacemaking efforts with groups such as the Afghan and Pakistani Taliban, whose central goal is to establish an Islamic constitution and who deny that the state they are fighting has Islamic credentials.

The book is structured around five chapters contained within three parts. Part I sets out by explaining the origins and theoretical foundations of Islamic constitutions and captures the universe of constitutional Islam. Chapter 1 introduces the religious theory of Islamic constitutionalism and examines the popularity of Islam in political life and how it originated along with constitution making in the Muslim world. Chapter 2 introduces a model Islamic constitution. Using this model constitution empirically illustrates the universe of constitutional Islamization, providing data on which countries and regions have adopted constitutional Islam and in what form. It also ranks these countries in an index according to their Islamicity and then observes how the incidence of all forms of Islam in a constitution correlates with demography, geography human rights and in particular, colonial history.

Part II deals with Islamic supremacy clauses. In Chapter 3, we delve into a deeper analysis of a particular form of clause that almost half of all Muslim countries have in their constitutions and which we argue is the most important Islamic clause in constitutions. The Islamic supremacy clause subjugates all law making to Islam, shari'a, or Islamic precepts. It traces the origins and incidence of this clause and its correlation to human rights in constitutional design. Chapter 4 uses case studies and some empirical analysis related to the Islamic supremacy clause.

In Part III, Chapter 5 draws upon the existing literature to analyze the effects of Islamic constitutionalism; that is, how the rights and Islamic supremacy clauses play out in court battles in Pakistan and Egypt; the fundamental question for that chapter is then, unsurprisingly, one of judicial decisions: in court cases, does constitutional Islam override constitutional rights as is sometimes popularly assumed?

Part I

Islamic Constitutionalism

Origins and Present

1.1 THE ATTRACTION OF ISLAM DURING DEMOCRATIZATION "MOMENTS"

In much of the Muslim world, the idea of incorporating Islam into the constitutional-legal framework has remained popular, partly due to historical and cultural reasons and ironically, also to some extent, as a reaction to or even partly as a consequence of Western apprehension of the matter.[1] This became evident after the Arab Spring. A recurrent slogan of protestors in the Arab Spring was "*ash-shab yurid isqat an-nizam,*" translated as "the people want to bring down the regime." The protestors in the Arab Spring certainly wanted democracy and rights.[2] Unlike the outsiders' fear of the rise of consti-tutional Islam, the protestors did not perceive this as a zero-sum choice where they would trade democracy for religion or vice versa. This meant that they did not desire secular government, which is often associated with repression, colonialism, and an assault on Islam in the popular imagination in Muslim countries.[3] Rather, the Arab Spring voiced protestors' demands for both Islam and democracy. Even though the Arab Spring movements were not inherently Islamist in nature, the protestors were clamoring for freedom and justice as "Muslims and not against religion."[4] While they wanted Islam, they also overwhelmingly desired democracy, rights, and the rule of law.[5] Such

---

[1] Magali Rheault and Dalia Mogahed, "Many Turks, Iranians, Egyptians Link Sharia and Justice" (Gallup, July 25, 2008) <www.gallup.com/poll/109072/many-turks-iranians-egyptians-link-sharia-justice.aspx> accessed January 12, 2022.

[2] John L. Esposito, Tamara Sonn, and John O. Voll, *Islam and Democracy after the Arab Spring* (Oxford University Press 2016) 1–25.

[3] Tariq Ramadan, *Islam and the Arab Awakening* (Oxford University Press 2012) 83.

[4] Ramadan, *Islam and the Arab Awakening* 15.

[5] See Richard Wike, "The Tahrir Square Legacy: Egyptians Want Democracy, a Better Economy, and a Major Role for Islam" (*Pew Research Center*, January 24, 2013).

demands deeply challenged some foreign governments' expectation that democratization in the Middle East would bring secular parties to power and encourage a separation of religion and state, similar to the West. Instead, Islamic parties rose to power when democratization took hold in the Middle East. Some commentators even skeptically began to refer to the Arab Spring as the "Islamist Spring."[6]

In fact, greater democracy in the Muslim world arguably created increasing space for Islam – symbolically and politically. And this is not surprising, since secularism, or the popular "anti-Islamic" conception of it (as is understood in the popular imagination) has never gained much legitimacy in much of the Muslim world. Although a bit broad-brushed, the *Economist* goes so far as to argue that "most Muslims do not believe in the separation of religion and state, as America and France do, and have not lost their enthusiasm for religion, as many 'Christian Democrats' in Europe have."[7] Given this popular cry for Islam, one of the dominant promises of the Islamists elected to power after the Arab Spring was the implementation of shariʿa in their respective societies. This phenomenon is not limited to the Arab Spring and has played out several times: For example, in the case of Iraq, "as the constitutional process became increasingly participatory and democratic, the constitution itself became increasingly Islamic in orientation and detail" and "more democracy meant more Islam."[8] In many Muslim-majority countries, many citizens desire Islam to have a role in state governance that goes beyond mere symbolism and rituals.

Why would bringing Islam and shariʿa into the constitution and political sphere be so popular in Muslim societies? Possibly because of colonial history and partially because many Muslims consider shariʿa, good governance, and rights as indivisible and complementary and difficult to divorce from each other. Indeed, in many countries, Muslims blame distance from Islamic teachings in society as responsible for much of the political decay, corruption and lack of accountability. This popular conception of Islam perceives shariʿa

---

[6] See Heather Maher, "Muslim Protests: Has Obama Helped Bring on an Anti-U.S. 'Islamist Spring'?" (*The Atlantic*, September 23, 2012); David Rohde, "The Islamist Spring" *Reuters* (April 5, 2012) (explaining that secular parties split and Islamists took control of politics in Tunisia and Egypt); John R. Bradley, *After the Arab Spring: How Islamists Hijacked the Middle East Revolts* (St. Martin's Press 2012) (arguing that democracy introduced by the Arab Spring ultimately benefited Islamists).

[7] "The Uprisings: Islam and the Arab Revolutions" *The Economist* (March 31, 2011) <www .economist.com/node/18486005> accessed June 19, 2020.

[8] Noah Feldman and Roman Martinez, "Constitutional Politics and Text in the New Iraq: An Experiment in Islamic Democracy" (2006) 75 Fordham Law Review 883, 884.

as a solution to the problems of the Muslim world. The Muslim Brotherhood's slogan – "Islam is the Solution" – quite aptly captures this understanding of Islam in popular imagination.[9] In fact, shari'a itself is then loosely analogized as a constitutional framework, holding rulers accountable to a higher order – God's law – for transgressions, rights violations, and corruption. Indeed, during the public consultations in the constitution-making process in Egypt in 1971, it was apparent that those who desired to incorporate Islam and human rights into the constitution associated the two as integral to each other.[10] In polls, it appears that the majority of Muslims who desired Islam to be a source of legislation saw it as a means to ensure rights. The positive rights associated with Islam in the popular imagination widely overlap with modern-day human rights norms – for example, the right to equality, checks on government, the right to a fair trial, eradication of corruption, and protection of minorities. In "secular" Turkey, less than a third of Muslims who want Islamic law to be a source of legislation perceive it to limit personal freedoms; thus, it could very well be that the demands for rights and Islam are motivated by the same forces.[11] In most Muslim countries, the recognition of secularism in the constitution has limited public appeal, and it is only limited to some elites who perceive it as necessary.[12] As Khalid Masud has commented, "Muslim thinkers found it very difficult to understand new ideas like secularism in isolation from [a history of] Christian (Western colonial) supremacy."[13] Rather than being understood as an alternative style of government, secularism is certainly feared as a means to completely rid the state of religion – to remove God from the public space – a goal that is intolerable for many Muslims. Further, secular-styled governments ranging from Nasser in Egypt to the Shah in Iran and Bourguiba in Tunisia happened to be very dictatorial regimes, which eroded the legitimacy of secularism in the Muslim world.

---

[9] Kristen Stilt, "'Islam is the Solution': Constitutional Visions of the Egyptian Muslim Brotherhood" (2010) 46(1) Texas International Law Journal 73–108.

[10] Kristen A Stilt, "Constitution in Authoritarian Regimes: The Case of Egypt" in Tom Ginsberg and Alberto Simpser (eds.), *Constitutions in Authoritarian Regimes* (Cambridge University Press 2013) 111–38.

[11] Rheault and Mogahed, "Many Turks, Iranians, Egyptians Link Sharia and Justice."

[12] Khaled Abou El Fadl, "The Centrality of Shari'ah to Government and Constitutionalism in Islam" in Rainer Grote and Tilmann J Röder (eds.), *Constitutionalism in Islamic Countries: Between Upheaval and Continuity* (Oxford University Press 2012) 35–62 (discussing the unviability of secularism in Muslim countries because of its symbolism as a Western intellectual invasion among other reasons).

[13] Muhammad Khalid Masud, "The Construction and Deconstruction of Secularism as an Ideology in Contemporary Muslim Thought" (2005) 33(3) Asian Journal of Social Science 363, 346.

Even in Turkey – the most secular of all Muslim-majority countries – the charm of secularism has been waning in the face of popular politics. Thus, in essence, while the idea of Islam and Islamic law conjures up negative connotations in the West, for Muslims, according to Professor Feldman, it is often Islam that, in fact, continues to "invoke the core idea of law in terms that resonate deeply with the Islamic past."[14] And polls routinely attest to the fact that vast majorities in Muslim societies desire to see Islam embedded in their constitutional and legislative framework regardless of the rational merits of such incorporation. That is, for many Muslims, Islam provides the symbolism and vocabulary of contestation against injustice and subjugation.

As a result, it is not surprising that democratization after the Arab Spring led Islamist parties to power. Contrary to regimes like that of Hosni Mubarak, the pre–Arab Spring Egyptian president, Islam and democracy served as the rallying call of Islamist parties from Tunisia to Egypt and Algeria to Pakistan. In a political landscape beset by authoritarianism, the parties promised both: constitutionalism and Islam. Indeed, the rise of political Islam in the 1970s – or the phenomenon commonly referred to as "Islamic fundamentalism" – was in itself partly a reaction to the secular reforms of oppressive Middle Eastern regimes.[15] Unsurprisingly, in societies where avenues for political expression were forcibly blocked, movements based on Islamic political philosophy represented the only opening left for protest.[16] As Fouad Ajami points out, "Islamist" movements have had significant resonance in the Arab world *precisely* because, in contrast to authoritarian secular regimes, they were "democratic" and representative; that is, "[they] invited men to participate . . . [in] contrast to a political culture that reduces citizens to spectators and asks them to leave things to their rulers. At a time when the future is uncertain, it connects them to a tradition that reduces bewilderment."[17] Ayubi also notes that "as the drive toward emancipation [became] increasingly and genuinely

[14] Noah Feldman, *The Fall and Rise of the Islamic State* (Princeton University Press 2008) 6 (discussing the increasing tendency of governments in Muslim-majority countries to declare themselves Islamic and apply shari'a).

[15] Sami Zubaida, *Law and Power in the Islamic World* (I.B. Tauris 2005) (arguing that political Islam is a reaction to secularizing reforms by "Europe and Christianity"); Fareed Zakaria, "Islam, Democracy and Constitutional Liberalism" (2004) 119(1) Political Science Quarterly 1, 11–12 (describing how the Arab world associates the failure of their governments with the failure of secularism and the West and how fundamentalism gave Arabs a language for dissent and opposition).

[16] Nazih NM Ayubi, "The Political Revival of Islam: The Case of Egypt" (1980) 12(4) International Journal of Middle East Studies 481, 487.

[17] Fouad Ajami, *The Arab Predicament: Arab Political Thought and Practice Since 1967* (Cambridge University Press 1982) 134.

popular" in the Muslim world, it also became more religious.[18] With this force in the backdrop, popular democracy after the Arab Spring brought Islamic parties to power with the mandate to ensure for religion, namely Islam, a distinct place in statecraft and the new constitution.

1.2 LIBERAL LEANINGS AND MORAL STANDINGS: ISLAMIC CONSTITUTIONALISM

Beginning in the 1970s, widespread calls for the implementation of Islamic law were observed in Muslim-majority countries.[19] Amid these demands, Muslim-majority countries privileged religion more robustly in their constitutions as compared to the previous ones. But despite the popularity of Islamic ideology as a part of political life, the question remains: Where and how did this demand for Islam become entrenched with constitutionalism in the Muslim world?

When the autocratic rulers in parts of the Muslim world faced fiscal stress and political tensions during the nineteenth century, reformers looked within the system to arrest the decline. The emulation of Western political ideas and norms was considered essential to reform aging Muslim polities. Accordingly, armed with a desire to ensure fiscal and political accountability and to keep the Islamic heritage intact, the reformers in the Muslim world began experimenting with the "technology" of European written constitutionalism. Since it confronted the European nation-state system in the nineteenth century, the Muslim world has frequently wrestled with a rather nuanced relationship between the norms of religion and the core ideas of modern constitutionalism. Confronted with a pervasive European orientalism that viewed the Ottoman Empire as the embodiment of despotism,[20] reformers and conservatives alike struggled to integrate religious modes of governance into a modern form. Beginning with Tunisia in 1861, states in the Islamic world adopted the *form* of Western constitutions.[21] Yet, in an attempt to develop an Islamic

---

[18] Ayubi, "Political Revival of Islam" 481, 485.

[19] Zubaida, *Law and Power* 1 (explaining the Islamic revival in the 1970s and calling for application of shari'a in system of government).

[20] Asli Cirakman, "From Tyranny to Despotism: The Enlightenment's Unenlightened Image of the Turks" (2001) 33(1) International Journal of Middle East Studies 49 (describing the tendency of European writers to describe the Ottoman government as despotic and tyrannical).

[21] Intissar Kherigi, "Tunisia: The Calm After the Storm" (*Aljazeera*, November 28, 2011) <http://www.cfr.org/tunisia/al-jazeera-tunisia-calm-after-storm/p26744> accessed June 19, 2020 (discussing that 150 years after the signing of the Arab world's first constitution in 1861, Tunisia finally has an independent, elected body to draw up a new constitution).

constitutionalist system, the reformers in Muslim countries sought to hold political authority accountable to Islamic law.[22] To balance the twin goals of adhering to constitutionalism and Islam, modern practices were carefully framed in Islamic idioms and presented as modest organizational tools.[23] Since then, the status of Islamic law, and specifically, its relationship with the man-made law, has tended to remain a central issue of constitutional design in the Muslim world. As a kind of natural, higher law that precedes the establishment of individual states, Islam is (and has been) thought of as a means to constrain and limit temporal authority in the Muslim world.[24]

Prior to experimentation with written constitutions, it was shari'a that historically functioned as a form of higher law that inspired constitutions in some parts of the Muslim world. For example, according to the doctrine of *siyasa shari'a*, which had an "enormous impact on the political philosophy of the Ottoman state"[25] to ensure the legitimacy of laws, "the ruler would have to consult with classical Islamic jurists and ... ensure that ... edicts must not require Muslims to perform acts that these jurists deemed forbidden and [did] not cause general harm to society by impeding the goals that Islamic jurists accepted as goals of the law."[26] Under this doctrine, governments in some parts of the Muslim world had the power to make and apply laws, as long as such laws did not violate shari'a and were in the public interest.[27] With such constraints upon government, scholars of Islam explicitly recognized the congruence between shari'a and natural law. Some even argued that shari'a

---

[22] Nathan J. Brown, *Constitutions in a Nonconstitutional World: Arab Basic Laws and the Prospects for Accountable Government* (State University of New York Press 2001) 20 (examining a treatise on government by the leading Tunisian politician of the constitutional period Khayr al-Din al-Tunisi, who wrote about the importance of restraining state power and accountability of the ruler); Cf. Fourth Draft of Constitution of Tunisia (2013) (on file with the authors) (as an example of a constitution without any provision on Islamic law).

[23] Nathan J. Brown and Abel Omar Sherif, "Inscribing the Islamic Shari'a in Arab Constitutional Law" in Yvonne Yazbeck Haddad and Barbara Freyer Stowasser (eds.), *Islamic Law and the Challenges of Modernity* (Altamira Press 2004) 55, 59 (using the examples of the Tunisian and the Ottoman constitutions to illustrate the reframing of Islamic vocabulary to fit constitutional practices).

[24] See Feldman, *Fall and Rise of the Islamic State.*

[25] Clark B. Lombardi and Nathan J. Brown, "Do Constitutions Requiring Adherence to Shari'a Threaten Human Rights? How Egypt's Constitution Reconciles Islamic Law with the Liberal Rule of Law" (2006) 21(1) American University International Law Review 379, 404–405.

[26] Lombardi and Brown, "Do Constitutions Requiring Adherence to Shari'a Threaten Human Rights?"

[27] Jan Michiel Otto, *Sharia and National Law in Muslim Countries* (Leiden University Press 2008) 11.

had certain features that might make it more constitutionalist than a positive, man-made constitutional order.[28]

While early Western scholarship traced the roots of constitutionalism to natural law doctrines in Christianity and Judaism, surprisingly, "Islam, despite its strong legal orientation, provoked no [similar] interest."[29] This is despite the fact, as Professors Esposito and Voll note, that the Islamic heritage contains a number of fundamental concepts that can support constitutionalism in the Islamic world, such as consensus, consultation, limits on arbitrary government power, limited sovereignty of the ruler, social contract, and separation of powers.[30] Nevertheless, some Western scholars perceived that Islam as a non-Western religion could not have espoused values compatible with those of the Enlightenment.[31] In contrast, in recognition of the constitutionalist functions that shari'a envisaged, some Muslim countries enacted positive legislation only for certain issues, while law and the limits of temporal authority in government on certain issues were organically derived from the various schools of Islamic law.[32]

Once it was decided that modernity required constitutional democracy in line with the European model, Islam's previous role in governance had to be realigned and reconfigured to fit the emergence of the "modern" nation-state. Islamic tools of governance were thus "modernized" and reframed, as constitution-makers in the Muslim world blended Islamic rhetoric into written constitutions or engaged in what we today refer to as "constitutional Islamization." Islam provided a familiar, indigenous anchor for rooting potentially alien change within the framework of society's own distinctive cultural

---

[28] Otto, *Sharia and National Law* 170.

[29] Brown, *Constitutions in a Nonconstitutional World* 108.

[30] John L. Esposito and John O. Voll, *Islam and Democracy* (Oxford University Press 1996) (discussing aspects of Islamic heritage that support democratization like consensus and consultation, constitutional opposition, and limits on arbitrary government); see also Rainer Grote and Tilmann J Röder (eds.), *Constitutionalism in Islamic Countries: Between Upheaval and Continuity* (Oxford University Press 2012) 20 (showing that Islamic heritage is compatible with constitutionalism like rule of law, consultation, separation of powers, and limited government); but see Elie Kedourie, *Democracy and Arab Political Culture* (Routledge 1992) 5 (for the idea that representation, elections, popular suffrage, the regulation of political institutions by laws laid down by a parliamentary assembly, of the guarding and upholding of these laws by an independent judiciary, and the secularity of state are all profoundly alien to the Muslim political tradition).

[31] Ramadan, *Islam and the Arab Awakening* 13 (showing that Western governments support Arab dictatorships rather than Islamist political movements).

[32] Paul Marshall, *Radical Islam's Rules: The Worldwide Spread of Extreme Shari'a Law* (Rowman and Littlefield Publishers 2005) (discussing the lack of legislation in many Islamic jurisdictions in favor of shari'a).

identity. As Schacht argues, even today, law "remains an important, if not the most important element in the struggle which is being fought in Islam between traditionalism and modernism under the impact of Western Ideas."[33]

1.3 A TALE OF FOUR MONARCHIES: TUNISIA, THE OTTOMAN EMPIRE, EGYPT, AND IRAN

In Tunisia, where the Muslim world's first modern constitution was written, Islam's role in the constitution-making process is particularly instructive. The insertion of Islamic rhetoric to formulate the constitution was seen as a strategic tool employed by reformers to ease the insertion of reforms perceived as "Western" into the political milieu and to legitimize these "alien" reforms in the eyes of the resisting religious elites and conservatives. Ideas about constitutionalism entered the political scene just as Western, European colonial dominance – especially in material and fiscal terms – was consolidating within the region. The British and French had growing privileges within the province of Tunis. They could even exercise consular jurisdiction over Tunisian nationals and religious minorities residing in Tunisia. Under this jurisdiction, Tunisians could be tried under a separate legal and justice system beyond the reach of Tunisian authorities. This legal exceptionalism for Tunisians created enormous resentment among the Muslim population. It was this colonial treatment embedded in an asymmetrical power structure that anchored the public's understanding of "European" and "Muslim" political thought. In this context, the narrative of "we are Islamic" found its ground steady. The Tunisian Constitution of 1861 (*Qanun al-dawla*) precisely reflected this political context by opening with reference to God and shari'a as guarantors of security. The King had to give an oath in the name of God to the Grand Council. The Constitution also established an advisory body of ulama and a shari'a court. The members of the Grand Council were also referred to in Islamic terminology, as *ahl al-hall wa-l-aqd* (the people who loosen and bind) and the public was referred to as *na'ayana* (our flock).[34] It is telling that the Constitution of Tunisia 1861 – the first constitution in the Muslim world – was drafted under the pressure of the British and French Consuls. Since Tunisia, like other Muslim countries such as Iran and Afghanistan, had become a pawn and a site of diplomatic tussle between European powers, the influence of external powers was inevitable. The Ottoman Sultan and the French and British turned Tunisia into their

---

[33] Joseph Schacht, *An Introduction to Islamic Law* (Oxford University Press 1964) 1.
[34] Brown, *Constitutions in a Nonconstitutional World* 16.

battlefield for economic and ideological assertions. Similar to the British and Russian influence in Iran, France and Britain competed for economic and political clout in Tunisia through economic concessions. They were also political rivals; the French wanted Tunisia to be isolated from the Ottomans while the British wanted to reinforce the relationship between the bey of Tunisia and the Ottomans. For the French, the constitution was a means to limit the authority of the government by converting the absolute monarchy into a constitutional monarchy. Alongside the French, there was also a cadre of Muslim reformers – Khayr al-Din most notable among them – desperate to see political accountability and the progression of their nation.[35] He advocated for checks on the rulers "either in the form of a heavenly *sharia* or a policy based on reason" and encouraged "the ulema [scholars] and the notables of the *umma* [Muslim community] to resist evil."[36] These reformers disliked the absolute power of the bey and desired a democratized and accountable legal and administrative system.

According to another reformer, Ahmad Ibn Abi al-Diyaf, the absolute power of the monarch had been very damaging for Tunisia, and shari'a was one tool, but not a sufficient one, to constrain rulers.[37] He argued that the absolute government not only infringes on shari'a by usurping the role of God but is also contrary to the dictates of reason because it is based on coercion and violence.[38] The *qanun* – or law – not derived from shari'a could be a valuable medium to set such limits. He accordingly developed the notion of a "government bounded by law." This was partly because the religious scholars – who historically had served somewhat as a check on the ruler – were not fulfilling their task of using temporal law to limit arbitrariness. Even the French Consul, writing to his superiors, described the Tunisian government as capricious and arbitrary, and reported the lack of Islamic principles of good governance in practice. To this end, Europeans and local Muslim reformers had a common agenda that would be achieved through modern constitutionalism. The constitution limited authority, improved governance, and provided rights to Tunisians. Over time, this Western-Islamic dichotomy, assisted by power asymmetries between the East and West, between the colonized and the colonizers, cemented into a deeper narrative of European – and today

---

[35] See Khayr al-Din al-Tunisi, *The Surest Path: The Political Treatise of a Nineteenth-Century Muslim Statesman* (Harvard University Press 1967).

[36] Brown, *Constitutions in a Nonconstitutional World* 16.

[37] See Ahmad Ibn Abi al-Diyaf, *Consult Them in the Matter: A Nineteenth-Century Islamic Argument for Constitutional Government* (L Carl Brown tr, University of Arkansas Press 2005).

[38] Ibn Abi Al-Diyaf, *Consult Them in the Matter* 53.

Western – values versus Islamic values.[39] In fact, the European press played on this apparent dichotomy between European or "liberal" values and Islam. In the popular European imagination, the constitution was a "proof that Islam could accept the values of the Enlightenment. The influential French *Journal des Debats* claimed the constitution as the sign of 'good progress' and a model for other Muslim countries. In its view, the constitution made the state 'civilized' and its Prince 'as liberal as he is enlightened.'"[40]

We see a similar pattern developing in the Ottoman Empire in the mid-nineteenth century. From 1826 to 1877, the Ottoman government desperately tried to modernize and revitalize its declining empire, which had stopped expanding geographically after failing to defeat European forces at Vienna. Among other problems, the economy was in decline and tensions were also mounting between different ethnicities. Pressure was mounting with regards to Europe's expanding and competing capitalism, which led European countries seeking new markets and zones of influence and required reforms necessary for capitalist expansion, such as suitable self-serving commercial laws. Consequently, a system of foreign privileges, immunity, and interventions arose in the Ottoman Empire. To finance modernization, the government had borrowed heavily, leading to further fiscal problems and foreign domination.[41] A group of reformers sought to restore the legacy of their nation and believed that the adoption of "Western" style governance – including a constitution – with Islamic characteristics would provide the most appropriate tools for improving the future of a chaotic, declining empire and constraining the power of the Sultan.[42] As "crisis followed crisis, the liberals became convinced that the safety, if not the very existence of the Empire, lay in a radical reshaping of its government structure. Above all they perceived a need to end the absolute rule of the sultan and to substitute a constitutional form of government."[43] Therefore, a series of "constitutional" reforms, called *Tanzimat* (literal meaning: reorganization), was promulgated in 1839. The objective of these reforms was to counter nationalist movements and foreign powers. *Tanzimat* was an adoption of European political modernity within Ottoman institutions and bureaucracy. The military establishment was the *Tanzimat*'s first priority. The second priority was the empire's administrative apparatus, which continued to remain the main focus of Ottoman reformers

[39] Brown, *Constitutions in a Nonconstitutional World* 16.
[40] Brown, *Constitutions in a Nonconstitutional World* 16.
[41] Brown, *Constitutions in a Nonconstitutional World* 21.
[42] Brown, *Constitutions in a Nonconstitutional World* 25.
[43] Brown, *Constitutions in a Nonconstitutional World* 25.

from 1839 onward, the year when the first *Tanzimat* edict (*Hatt-i-Sharif of the Gulhane*) was issued. Among other changes, the reforms attempted to integrate non-Muslims and non-Turks by enhancing their civil liberties and granting them legal equality. In 1869, laws were promulgated to regulate "Ottoman affiliation" (meaning citizenship) and reorganize the judiciary, which was previously divided between Islamic, communitarian, and secular courts. Similarly, matters relating to trade, official transactions, and registration of land and municipalities were regulated through some additional laws.

The constitution was perhaps *the* major tool of reform. To draft the constitution, a committee comprising senior officials, military leaders, and ulama was created. The draft prepared by the committee had substantial similarity with the Belgian Constitution of 1831 and the Prussian Constitution of 1850.[44] The Constitution introduced measures to keep a check on absolute rule. The Sultan could not unilaterally enact laws or amend the Constitution. The Constitution created a legislative body and guaranteed personal liberty, religious freedom, free education, and equality before the law irrespective of religion, caste, or creed. It also instituted a weak bicameral parliament with both an elected house and an appointed senate. Ministers were responsible principally to the Sultan, but parliament could also try them for criminal offenses, with the Sultan's permission. Yet, the Islamic idiom was a recurring feature in the Constitution. Article 4 appointed the Sultan the protector of the Muslim religion under the title of the Supreme Caliph. Article 11 proclaimed Islam the state religion. Further, the Sultan was tasked with carrying out provisions of Islamic law (Article 7). Affairs relating to the shari'a were also the exclusive prerogative of shari'a tribunals. It was quite apparent that part of the reason for using Islam in the Constitution was that drafters wished to legitimize positive, man-made legislation – a feature of modern political systems – alongside divine shari'a.[45] In fact, when the Constitution was resurrected in 1908, it required the Sultan to swear an oath to shari'a in addition to the nation, Constitution, and homeland.

Similar to Tunisia and the Ottoman Empire, Egypt also suffered from financial bankruptcy and European dominance in its political and economic spheres.[46] The extent of imperial dominance was such that French and British ministers had been inducted into the Egyptian cabinet. As political and military resentment intensified, the ruler or khedive, keen to counter European influence, encouraged the constitution-making process. Amid these

---

[44] Brown, *Constitutions in a Nonconstitutional World* 21.
[45] Brown, *Constitutions in a Nonconstitutional World* 24.
[46] Brown, *Constitutions in a Nonconstitutional World* 26–27.

circumstances, a group of reformers – from the political elite mainly – saw the Constitution as a way to make government more accountable and responsible. This movement led to the promulgation of the Constitution in 1882.

During that period, Iran was the fourth Muslim country to enact a formal constitution. It is the first constitution to contain the most robust constitutional entrenchment of Islam. In Iran, the constitution was written in circumstances similar to Egypt, Tunisia, and the Ottoman Empire. Much to the resentment of its citizens, Iran had become economically and militarily weak during the nineteenth century. Reliance on cash crops, an increasing export of raw materials, and the growing rate of unemployment had all contributed to a poor economic situation that energized debates about modernization and lessening the impact of European commerce on Iran's economy.[47] Externally too, Iran had become significantly dependent on European powers, namely, Britain and Russia. Rather than resisting foreign domination, the monarchs of the Qajar dynasty had succumbed to British and Russian pressure. Consequently, by the late nineteenth century, Iran was essentially "a prisoner of imperial interests."[48]

The resentment against imperial powers intensified; an uprising that came to later be known as the Constitutional Revolution erupted. The central demand of protestors in the Constitutional Revolution was for the rule of law and establishment of representative government. Since 1860, there had been a recurring demand among many Iranians for a House of Justice (*adalatkhana*) that would dispense justice with fairness as against Qajars' arbitrary justice.[49] After months of incessant agitation across Iranian society, including clergy, traders, peasants, and merchants, the Iranian monarch, Muzaffar al-Din Shah, signed a proclamation for constitutional government in August 1906. This declaration marked Iran's transition from absolute monarchic to parliamentary government. It recognized the people as the source of political power, contained numerous rights, and set up a division

---

[47] Janet Afary, *The Iranian Constitutional Revolution, 1906–11: Grassroots Democracy, Social Democracy and the Origins of Feminism* (Columbian University Press 1996) 17 (detailing the origin of the Constitutional Revolution of 1906 in the structural and ideological transformations at the turn of the century, resulting from decades of economic change and damaging European influence).

[48] Ali Geissari, "Constitutional Rights and the Development of Civil Law in Iran, 1907–41" in HE Chehabi and Vanessa Martin (eds), *Iran's Constitutional Revolution: Popular Politics, Cultural Transformations and Transnational Connections* (I. B. Tauris 2010) 69–71.

[49] Afary, *The Iranian Constitutional Revolution, 1906–11* 57.

of power.[50] But the Constitution of 1906 did not contain a bill of rights and it did not clearly define the authority of the executive, legislature, and judiciary. Therefore, work on a supplementary constitution started promptly to solidify the gains from the Constitutional Revolution and fill gaps in the constitution. Accordingly, in 1907, a supplementary constitution was completed. This new constitution contained an extensive bill of rights, guaranteeing protection to life, property, privacy regarding letters and telegrams, and the right to a fair trial. Unlike the Constitution of 1906, Islam was entrenched deeply in the 1907 draft through a very strong Islamic supremacy clause. The majlis delegates had agreed that a committee of leading clerics would review and rewrite the provisions of the Constitution that conflicted with Islamic law.[51] To this effect, Article 2 of the 1907 supplementary constitution called for the establishment of a Council of Clerics entrusted with the Islamic review mechanism. It further provided that the laws ratified by the majlis could not be at variance with the shari'a. Article 2 also declared that "laws passed by [the National Assembly] must never to all ages be contrary to the sacred precepts of Islam and the laws laid down by the Prophet." This was the first repugnancy clause in the constitutional history of Muslim countries and it thus bears credit for introducing the very language of repugnancy that migrated transnationally into future constitutions of several Muslim-majority states. The clause was certainly an innovation, not just among the handful of relatively independent Muslim-majority states that actually had a written constitution at the time – Tunisia, Egypt, and the Ottoman Empire – but also in other constitutions of the world.

---

[50] See Asghar Schirazi, *The Constitution of Iran: Politics and the State in the Islamic Republic* (I. B. Tauris 1998) (discussing the Constitutional Revolution that produced the first Iranian constitution that separated judicial, executive, and legislative branches of government).

[51] Afary argues that the concept of "freedom" was generally ignored in the 1907 Constitution. This is not surprising "since many members of the *ulama* continued to oppose the notion of freedom, and the word soon adopted a highly pejorative connotation. Freedom, including the right to be different and to act differently from other people, was equated with non-religiosity, immorality, lack of chastity, and licentious behavior. With regards to gender, words such as freedom and liberation had come to have a doubly negative connotation. For example, a 'free woman' meant a vulgar, immoral, and sexually promiscuous one." Afary, *The Iranian Constitutional Revolution, 1906–11* 220.

2

What is an Islamic Constitution?

It is certainly not surprising that the idea of an "Islamic" politico-constitutional order remains popular to this day. Since the time of early constitutional experiments in the Muslim world, the issue of incorporation of Islam in constitutions has tended to remain a central issue of constitutional design, both for the Muslim world and for Western observers. As soon as Muslim countries started to gain independence during the twentieth century, they were keen not only to write constitutions signaling their sovereignty and independence and providing a framework of governance but also to incorporate Islam into these constitutions. After independence from Britain in 1947, the debates in the Constituent Assembly of Pakistan centered on the question of divine or public sovereignty and the legal status of Islam in the political system. Likewise, in Syria, at around the same time, similar debates took place about incorporating Islam within the constitutional framework. Most constitutions in Muslim-majority countries contain certain notions of Islam and shari'a ranging from the stricter versions in Iran and Pakistan to the more lenient ones in Algeria, Bangladesh, and Malaysia. Even today, for governments in the Muslim world, the adoption and application of Islamic law in the legal system is not only an indicator of the religiosity of a Muslim country, and its leaders, but also allows for a veneer of legitimacy of rule, for both democrats and dictators alike. However, shari'a, or the application of it, is not *all* that defines constitutional aspirations in Muslim countries, nor is it true that Islam is the sole source of political legitimacy for Muslims. Yet it certainly remains an extremely important feature of a constitutional order for many Muslims.

Credit for the empirical findings and analysis in this chapter largely goes to Moamen Gouda and Tom Ginsburg, with whom Dawood Ahmed has already published work on this topic. Much of this work is included, with edits, in this chapter.

During the Arab Spring, the Islamist parties promised, directly or indirectly, an Islamic constitution. The promise of Islam in the political life of a nation-state seems to be a recurring theme in constitutionalism. Historically, many regimes, beginning with Tunisia in 1861, have promised to incorporate Islam into the constitutional order. Questions remains as to the extent and manner states have succeeded in materializing these promises. Yet what is an Islamic constitution and how can we measure whether a constitution lives up to the claim of being Islamic? This chapter explores answers to these questions by measuring the role of Islam in the constitutions of Muslim countries.

2.1 THE AL-AZHAR ISLAMIC CONSTITUTION

There are myriad ways in which Islam can be given a place in the constitutional order, some more central than others. From being *a* or *the* source of legislation to the criterion for declaring the laws void for repugnancy, Islam has been employed to stipulate the qualification for head of the state and make reference to Islamic values in the preamble. Even more so, Islamic principles have been made the normative basis of constitutional rights.

The debate about Islamic constitutionalism and democracy in Muslim countries dates back to the Tunisian experience of constitutionalism in 1861. Since then, Muslim countries have been grappling with constitutionalism and Islam or creating an Islamic constitution. While there is no single conception of an Islamic constitution, there are countless opinions about what makes a society "Islamic." While it is true that the members of the Organization of Islamic Cooperation (OIC), an intergovernmental organization representing Muslim-majority countries worldwide,[1] except for Saudi Arabia, have formal written constitutions, underlying principles categorizing them as Islamic constitutions are yet to be evaluated. Definitional work on "Islamic constitution" is the most crucial aspect before proceeding to compare the Muslim world's constitutions for their Islamicity, ranking them and assessing their status based on rights and democracy. It is only possible if we have a model against which we can compare all constitutions enacted in the Muslim world. For the purposes of this analysis, there is one prototype: a model Islamic constitution

---

[1] Under the OIC Charter, Article 3(2), the criteria for membership are that a country has a "Muslim majority" and that the council of foreign ministers approves the new member by consensus. The membership of countries with a Muslim minority (e.g., Benin, Cameroon, Gabon, Guyana, and Uganda) is therefore not in accordance with the provisions on membership of the OIC Charter. Nevertheless, all OIC members are included in our sample for consistency.

that al-Azhar University in Egypt drafted for governments in the Muslim world to emulate.

Al-Azhar University, based in Cairo, is widely considered one of the most scholarly authoritative institutional bodies on Sunni Islam globally. It is often considered the chief center of Arabic literature and Islamic learning in the world. Founded over 1,100 years ago by the Fatimid dynasty as a madrasa, or center of Islamic learning, it is one of the oldest and most respected Sunni religious institutions in the world. The head cleric of al-Azhar, the Grand Imam of al-Azhar, also known as the Grand Sheikh of al-Azhar, is considered by some Muslims as the highest authority in Sunni Islamic thought and Islamic jurisprudence.[2] Despite its subordination to the Egyptian state in recent decades, it is still recognized as an important learning center for Muslims The madrasa was initially one of the relics of the Isma'ili Shi'a Fatimid dynasty of Egypt, descended from Fatimah, daughter of Prophet Muhammad, and Ali, son-in-law and cousin of Prophet Muhammad. By bringing together diverse disciplines under the same roof, it was one of the first universities in the world and the only one to survive as a modern institute. In 1961, al-Azhar was officially established as a "modern" university under the government of Egypt's second president Gamal Abdel Nasser when a wide range of secular faculty members were added for the first time. Before then, the *Encyclopedia of Islam* classified al-Azhar as a madrasa, center of higher learning, and, since the nineteenth century, as a religious university, but not as a university in the secular academic sense, overlooking its modern "transition from madrasa to university." Even outside the Muslim world, al-Azhar is known as the voice of moderate Islam.

In October 1977, the Islamic Research Academy (IRA) hosted a major meeting at al-Azhar University in Cairo. A decision was taken there to draft a model Islamic constitution that could be used as a framework by any country that wished to model itself on the basis of Islamic constitutionalism and shari'a. All parties agreed that the content of the Islamic Constitution drafted must not only be compliant with shari'a, but it should especially be cognizant of differing Islamic schools of jurisprudence. Soon thereafter, the Grand Sheikh of al-Azhar issued a decree on January 5, 1978, whereby a High Committee of experts was formed for the purpose of drafting this Islamic Constitution. A year later, the final version of this Constitution was published

---

[2] Clinton Bennett, *Muslims and Modernity: An Introduction to the Issues and Debates* (Bloomsbury 3PL 2005) 220.

in the autumn of 1978 in al-Azhar's official magazine.[3] However, "this Islamic constitution was forgotten."[4]

After being neglected for more than three decades, the al-Azhar Constitution showed up at Cairo's Tahrir Square during the 2011 uprising. An original Arabic scanned copy of the Constitution along with an English translation was in fact published on July 13, 2011 on Tahrir Documents, a website dedicated to archiving, translating, and electronically publishing activist papers from Cairo's Tahrir Square.[5] Later, an Egyptian newspaper announced that Salafis (adherents of one of the most puritanical strains of Islam), along with the former Grand Mufti of Egypt Nasr Farid Wasel and a group of renowned Islamic scholars, had already started preparing a draft constitution for Egypt based on the shari'a. Their coalition, called the Islamic Legitimate Body of Rights and Reformation (ILBRR), was essentially aimed to advance the country toward an Islamic model of governance.[6] More importantly, Mohamed Yousry, a Salafi scholar and the secretary general of the ILBRR, pointed out that the main model to frame the new constitution was the al-Azhar Constitution.[7] Apparently, all the Islamic movements in Egypt agreed upon this Constitution as the model Islamic constitution. One commentator even suggested the al-Azhar Constitution could pacify disputes between the various stakeholders as to what was Islamic or not.[8]

---

[3] Reinhard Schulze, "Citizens of Islam: The Institutionalization and Internationalization of Muslim Debate" in Christopher Toll and Jakob Skovgaard-Petersen (eds), *Law and the Islamic World: Past and Present* (Munksgaard 1995) 167–85 (narrating what has happened after the Islamic constitution was introduced, "the [IRA]-proposal was not discussed openly. The [IRA]-session of 1979 could not be held, as most participants from the *duwal al-rafd*, i.e., from those states that rejected the Egyptian-Israeli peace treaty of 1978, were not allowed to travel to Cairo. Again, divergent political views prevented the jurists from defining a legal conception of the Muslim nation (*Umma*). The main problem, of course, was to what extent an Islamic constitution should be the legal framework of the *Umma*; mostly it was postulated that an Islamic constitution should be the model of nation-state constitutions. It should prescribe an Islamic form of government and jurisdiction without questioning the sovereignty of the nation-states").

[4] Hamdi Dabash, "Al-Azhar and Salafi Scholars Prepare Islamic Constitution" Egypt Independent (July 7, 2011) <http://www.egyptindependent.com//news/al-azhar-and-salafi-scholars-prepare-islamic-constitution> accessed August 11, 2014.

[5] See generally, Moamen Gouda, "Islamic Constitutionalism and Rule of Law: A Constitutional Economics Perspective" (2013) 24(1) Constitutional Political Economy 57.

[6] Gouda, "Islamic Constitutionalism and Rule of Law" 57.

[7] See Dabash, "Al-Azhar and Salafi Scholars Prepare Islamic Constitution."

[8] Gouda, "Islamic Constitutionalism and Rule of Law" 57.

2.2 ANALYZING THE "ISLAMIC CONSTITUTION"

The model Constitution consists of a preamble and nine sections, encompassing ninety-three subsections. It sets out, inter alia, principles related to operation of the economy, independence of the judiciary, and fundamental rights, including the right to work; freedom of expression, religion, and thought; freedom to join trade unions; and freedom of the press. It provides for a presidency and the means to appoint the president (imam). Interestingly, in Article 81, it also provides for the establishment of a "Supreme Constitutional Court ... having the jurisdiction to decide upon the conformity of laws and regulations to the rulings of Islamic shari'a and the provisions of this Constitution." It also deals with other matters such as the procedure of constitutional amendments, accountability of the president, equality before law, and administrative matters, such as the location of the capital city and design of the national flag. The Constitution makes the president accountable to the judiciary. However, the most apparent feature of this model Constitution is the frequent referencing of Islamic clauses. For example, Article 1 opens with a statement expressing the unity of the Muslim political community globally. Article 1b reads: "Islamic shari'a is the source of all legislation." Article 65 states: "Judges are subject only to the Islamic shari'a in their judgments." Article 61 provides that "the judiciary shall rule justly in accordance with the rule of Islamic shari'a." Article 12 further stipulates that "the state is required to teach Muslims the fundamentals of religion, including: religious obligations, the Prophet's biography, and the biography of the Caliphs. This study should be comprehensive throughout all years of education." The Constitution requires the economy to "be based upon the principles of Islamic shari'a, which guarantees human dignity and social justice" (Article 18). Under this Constitution, usury is forbidden (Article 23). The rights are subject to shari'a. For example, freedom of religion and thought, the freedom to work, the freedom to express opinion directly or indirectly, the freedom to establish and participate in trade union associations, personal freedom, and the freedom of movement and congregation "are all basic and natural rights that are protected within the framework of the Islamic shari'a" (Article 29). As for the head of state, Article 47 makes it clear that "candidates for the presidency must be a Muslim, male, past the age of majority, of sound mind, pious, and knowledgeable about the rules of Islamic shari'a." More importantly, Article 83 provides that "[t]he state shall have a Shura council" which, among other important tasks, reviews legislation to ensure "it is consistent with rulings of Islamic shari'a."

The al-Azhar Constitution is clearly not short of Islamic credentials and rhetoric. It categorically privileges Islam as an overarching principle of the constitutional and legal order. Given its short length, the Constitution is, however, sparse on some important matters. For example, it remains silent on the procedure for impeachment of the president (imam), the status of international law, eligibility criteria of a member of parliament (presumably the *shura* council, although this is not clear), appointment procedure of ministers, role of parliamentary/election commissions, establishment and regulation of the armed forces and police, the procedure for enacting legislation, the method of appointing judges on the Supreme Constitutional Court, and so forth. The model Constitution also refrains from allocating the interpretative authority of shari'a to a particular person or institution.[9]

It seems that much has been deliberately left out by design because the intention of the framers was to perhaps only provide a template of an "Islamic" constitution that could be molded by each state according to its particular circumstances. To this end, it was recognized that going into specific details would be problematic not only because Islamic doctrine may not have had much to say about a particular issue (e.g., the method of appointment of judges or the procedure of impeachment of the president [imam]) but also because greater detail and specificity might have engendered more divisiveness and harmed the overall project.

2.2.1 *Measuring Islamic Constitutions: Method*

To compare and conclusively answer the question of incorporation of Islam within modern constitutions, we need to first know the defining characteristics of Islamic constitutionalism. The al-Azhar Constitution serves as the template for this exercise. We identified thirty "Islamic clauses" in the al-Azhar Constitution and constructed a survey based on these clauses.[10] (Table 2.1

---

9   It must be acknowledged that al-Azhar's model constitution differs from modern liberal constitutions in the sense that Islam (shari'a) becomes a kind of "grundnorm" below which lie other ideals of the constitution, including human rights, provisions on religious and gender equality, and so forth. This is not to say that the model constitution does not provide for rights and other democratic features or does not strive to modernity or equality. It probably does, but to the extent that it seeks to reconcile modernity with tradition, it also makes certain liberal features often taken for granted in liberal constitutionalism – such as women's rights, the right for women to hold public office, and so forth – vulnerable to human and possibly subjective interpretation of Islamic principles, which may or may not support a liberal society.

10 We found that while the al-Azhar Constitution captured an overwhelming number of the Islamic clauses found today, there were some important ones that were contained in the constitutions of several Muslim countries yet were lacking in the al-Azhar constitution; for

TABLE 2.1. *Islamic articles in the al-Azhar Constitution*

Questions	Corresponding articles in al-Azhar Constitution
A. General characteristics	
Q1. [STATEREL]- Does the constitution state that Islam is the state religion?	Article 1b
Q2. [PREAMBLE]- Does the Preamble reference Islamic idiom?	Preamble
Q3. [UNITY]- Is there reference to the unity of OR association with the Muslim world or any mention of *ummah* (Islamic political community)?	Articles 1–3
Q4. [JIHAD]- Is there a reference to jihad or defense of the faith?	Article 56
Q5. [CALENDAR]- Does the constitution reference an Islamic calendar and/or holidays?	Article 15
Q6. [HDMUSLIM]- Does the head of state or government have to be Muslim?	Article 47
Q7. [CTZMUSLIM]- Should all citizens be Muslims?	No mention of non-Muslims in al-Azhar Constitution
Q8. [JDMUSLIM]- Is it stated that judges of the highest court need to be Muslim?	Articles 61 and 65
Q9. [OATH]- Does it mention Islamic idiom in the presidential and/or ministerial or parliamentary oath?	Article 48
Q10. [MORAL]- Are Islamic morals given some constitutional foundation?	Article 7
Q11. [AMENDMENT]- Are the provisions related to Islam unamendable?	Preamble, Article 1b
Q12. [ADVISORY]- Does the constitution mention a religious council that is advisory?	Article 83
Q13. [AUTHORITY]- Does the source of authority or power stem from any religious notions?	Articles 55, 56, and 57
Q14. [ACCOUNTABILITY]- Is government accountable to or to rule in accordance with the laws and limits of Islam?	Article 7
B. Rights	
Q15. [RIGHTS1]- Does the constitution make the enjoyment of any rights or freedoms subject to shari'a requirements?	Article 29
Q16. [WOMEN]- Is there a clause stating that women should serve their husband or that serving the family should be their priority?	Article 8

Questions	Corresponding articles in al-Azhar Constitution
C. Executive	
Q17. [DUTY]- Does the head of state/government have some religious duties/symbolism?	Article 47
Q18. [HDKNOWLEDGE]- Does the head of state or government need to possess Islamic knowledge?	Article 47
Q19. [PLEDGE]- Is the head of state/government appointed through a pledge of allegiance (*bai'ah*)?	Article 48
D. Legislation	
Q20. [SOURCE]- Is Islam identified as a source of legislation?	Article 1b
Q21. [SUPREMACY]- What is the degree of supremacy of Islam? Code the intensity (asked only if SOURCE is answered 1).	Article 1b
Q22. [REPUGNANCE]- Does the constitution state that no laws can be repugnant to Islam?	Articles 83 and 92
E. Judiciary	
Q23. [JUDICIARY]- Is there an explicit provision requiring the judiciary to apply shari'a or refuse to apply laws that contradict it?	Article 81
Q24. [JDKNOWLEDGE]- Is it stated that judges of the highest court need to have Islamic knowledge?	Article 65
Q25. [COMPLIANCE]- Does the constitution mention a religious council or judicial court that has the power to review legislation (ex ante or ex post) to declare shari'a compliance?	Article 83
F. Economy	
Q26. [ECONOMY] - Does it provide that the economy/ trade or banking will be in accordance with Islam?	Article 23
Q27. [INTEREST]- Does the constitution ban interest rate (*riba*) (asked only if ECONOMY is answered 1)?	Article 23
Q28. [ALMS]- Does it make provision for the state to recognize or organize alms/charity/zakat/waqf?	Article 26
G. Other issues	
Q29. [CRIME]- Does the constitution make any explicit provision that Islamic criminal penalties (amputations, stoning) will be implemented?	Articles 56, 59, 69, 71, 72, and 79
Q30. [EDUCATION]- Does the constitution make provision for the state to provide Islamic (or religious) education?	Articles 10 and 11

presents a list of thirty questions/clauses that were found to represent constitutional Islamization and the corresponding articles in al-Azhar's model constitution). The next step was to use these Islamic clauses as a basis for comparison among the constitutions of Islamic countries. To define our sampling pool of Islamic countries, and in the interest of including every Muslim-majority country or at least those containing a sizable Muslim population (such as Cameroon and Benin), we focused on the members of the OIC, the second largest intergovernmental organization after the United Nations with a membership of fifty-seven states spread over four continents. The OIC includes virtually every Muslim-majority country as a member, along with many countries with large Muslim minorities, such as India. The OIC claims that it is "the collective voice of the Muslim world" and its role is to "safeguard and protect the interests of the Muslim world in the spirit of promoting international peace and harmony among various people of the world."[11]

To collect the constitutions of these countries for coding, we drew on constitutional texts from Constitute, a joint project by Google and the Comparative Constitutions Project to catalog the formal contents of the world's written and operative constitutions. We analyzed the current constitution of each of the fifty-six OIC members (excluding Palestine from the analysis since it is not yet recognized as a state internationally). For the countries located in the Middle East, the Arabic texts were also read to ensure that all nuances regarding Islamicity are covered. Using the thirty Islamic clauses as a benchmark, the OIC-member constitutions were then coded, rechecked by another coder, and eventually comprised into a unique data set of Islamic constitutions, also known as the Islamic Constitutionalism Index.[12]

2.2.2 *Empirical Findings on Islamic Clauses*

Analysis of the data shows that constitutional Islamization is a common feature in the constitutions of Muslim-majority countries. A small number

example, the al-Azhar Constitution did not contain clauses declaring Islam as a state religion nor repugnancy clauses that stated that no law can be enacted that was repugnant to Islam. The references had to be explicitly "Islamic" to be counted in our survey instrument; this ensured rigour. That is, references to God or religion in general did not classify as Islamic within our instrument. For example, the Indonesian Constitution references God, but since it is not a specifically Islamic reference, we do not count this as an Islamic clause. Also see, Dawood Ahmed, Moamen Gouda, and Tom Ginsburg, "Islamic Constitutionalism Project" (SHARIAsource, Harvard Law School, 2018) <https://beta.shariasource.com/projects/islamic-constitutionalism> last accessed May 1, 2021.

[11] *Organisation of Islamic Cooperation* <http://www.oic-oci.org/oicv2/home/?lan=en>.

[12] Ahmed, Gouda, and Ginsburg, "Islamic Constitutionalism Project."

of Muslim-majority countries describe themselves as secular, most notably the Central Asian countries, Turkey, and Mali. We do not find Islamic clauses in the constitutions of countries that are not Muslim majority (i.e., not having Muslims as more than 50 percent of the population). Some countries, such as Uzbekistan and Sierra Leone, are completely silent on the treatment of religion in the constitution; that is, they do not declare Islam nor secularism as a constitutional principle. Conversely, over half (27), or almost 60 percent of the 45 Muslim-majority countries in the world express some relationship to Islam in their constitutions;[13] that is, they have undergone some degree of constitutional Islamization. This is an important finding – Islam plays a major role in the constitutions of most Muslim-majority countries. Nevertheless, there is tremendous variation in the degree and mode to which these constitutions are Islamized.

The state religion clause (i.e., declaring Islam to be the religion of the state) is the most popular in highlighting the Islamic character of the constitution within Muslim-majority countries. A staggering twenty-three of the twenty-five constitutions referring to Islam across the jurisdictions contain these clauses. Similarly, the clauses referring to Islam as the source of law are also widely incorporated: eighteen countries have employed this clause in their constitutions. The constitutions of six Muslim-majority countries contain repugnancy clauses (sometimes in addition to a source of law clause, e.g., in the case of the Iraqi Constitution) that stipulate that no laws can be passed that contradict Islam. In Iran, the constitution states that judges should refrain from executing laws that violate Islam. Similarly, the Basic Law of Saudi Arabia states: "the judges bow to no authority other than that of Islamic shari'a" (Article 46). Other popular clauses are those that require the head of the state or government to be a Muslim (fifteen constitutions contain such a requirement). A number of constitutions provide for Islamic language in the oath of constitutional offices. The Pakistani Constitution of 1973 even requires members of parliament to be those "who do not violate Islamic injunctions" (Article 62[d]). Some constitutions, including that of Iran and Yemen, even

---

[13] Pew lists forty-nine Muslim-majority countries. We have not included in our sample four countries – Kosovo, Mayotte, Palestine, and Western Sahara; hence our sample of Muslim-majority countries is forty-five and not forty-nine. Kosovo is not a UN member or non-member state. None of these four states are recognized as states. In any case, the constitution of Kosovo does not contain any Islamic clause. The provisional constitutions of Palestine and Western Sahara do contain some references to Islam. Mayotte does not have a constitution. Hence, even if we include these countries, the results would even out. "Number of Muslims in Western Europe" *(PEW Research Center*, December 2, 2014) <http://features.pewforum.org/muslim-population/>.

provide that the head of the government (in addition to the head of the state) should be a Muslim. Some constitutions – like those of Pakistan, Mauritania, Morocco, Egypt, and Algeria – provide for an advisory religious body, while in Iran, the body is not simply advisory but has significant powers, including that of reviewing legislation to assess whether laws violate Islamic principles. The Pakistani Constitution as amended in 1980 also provides for a Federal Shariat Court that can "examine and decide the question whether or not any law or provision of law is repugnant to the injunctions of Islam, as laid down in the Holy Quran and Sunnah of the Holy Prophet" (Article 203 C). In terms of rights, the Afghan and Bahrain constitutions limit some constitutional rights to what is permitted under Islam, whereas, in Iran, Saudi Arabia, and the Maldives, all rights are subject to Islam. Some constitutions include recognition of Islamic holidays. Some countries have gone so far as to make provisions related to Islam unamendable. Interestingly, in terms of analogizing Islam and shariʻa as "natural law" limits on earthly authority of rulers, as was perceived to be the case in premodern times, only the Saudi Basic Law explicitly provides that the king "shall undertake to rule according to the rulings of Islam" (Article 25). In the Maldives, the President can be removed if they are in "direct violation of a tenet of Islam" (Article 100). There are more Islamic clauses that we found related to jihad, the provision of charity, and the provision of religious education, but these were rare. One very rare yet very important clause we found was in the constitution of the Maldives; under Article 9(d) of the Maldives's constitution, one cannot be a citizen unless he or she is a Muslim.

2.3 ISLAMIC CONSTITUTIONS INDEX: RANKING ISLAMIC CONSTITUTIONS

The survey of Islamic clauses in the constitutions across the Muslim-majority countries provides us with a snapshot of Islamic constitutions.[14] It allows us to see which clauses are most popular – for example, state religion, Muslim head of state, and source of law clauses. Yet, without further comparative analysis, surveying Islamicity of constitutions does not in itself provide answers to such questions as: Which is the most Islamic constitution in the world, and which is the least? To answer such questions, we created the Islamic Constitutions Index (ICI), which ranks all the OIC members' constitutions for their

---

[14] Ahmed, Gouda, and Ginsburg, "Islamic Constitutionalism Project."

Islamicity. The ICI measures Islamic constitutionalism and distinguishes between OIC members that have Islamic constitutions and those that do not. Each country's score on the Index is the total number of Islamic clauses in its constitution. We developed a special scoring methodology. If the supremacy article refers to Islam/Islamic law/shari'a, two points are added. One point is scored if the article refers to "principles" of Islam/Islamic law/shari'a. The reason behind this is that a direct reference to Islam or shari'a would be valued more than a reference to "principles," which might refer to general principles in Islam, such as justice, equality, and modesty. In addition, an extra point is added if the supremacy article states that Islam (or its principles) is "a" source of law or that if there is no other law governing a matter, then Islamic law will apply. Further, two points are added if Islam is "a" primary or basic or foundational source of law. Finally, if the supremacy article states that Islam (or its principles) is "the" source (or the only source) of law, three points are added. The reason behind this scoring theme is that we perceive "supremacy" clauses that provide for laws' compliance with Islam or that privilege Islam as an important source of legislation as the most powerful in terms of Islamicity, more so than any other clause – even the "state religion" clauses.[15] These supremacy clauses also have a tendency to allow courts to undertake what Feldman labels an "Islamic judicial review," the purpose of which is "not merely to ensure [legislation's] compliance with the constitution but rather, to *guarantee* that it does not violate Islamic laws or values."[16] Both types of clauses imply the supremacy of – or at the very least create a privileged space for – Islam and Islamic law within the normative constitutional-legal order.[17] The formulation of a supremacy clause in the form of a repugnancy clause would arguably imply a more robust ability to challenge legislation on the basis of the violation of a "superior" normative order grounded in Islam. The source of law clause, depending on the degree to which it entrenches Islam, that is, as "a" or "the" source, could also potentially serve this function. Indeed, as Brown and Sherif opine, even simply privileging Islam as "a"

---

[15] Dawood Ahmed and Tom Ginsburg, "Constitutional Islamization and Human Rights: The Surprising Origin and Spread of Islamic Supremacy Clauses" (2014) 54(3) Virginia Journal of International Law 615.

[16] Noah Feldman, *The Fall and Rise of the Islamic State* (Princeton University Press 2008) 2 (discussing the increasing tendency of governments in Muslim-majority countries to declare themselves Islamic and apply shari'a).

[17] See Nathan J Brown and Abel Omar Sherif, "Inscribing the Islamic Shari'a in Arab Constitutional Law" in Yvonne Yazbeck Haddad and Barbara Freyer Stowasser (eds), *Islamic Law and the Challenges of Modernity* (Altamira Press 2004) 55–80 (citing examples of constitutional texts of Arab countries which cite shari'a as a source of law and the effect of these provisions).

source of law – the weakest formulation of a supremacy clause – in the
constitution means that it becomes possible for many to argue that Islam
authoritatively forms the "fundamental legal framework."[18]

Using their total scores, we ranked all countries according to their
Islamicity. The more a constitution promises with respect to Islam, the more
Islamic it is and the higher its ranking. Thus, a score of zero indicates that the
country in question has not undergone any degree of constitutional
Islamization, while scores above zero illustrate Islamization. The higher the
number, the greater the Islamic credentials of that country's constitution.

Table 2.2 demonstrates the ranking of the constitutions of OIC countries
according to the degree of Islamicity.

TABLE 2.2. *Islamic Constitutions Index*

Rank	Countries	Sum
1	Iran 1979 (rev. 1989)	26
2	Saudi Arabia 1992 (rev. 2005)	23
3	Maldives 2008	17
4	Pakistan 1973 (reinst. 2002, rev. 2012)	16
5	Somalia 2012	14
6	Afghanistan 2004	13
7	Yemen 1991 (rev. 2001)	13
8	Bahrain 2002	11
9	Iraq 2005	11
10	Algeria 1963 (rev. 2008)	9
11	Mauritania 1991 (rev. 2012)	9
12	Sudan 2005	9
13	Egypt 2014	8
14	Libya 2011	8
15	Oman 1996 (rev. 2011)	8
16	Qatar 2003	8
17	Kuwait 1962 (reinst. 1992)	7
18	Morocco 2011	7
19	United Arab Emirates 1971 (rev. 2004)	7
20	Comoros 2001 (rev. 2009)	6

[18] Brown and Sherif, "Inscribing the Islamic Shari'a" 63.

Rank	Countries	Sum
21	Brunei 1959 (rev. 1984)	5
22	Malaysia 1957 (rev. 1996)	5
23	Syria 2012	5
24	Tunisia 2014 (Draft translation)	5
25	Jordan 1952 (rev. 2011)	4
26	Bangladesh 1972 (reinst. 1986, rev. 2011)*	2
27	Djibouti 1992 (rev. 2010)	1
28	Albania 1998 (rev. 2008)	0
29	Azerbaijan 1995 (rev. 2009)*	0
30	Benin 1990*	0
31	Burkina Faso 1991 (rev. 2012)*	0
32	Cameroon 1972 (rev. 2008)*	0
33	Chad 1996 (rev. 2005)*	0
34	Côte d'Ivoire 2000*	0
35	Gabon 1991 (rev. 1997)*	0
36	Gambia 1996 (rev. 2004)*	0
37	Guinea 2010*	0
38	Guinea-Bissau 1984 (rev. 1991)*	0
39	Guyana 1980 (rev. 1995)*	0
40	Indonesia 1945 (reinst. 1959, rev. 2002)	0
41	Kazakhstan 1995 (rev. 1998)*	0
42	Kyrgyz Republic 2010*	0
43	Lebanon 1926 (rev. 2004)	0
44	Mali 1992*	0
45	Mozambique 2004 (rev. 2007)*	0
46	Niger 2010*	0
47	Nigeria 1999*	0
48	Senegal 2001 (rev. 2009)*	0
49	Sierra Leone 1991 (reinst. 1996, rev. 2008)	0
50	Surinam 1987 (rev. 1992)	0
51	Tajikistan 1994 (rev. 2003)*	0
52	Togo 1992 (rev. 2007)*	0
53	Turkey 1982 (rev. 2002)*	0
54	Turkmenistan 2008*	0
55	Uganda 1995 (rev. 2005)*	0
56	Uzbekistan 1992*	0

Source: Ahmed, Gouda, and Ginsburg, "Islamic Constitutionalism Project."

The rankings illuminate the world of constitutional Islamization. The top rankings of Saudi Arabia and Iran also confirm popular perceptions in some sense. However, contrary to the popular imagination, Somalia and the Maldives also do not lag far behind Iran and Saudi Arabia. The results for Turkey and the Central Asian countries are not surprising. These countries have expressed deep commitments to secularism in their constitution, and some regimes in these countries have often suppressed the free exercise of Islam.[19]

The Index, most importantly, allows for differentiation between various degrees and layers of constitutional Islamization. It illustrates that "constitutional Islamization" is not a monolithic phenomenon. Rather, its occurrence immensely varies across the globe. Some countries have much more "Islamic" constitutions than others and some Islamic clauses matter much more than others in terms of their potential effects in the country's normative constitutional order. For instance, although the Saudi Basic Law makes many references to Islam, it is really the Iranian Constitution which is more "Islamic" in substance. Our analysis and Index add more nuance and sophistication to our understanding of the world of Islamic constitutions. Most importantly, it allows us to test various questions that provide novel insights into the issues related to Islam, democracy, and human rights. Most of these questions remained untested empirically until this was explored by Ahmed and Gouda.

2.4 CORRELATIONS

2.4.1 *Population and Geography*

The Index in Table 2.2 illustrates that 60 percent of countries with a Muslim majority have constitutions that are Islamized. There are also countries with large Muslim majorities that have no degree of constitutional Islamization. To this end, eighteen Muslim-majority countries, including Azerbaijan, Mali, and the Kyrgyz Republic, either explicitly demarcate state and religion in their constitutions or make no mention of Islam. Countries that have the most Islamic constitutions, including Iran, Saudi Arabia, Pakistan, and the Maldives, also have a religiously homogenous population with over 90 percent Muslims. It means the trend unsurprisingly remains: the higher the percentage of Muslims in the country's population, the more "Islamic" its constitution will be. The density of Muslim population, however, is not directly

---

[19] "*" denotes all Muslim-majority countries that have explicitly declared secularism as a constitutional principle. Bangladesh is quite interesting; it adopts secularism as a constitutional principle but also makes Islam the state religion.

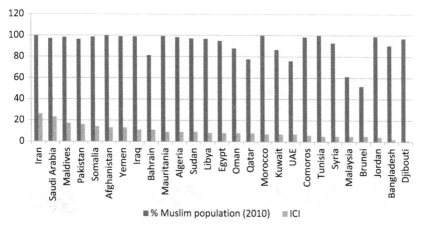

FIGURE 2.1. Levels of Islamicity vs Muslim population percent

correlated with the level of Islamicity in a constitution, but it certainly increases the probability of constitutional Islamization. We also find that the Central Asian countries, in contrast to the majority of Muslim states, show zero constitutional Islamization with a very low demand for shari'a to be the official law of the land.[20] On the other hand, in the Middle East and North Africa, where polls show a high demand for Islamic law to be applied, there are also relatively high degrees of constitutional Islamization. This illustrates that democratic demand perhaps does partly influence the degree of adoption of Islamic clauses in constitutions.

See Figure 2.1 for a side-by-side comparison of Islamicity vs Muslim population. The comparison excludes the countries that have zero Islamicity in their constitution.

Taking geography into consideration, there seems to be significant variance of Islamicity among different geographic regions. The Central Asian countries and European Muslim-majority states have zero constitutional Islamization. In Southeast Asia, Malaysia's constitution is Islamized to some degree, so is that of Brunei. Even though Indonesia's constitution is not Islamized, it does make references to "God." In South Asia, the constitution of every Muslim country – Bangladesh, Pakistan, the Maldives, and Afghanistan – is Islamized. In the Middle East and North Africa too, the constitution of every Muslim country, with the exception of Lebanon, is Islamized. Africa presents some mixed results: some Muslim countries (e.g., Sierra Leone) are silent on the

[20] "Beliefs About Sharia" (*Pew Research Center*, April 30, 2013) <www.pewforum.org/2013/04/30/the-worlds-muslims-religion-politics-society-beliefs-about-sharia/> accessed June 20, 2020.

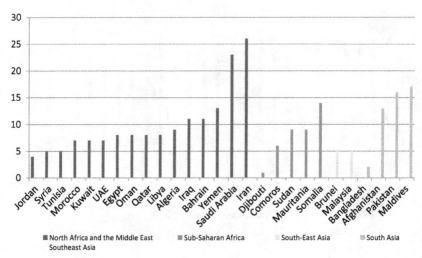

FIGURE 2.2. Levels of Islamicity and regions

place of Islam in the constitution. Others (such as Mali and Senegal) expressly declare a commitment to secularism, while some states (including Somalia and Djibouti) have undergone constitutional Islamization. Further, the constitutions of Muslim countries in South Asia and the Middle East and North Africa register the highest levels of Islamicity. This variance in Islamicity based on geographical location is perhaps due to a number of factors, including colonial history, as is explored in in the following pages; distance from the epicenter of Islam (Mecca/Medina in Saudi Arabia); the means by which Islam spreads; the agents of religious spread (i.e., military vs traders); and so forth.

See a geographical illustration of constitutional Islamization in Figure 2.2 and notice the absence of Central Asian and many African countries that have a Muslim majority.

2.4.2 *Islam and Human Rights*

The interaction between constitutional Islamization and human rights has time and again remained under contestation in the popular imagination. Western constitutionalist thought has generally tended to view the Islamic world as the "antithesis of constitutional government."[21] This narrative has

---

[21] Nathan J Brown, *Constitutions in a Nonconstitutional World: Arab Basic Laws and the Prospects for Accountable Government* (State University of New York Press 2001) (discussing the perceived incompatibility of the Islamic world and constitutionalism by Western scholars such as Montesquieu).

penetrated not only academic but also policy thinking in the United States and Europe. The House of Lords in the United Kingdom stated that shariʻa was "wholly incompatible" with human rights legislation.[22] A number of US states have also attempted to enact laws that forbid state courts from considering Islamic law when deciding cases.[23] Similarly, during the drafting of the Iraqi constitution, there was much discomfort within Washington about the possible inclusion of Islamic law in the constitution.[24] Voll notes that, in these concerns, there is an implicit assumption that an "Islamic" state, even if democratically established, would be transformed into an illiberal and undemocratic "theocracy."[25]

Using the data of the Comparative Constitutions Project, the relation between the Islamicity of a constitution and the number of constitutional rights is investigated in Table 2.3.

In general, there seems to be no direct correlation between the number of rights in a constitution and its *degree* of Islamicity; in fact, it seems that constitutions with a high degree of Islamicity sometimes have a larger number of rights than *less* Islamic constitutions. For example, the Maldives's constitution has a very high Islamicity index, yet it also has the second highest number of rights (out of 45 Muslims countries), more than many Muslim countries that have less Islamic constitutions. Nevertheless, constitutions of Muslim-majority countries that have zero levels of Islamicity, on average, contain a higher number of rights than constitutions of Muslim countries that have *some* level of Islamicity. This certainly does not necessarily mean the Islamicity caused a smaller number of rights or that it is in tension with rights. Indeed, the next chapters demonstrate that sometimes the adoption of Islamic supremacy clauses assists and legitimizes the insertion of rights in a constitution. Certainly, there are many more factors that would dictate the adoption

---

[22] Afua Hirsch, "Sharia Law Incompatible with Human Rights Legislation, Lords say" Guardian (October 23, 2008) <www.guardian.co.uk/world/2008/oct/23/religion-islam> accessed June 20, 2020.

[23] "Oklahoma Sharia Law Blocked by Federal Judge" Huffington Post (May 25, 2011) <http://www.huffingtonpost.com/2010/11/08/oklahoma-sharia-law-struck-down-_n_780632.html> accessed June 20, 2020 (discussing the legal debate around Oklahoma's attempt at banning state courts from considering Islamic law when deciding cases). Thirteen US states have introduced bills to circumvent the application of sharia. See Zaid Jilani, "At Least 13 States Have Introduced Bills Guarding Against Non-Existent Threat of Sharia Law" Think Progress (February 8, 2011) <http://thinkprogress.org/politics/2011/02/08/142590/sharia-states/?mobile=nc.>.

[24] L Paul Bremer III, *My Year in Iraq: The Struggle to Build a Future of Hope* (Threshold Editions 2006) 224 (for a discussion of Iraqi constitutional process and role of Grand Ayatollah Sistani).

[25] John O Voll, "Islam and Democracy: Is Modernization a Barrier" (2007) 1(1) Religion Compass 170, 171.

TABLE 2.3. *Islamicity of constitutions and rights*

Countries	ICI	Rights
Iran 1979 (rev. 1989)	26	44
Saudi Arabia 1992 (rev. 2005)	23	13
Maldives 2008	17	72
Pakistan 1973 (reinst. 2002, rev. 2012)	16	43
Somalia 2012	14	N/A
Afghanistan 2004	13	36
Yemen 1991 (rev. 2001)	13	32
Bahrain 2002	11	43
Iraq 2005	11	51
Algeria 1963 (rev. 2008)	9	36
Mauritania 1991 (rev. 2012)	9	30
Sudan 2005	9	48
Egypt 2014	8	N/A
Libya 2011	8	35
Oman 1996 (rev. 2011)	8	39
Qatar 2003	8	32
Kuwait 1962 (reinst. 1992)	7	N/A
Morocco 2011	7	51
United Arab Emirates 1971 (rev. 2004)	7	30
Comoros 2001 (rev. 2009)	6	23
Brunei 1959 (rev. 1984)	5	2
Malaysia 1957 (rev. 1996)	5	30
Syria 2012	5	41
Tunisia 2014 (Draft Translation)	5	N/A
Jordan 1952 (rev. 2011)	4	28
Bangladesh 1972 (reinst. 1986, rev. 2011)*	2	47
Djibouti 1992 (rev. 2010)	1	25
Albania 1998 (rev. 2008)	0	75
Azerbaijan 1995 (rev. 2009)*	0	70
Benin 1990*	0	42
Burkina Faso 1991 (rev. 2012)	0	52
Cameroon 1972 (rev. 2008)*	0	32
Chad 1996 (rev. 2005)	0	44
Côte d'Ivoire 2000*	0	35

Countries	ICI	Rights
Gabon 1991 (rev. 1997)*	o	33
Gambia 1996 (rev. 2004)	o	61
Guinea 2010	o	43
Guinea-Bissau 1984 (rev. 1991)*	o	46
Guyana 1980 (rev. 1995)*	o	55
Indonesia 1945 (reinst. 1959, rev. 2002)	o	31
Kazakhstan 1995 (rev. 1998)	o	56
Kyrgyz Republic 2010	o	68
Lebanon 1926 (rev. 2004)	o	13
Mali 1992	o	42
Mozambique 2004 (rev. 2007)*	o	63
Niger 2010	o	46
Nigeria 1999*	o	55
Senegal 2001 (rev. 2009)	o	31
Sierra Leone 1991 (reinst. 1996, rev. 2008)	o	55
Surinam 1987 (rev. 1992)	o	46
Tajikistan 1994 (rev. 2003)	o	64
Togo 1992 (rev. 2007)*	o	48
Turkey 1982 (rev. 2002)	o	66
Turkmenistan 2008	o	54
Uganda 1995 (rev. 2005)*	o	69
Uzbekistan 1992	o	53

of rights; for example, rights have become more ubiquitous in constitutions adopted recently – that is, time is a factor.

2.5 COLONIAL HISTORY AND ISLAMIZATION

Perhaps the most interesting and novel observation is the existence of a relationship between colonialism and constitutional Islamization. Although the two states that have the most Islamic constitutions, Iran and Saudi Arabia, were never colonized, in general, we find that Muslim-majority countries that were colonized by the British witness relatively higher levels of Islamization in their constitution than countries that were colonized by the French and Soviets. Indeed, no country in the French colonial tradition has adopted the

Islamic repugnancy clause (which makes all laws repugnant to Islam void and could arguably be thought of as the strongest entrenchment of Islam in a constitution). In contrast, no Muslim-majority country in Central Asia that was colonized by the Soviets has adopted any Islamic clauses in its constitution. It can be argued that the colonial structures have enduring legacies on legal systems, long after the colonial power had vanished.[26]

Some scholars suggest that there are correlations between economic outcomes, legal rules, and legal origin. Legal origin means whether a country's legal system is based on British, French, German, or Scandinavian civil law and the important implications for economic outcomes. That is, European powers imposed their legal system on their colonies and depending on the colonizer, this would result in a common law or civil law system being inherited, which in turn would affect economic outcomes. The argument goes that countries that received civil law as compared to common law may achieve different economic results.[27] This work was expanded by the focus on "colonial history" as an important factor; that is, countries had different outcomes not simply because of the legal system they inherited but also the differing attitude of the colonizer to educational policy, health policy, and local administration and self-government; it seeks to show that the identity of the colonizer is a predictor of postcolonial growth rates.[28] We take this analysis further to ask the important question of whether Islamization of Muslim countries is partly dependent on colonial legacy.

That is, can the identity of the dominant colonizer predict, at least partly, postcolonial political entrenchment of Islam within the public space? It is true that colonial structures may have enduring legacies on legal systems, long after the colonial power has packed up and moved home. Figure 2.3 certainly suggests to some degree that states that were colonized by the British have, to a certain extent, experienced higher levels of constitutional Islamization vis-à-vis states that were colonized by the French.[29] Certainly, the British and the

---

[26] Daniel M Klerman and others, "Legal Origin or Colonial History?" (2011) 3(1) Journal of Legal Analysis 379, 380.

[27] Rafael La Porta, Florencio Lopez-De-Silanes, and Andrei Shleifer, "The Economic Consequences of Legal Origins" (2008) 46 Journal of Economic Literature 285; Edward Glaeser and Andrei Shleifer, "Legal Origins" (2002) 117 (4) Quarterly Journal of Economics 1,193.

[28] Klerman and others, "Legal Origin or Colonial History?" 379, 380.

[29] Soviet colonized states (and others e.g., Mali and Senegal) are not included in Figure 2.3 as they have no Islamic clauses in their constitutions. Some qualifications should be made to the categorization of the states: (i) some states (e.g,. Syria) were colonized for short periods of time and hence the impact of colonial structures may have been significantly less prevalent than in states such as India, (ii) some states (e.g., Qatar) were Ottoman territories before they became

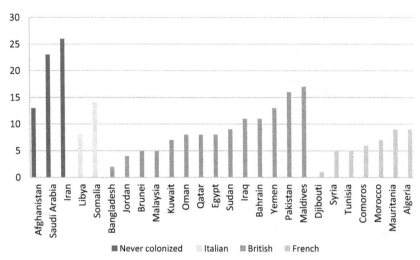

FIGURE 2.3. Constitutional Islamization and colonization (British, French, and Italian)

French – two of the three major foreign powers – ruled over vast Muslim territories and significant parts of Africa, Asia, and the Arab world during the colonization process.[30] As David Motadel observes,

In the heyday of empire, European powers ruled over most parts of the Islamic world. No ruler on earth governed more Muslim subjects than the British monarch. The British, French, Russian, and Dutch empires each accommodated more Muslims than any independent Muslim state. European politicians and colonial officials believed Islam to be of considerable political significance and were quite cautious when it came to matters of the religious life of their Muslim subjects. Governing the religious affairs of Muslims became a crucial aspect of imperial rule. In the colonies, European officials regularly employed religious leaders and Islamic institutions to

European protectorates and hence may have seen very little European infringement on Muslim legal structures, and (iii) although some states (e.g., Egypt and India) were colonized by one dominant state (e.g., Britain), they may have been influenced by short periods of colonization by other powers during different periods.

[30] SV Nasr, "European Colonialism and the Emergence of Modern Muslim States" in John L Esposito (ed) *The Oxford History of Islam* (Oxford Islamic Studies Online) <www.oxfordislamicstudies.com/article/book/islam-9780195107999/islam-9780195107999-chapter-13> (accessed April 6, 2021) (arguing that the colonization of Muslim territories began with the rise of European empires, the conquest of India, and the scramble for Africa in the nineteenth century. Its last phase included the division of the Arab territories of the Ottoman Empire after World War I. The Dutch ruled over territories that later became Indonesia, and the Germans, Spanish, Portuguese, and Russians held Muslim territories in East Africa, the Philippines, Malaya [what is now known as Malaysia], the Caucasus, and Central Asia).

enhance imperial authority. At the same time, the European empires were challenged by religious resistance movements and Islamic insurgency.[31]
Yet, as he adds, despite this,

> Religious life in the European empires was shaped not by Christian mission-aries but by adherents of non-Christian religions. European emperors and empresses ruled over Muslims, Sikhs, Buddhists, Hindus, and followers of numerous African religions. Religious affiliation was an important lens through which colonial officials viewed their subjects. Across the world, the governing of religion was a pivotal concern of imperial authorities. In the European empires, nowhere was this perceived to be of greater importance than in Islamic areas, as Muslims were usually considered especially sensitive subjects and prone to revolt.[32]

The colonial era ended after World War II, when Britain and France with-drew from the majority of their colonial territories and Muslim states began to emerge from 1947 onwards (although some, such as Iran or Afghanistan, had always remained independent, albeit nominally). The emergence of Muslim states involved negotiated withdrawals of colonial powers, as was the case in Malaya, India, and the Persian Gulf emirates, as well as brutal and bloody wars of independence, as in Algeria, and of course, new constitutions. The decol-onization also occurred in spurts, as European powers sought to protect their economic interests following their political and military withdrawals in a changing global environment. Iran in 1953 and Egypt in 1956 were, arguably, examples of the reassertion of colonialism, which nevertheless marked the gradual yet effective end of direct European rule over Muslims.

To be sure, the states that are the subject of data collection in this chapter have different histories, cultural setups, political histories, economic circum-stances, knowledge networks, geographic dynamics, and legal systems, all of which will no doubt affect the Islamic content of the constitution within public life. Accordingly, we do not argue that colonial origins are the key determinant of Islamic constitutional legacy – to make such a claim would require more work. Yet many of the states, with the notable exceptions of Saudi Arabia and Iran seem to have been colonized by one or more foreign powers to some degree at some point prior to independence. Thus, it is perhaps not wrong to assert that colonial history seems to have some bearing on Muslim countries' constitutional experimentation with Islam. As Vali Nasr points out,

---

[31] David Motadel, "Islam and the European Empires" (2012) 55 The Historical Journal 831.
[32] Motadel, "Islam and the European Empires" 831.

The legacy of colonialism is key in explaining both the diversity and the unity of different experiments with state formation in the Muslim world. Just as Islam, ethnic identity, social characteristics, and other indigenous religious and cultural factors can explain the commonalities between Muslim states – and conversely, economics, ideology, and leadership can explain divergences – colonialism too can explain the points of convergence and divergence in experiences with state formation across the Muslim world.[33]

Although various colonizers had similar aims, they implemented wholly different policies and approached their mandates differently. That is, although their means and effects varied with regards to the treatment of Islam, European colonial powers partook in several measures ranging from codification to modifying or co-opting Islamic institutions like mosques, law courts, and religious educational institutions (madrasas) in the colonial state and inquiring into the control and regulation of religious rituals like the pilgrimage to Mecca. In effect, European authorities institutionalized Islam as a part of the "modern state," so as to control and utilize it.[34] And, in doing so, as one scholar writes, quoting the example of Nigeria and the British, "The introduction, or imposition as some say, of the English common law, ideas and institutions into Nigeria has had tremendous influence in changing the pre-colonial Islamic legal system ... as a result of the colonial encounter, Islamic law has been transformed."[35] Yet where Islamic "law" was well established, the colonial regime could not simply eliminate it and, instead, had to adopt creatve mechanisms to modify it; to disband it completely would have invited significant resistance.[36]

Accordingly, while countries as diverse as Uzbekistan, Saudi Arabia, and Pakistan are all overwhelmingly Muslim, it is also their remarkably different experience (or inexperience) of colonial interactions that have had some influence in shaping the levels of Islam in their constitutional framework. The following section, exploring the history of British, French, and Soviet treatments of Islam in India, West Africa/Algeria, and Central Asia, respectively, seeks to show that there was indeed significant variation in terms of how colonial powers treated Islam in their colonies, and this may have contributed to the different paths various countries adopted in terms of Islamization. That is, while the space for Islam and Islamic law stayed very much intact (although

---

[33] Nasr, "European Colonialism and the Emergence of Modern Muslim States."
[34] Motadel, "Islam and the European Empires" 833.
[35] Auwalu Hamsxu Yadudu, "Colonialism and the Transformation of the Substance and Form of Islamic Law in the Northern States of Nigeria" (1991) Journal of Law and Religion 17, 22.
[36] Allan Christelow, *Muslim Courts and the French Colonial State in Algeria* (Princeton University Press 1985) 6.

heavily modified in substance) under British colonization, the French tried
rather more aggressively to impose their own "secular" vision. In contrast, a
decimating, brutal treatment of Islam and Islamic institutions occurred under
Soviet colonialism. This variation in treatment and space given to Islam in
public life could explain modern-day variations in the scope of constitutional
Islamization and, perhaps, Islamic law seen in Muslim-majority countries
today. That is, while the accommodation of Islamic institutions and laws
within British India and other colonies may have allowed Islam to remain,
and indeed prosper as, an active part of public life, the subjugation of the same
by the Soviets (and less so the French) left little space for Islam in their
colonies, thus explaining its limited importance within the constitutional
sphere of countries colonized by the French and Soviets.

2.5.1 *British Colonialism in India*

At its peak, the British Empire was the foremost global power. By 1922, it held
sway over about 458 million people – one-fifth of the world's population at the
time. As a result, its political, legal, linguistic, and cultural legacy is widespread. Although several territories where the British ruled include sizable
Muslim populations, including British Malaya, Sudan, Kenya, and Nigeria,
British India was perhaps the most significant in terms of Muslim population
and is thus the key focus of this section (although Nigeria is discussed later,
primarily to compare the French treatment of Islam in that same region). The
Dutch Republic, England, France, and Denmark-Norway all established
trading posts in India in the early seventeenth century, but it was only in the
eighteenth century that Britain ascended as the sole European power, rapidly
expanding its indirect power until after the Indian Uprising of 1857, when the
British Crown began direct rule from 1858 to 1947. At that time, the British
began to rule over a Muslim community unified at best by a few common
rituals and the beliefs and aspirations of a majority but not the totality of its
scholars. Yet Muslims constituted but a fifth of British India's population – a
minority unevenly distributed and territorially consolidated in Sind and the
Western Punjab.[37]

   The British, unlike the French and Soviets, adopted a relatively neutral
stance toward religion: Indeed, as Motadel notes, in India, while this active
religious neutrality of the colonial state left the public sphere open for
missionary activities of Christian organizations, "missionaries often acted

---

[37] Peter Hardy, *The Muslims of British India* (Cambridge University Press 1972)

outside of colonized territories, imperial rulers usually pursued a policy of religious neutrality and non-interference and refused to give missions special status in the colonies in order to avoid religious unrest."[38] That is, the colonial state attempted not to interfere with native religions and adopted a "secularity" in India that was much stronger than in Britain itself. It considered the separation of church and state essential to their ability to govern India as "externality and neutrality became the tropes of a state that tried to project itself as playing the role of a transcendent arbiter in a country divided along religious lines."[39] To be clear, secularism was introduced not as a coherent and positive doctrine but rather as a strategy of colonial rule, where the religious neutrality of the state meant noninterference in matters of the religion and customs of the native subjects; colonial codification of religious laws, for example, limited the authority of religious institutions in the realm of law – for example, by imposing the structure of English common law, thereby producing so-called Anglo-Hindu law for Hindus and Anglo-Muhammadan law for Muslims.[40]

As part of this approach, one of the goals of the British was to preserve and transform "Islamic law" as it was understood in India. In 1772, Hastings Regulations reaffirmed the principle whereby religious law would be applied to Hindus and Muslims on issues of inheritance, marriage, caste, and other religious customs and institutions. Lord Cornwallis, governor-general between 1786 and 1793, further extended Hastings's preservationist policy so as to avoid "collision with the habits and prejudices" of local people.[41] The British realized that the implementation of religious norms that might win the allegiance of elite groups was essential to exert control, minimize resistance, and collect tax revenues and debt;[42] accordingly, they preserved "indigenous law" because their early colonial state was in a precarious position. By giving the impression that Muslims were regulated under Islamic law, "the British literally erased the fact that they had displaced Mughal suzerainty."[43] These views led to significant accommodation in that the policy was that "indigenous

---

[38] Motadel, "Islam and the European Empires" 832.
[39] Peter Van Der Veer, "Secrecy and Publicity in the South Asian Public Arena" in Armando Salvatore and Dale E Eickleman (eds), *Public Islam and the Common Good* (Brill 2004) 33.
[40] Abdullahi Ahmed An-Na'im, *Islam and the Secular State: Negotiating the Future of Shari'a* (Harvard University Press 2008) 147.
[41] Eric Stokes, *The English Utilitarians and India* (Oxford University Press 1990) 23.
[42] Elisa Giunchi, "The Reinvention of Shari'a under the British Raj: In Search of Authenticity and Certainty" (2010) 69 The Journal of Asian Studies 1,119, 1,126.
[43] Scott Alan Kugle, "Framed, Blamed and Renamed: The Recasting of Islamic Jurisprudence in Colonial South Asia" (2001) 35 Modern Asian Studies 257, 267.

law should be applied to the extent that it was more 'consonant to the ideas, manners and inclinations' of the population than other legal systems … expecting the local population to adhere to an external value system would be, in fact, both irrational and unjust."[44] Giunchi writes that the British also had respect for India: They thought that India had been the seat of a great civilization that had undergone, like all other civilizations, progressive deterioration; the idea was that decline could be reversed by going back to the "pristine authenticity of Indian civilization, which was to be found in its religious texts."[45] Giunchi observes,

> Legal transformation was indeed marked, at least until the second half of the nineteenth century, by a certain idealization of the Orient and by a parallel discontent with British society. Reliance on religious texts rather than unwritten customs also responded to practical motives – the need to ascertain legal rules quickly; to limit the complexities of local mores, in the assumption (which was to prove wrong) that textual sources contained clear-cut rules; and to forge an alliance with the religious establishment, thus ensuring the loyalty of a population that was imagined as deeply religious.[46]

Respecting local customs and legislation in India, however, created a paradox for the colonial power when these norms either clashed with the laws of England or, for one reason or another, were "morally" repugnant in their view. In the interests of colonial order, a hierarchy needed to be established. Thus, the British implemented two types of repugnancy doctrines. First, the imperial government reserved the ability to disallow legislation in the colonies that was "repugnant to the laws of England."[47] That is, legislation could be declared invalid if it was deemed inconsistent with the laws of England. This was the case, for example, in Australia, Canada, and New Zealand. Second, and more importantly for present purposes, in other colonies and certainly throughout Africa, magistrates had the power to refuse the application of customary laws if, essentially, they offended "civilized standards." This doctrine was justified on the basis that it would eradicate unjust customs.[48]

---

[44] Giunchi, "Reinvention of Sharī'a under the British Raj" 1,124.
[45] Giunchi, "Reinvention of Sharī'a under the British Raj" 1,124.
[46] Giunchi, "Reinvention of Sharī'a under the British Raj" 1,124.
[47] Damen Ward, "Legislation, Repugnancy and the Disallowance of Colonial Laws: The Legal Structure of Empire and Lloyd's Case (1844)" (2010) 41 Victoria University of Wellington Law Review 381, 382.
[48] Bonny Ibhawoh, *Imperialism and Human Rights: Colonial Discourses of Rights and Liberties in African History* (State University of New York Press, 2007) 60.

Although the specific wording of the clause varied between colonies,[49] the gist was that customary laws were acceptable to the colonial administrators only if they were not repugnant to natural justice, equity, and good conscience and if they were not incompatible either directly or by implication with any law for the time being in force.[50]

The British also took the decisive step toward implementing a modern legal system for Islamic law, initiating a process that might be called the expropriation of law, which made the power to find, declare, and apply law a monopoly of government, whereas previously, a number of varied laws and customs had applied to the population at large.[51] The British view was that laws should be fixed and predictable. This allowed them to take control of Islamic law as they announced the need to publish codes of Islamic (and Hindu) laws so as to shift power from the local legal experts into the further control of English experts.[52] Only those sources could be used in the courts that had been processed through translation and codification. In order to systematize these compilations, selected cases were elevated into general principles and propositions, which could suffice as precedent for all later decisions. The greater the distance of a text from the original sources, the greater its frequency of use in courts. The British did not see their changes to Islamic law as codification; rather, they assumed that Islamic law had already been codified centuries ago, when "the door of ijtihad was closed."[53] By assuming the reality of taqlid, the British essentially created stagnation and enforced it, and this stagnation continues even today.[54] As Giunchi notes, in doing so, de facto, it was the colonial administrators and scholars who, driven by their stereotypes as well as by their needs, in effect made Islam a rigid law-centered entity in the lives and minds of the colonized peoples. For an Islamic norm to be considered valid, it had to be "ancient, certain and invariable" – the characteristics that had been initially assigned to religious texts – in addition to not contravening express law

---

[49] Gerald Caplan, "The Making of 'Natural Justice' in British Africa: An Exercise in Comparative Law" (1964) 13(1) Journal of Public Law 120.

[50] Bethel Chuks Uweru, "Repugnancy Doctrine and Customary Law in Nigeria: A Positive Aspect of British Colonialism" (2008) 2 African Research Review 286, 292. The repugnancy doctrine in Nigeria emerged from the decision in the case of *Eshugbaye Eleko v Government of Nigeria* (1931). In that case, Lord Atkin held, "The court cannot itself transform a barbarous custom into a milder one. If it stands in its barbarous character it must be rejected as repugnant to natural justice, equity and good conscience."

[51] Marc Galanter, "The Displacement of Traditional Law in Modern India" (1968) 24 Journal of Social Issues 65, 67.

[52] Kugle, "Framed, Blamed and Renamed" 271.

[53] Kugle, "Framed, Blamed and Renamed" 297.

[54] Kugle, "Framed, Blamed and Renamed" 297.

and British ideas of morality encapsulated in the formula of justice, equity, and good conscience.[55] This similar kind of experiment was also conducted on "Hindu" law or "Anglo-Hindu" law; thus Anglo-Hindu law was born, which Derrett and others have referred to as a bogus system.[56] And it seemed to have worked well. M. P. Jain observes,

> Hastings's policy of preserving the indigenous Indian laws came to be increasingly appreciated and eulogised. It came to be recognised that to ensure stability of the British Government in India, it was of fundamental importance that affections of the Indians should be conciliated, and that nothing could be more effective from this point of view than tolerance in matters of religion, and adoption of such indigenous institutions of the country as did not clash with the laws and interests of the conquerors.[57]

This restructuring of Islamic law into a fixed system rather than a disparate and diverse set of customs and rules is in some respects a natural precursor to it being "constitutionalized" and "legalized" today, as Islamic law became "a reified and static entity captured in a paradox, [as] the shariah was largely codified by the British act of wresting political power away from Muslims"[58] even as "[British notions of 'justice and right'] opened the floodgate to conceptual invasion by English presuppositions and utilitarian ideals ... in fact, by the close of the eighteenth century, we cannot really call Indian law 'Islamic.' Rather, the hybrid and oxymoronic term 'Anglo-Muhammadan' is more accurate."[59]

This reconstruction of shari'a in the Anglo-Muhammadan legal system, in particular, transformed what had been a morally driven and contextual method of reasoning into a "system."[60] This approach, inadvertently perhaps, also contributed a great deal to rising religious consciousness among Muslims and Hindus in India. Neutrality and "secularization" led to Hindu and Muslim forms of modernism leading to the establishment of modern Hindu and Muslim schools, universities, and hospitals, superseding or marginalizing precolonial forms of education. Ironically, it is this "Anglo-Muhammadan system" of Islam that has now spread into the wider political consciousness of

---

[55] Giunchi, "Reinvention of Shari'a under the British Raj" 1,132–33.
[56] Werner Menski, *Hindu Law: Beyond Tradition and Modernity* (Oxford University Press, 2009) 165.
[57] MP Jain, *Indian Legal History* (5th ed, M. M. Tripathi Pvt Ltd, 1990) 580.
[58] Kugle, "Framed, Blamed and Renamed" 258.
[59] Kugle, "Framed, Blamed and Renamed" 266.
[60] Giunchi, "Reinvention of Shari'a under the British Raj" 1,120.

Muslims in South Asia as Muslims ironically accepted this definition of "Islam" as a vehicle to agitate for political rights and nationalist agendas.[61]

Thus, far from having a secularizing influence on Indian society, the modernizing project of the British state in fact gave modern religion a strong new impulse as Hindus and Muslims became conscious of their "religious" identity that subsequently provided impetus to the demands for nations divided on religious lines and "Islamic" and "Hindu" communities, which eventually culminated in calls for Islamizing the constitution, entrenching Islamic law/parties, developing an "Islamic state," and so forth. Indeed, paradoxically, this earlier migration of a "diverse" system of Islamic law to a fixed, written, codified body by the British is now the rallying cry of those who wish to "Islamize" constitutions in countries like Pakistan; they reminisce about a glorious past where Islamic law was applied and justice prevailed with little awareness that this idea of a fixed "Islam" in political and legal life is very much a product of British colonialism.

A reified understanding of Islam continued to be reinforced in the modern era, which adopted its form but could not fulfill its promises. The British did not understand the consequences of their actions, nor did they have to bear them.[62] Today, it has not only given birth to but changed the boundaries of the debate revolving around Islam in constitutional life. The debates in the Constituent Assembly of Pakistan reveal that even in the early 1950s, Islam was widely seen by the political class as an ideology containing a set of norms to be applied. Upholding shari'a became part of the state's search for legitimation and unity and allowed it to cement its alliance with religious groups in the face of increasing Islamist and ethnic challenges, while at the same time preserving its legal structure, which was heavily influenced by British procedural norms. Further, even leading Islamic intellectuals such as Maulana Maududi understood the term shari'a to mean exactly this fixed system of state-driven and -enforced law inherited from the British.[63] Thus, it is right, as Giunchi notes that "while in Mughal times, the legitimacy of the rulers derived from formal abidance to Islam and from patronizing religious institutions and holy men, in Pakistan, the government's legitimacy became increasingly associated with the *actual implementation of Islamic law*, where the latter was interpreted as a set of norms extrapolated selectively from the doctrine . . .."[64]

[61] Menski, *Hindu Law* 303.
[62] Kugle, "Framed, Blamed and Renamed" 312–13.
[63] Kugle, "Framed, Blamed and Renamed" 309.
[64] Giunchi, "Reinvention of Shari'a under the British Raj 1,135–36.

As An-Naim also notes, "British colonial rule – specifically, colonial legislation and the administrative classification of Indians into religious categories –
is usually cited as the key historical frame for the emergence of communal
consciousness among Hindus and Muslims."[65] That is, the period of British
rule gave firmer edges to Muslim identities. There was a sharpening of the
distinction between Muslim and non-Muslim and the development of a
separate Muslim political identity against the claims of an all-inclusive
Indian national identity.[66] So in effect, British perceptions of Indian society,
British fears, and British styles of rule all played their part in making possible
the formal recognition of a Muslim political identity that would be relevant for
a modern state's formation and constitutional politics.[67]

2.5.2 *French Colonialism in West Africa and Algeria*

France colonized several Muslim-majority regions, most notably in Africa: it
controlled the Maghreb through the colony of Algeria, held the protectorate
of Tunisia, and had an emerging sphere of influence in Morocco. While
French control of Muslim regions began with the invasion of Egypt in 1798
(at which point Napoleon controlled Egypt for a period of two years), it was
only after the invasion of Algiers in 1830 that the French had acquired Muslim
subjects and developed institutions for governing them. Later, pursuant to the
Anglo-French Agreement of 1890, France also took over northwestern Africa –
the area that became French North and West Africa.[68]

While the British interfered in Islamic political content, in particular, by
"restructuring" Islamic law and indirectly preempting Muslim consciousness
and giving substance to what is today meant to be the idea of "Islamic law,"
they did not, for the most part, appear to be hostile to Islam or attempt to rid
the colony of it. Indeed, as explained earlier, they expressed a significant
degree of tolerance and noninterference toward the Islamic faith. This con-
trasted significantly with French treatment of Islam in their colonies. French
colonialism continually undermined and destroyed Islamic structures in West
Africa. Scholars of imperialism in West Africa have often characterized
French policies as interventionist and unaccommodating, contrasting them
with British policies of noninterference and accommodation. This can be

---

[65] An-Naim, *Islam and the Secular State* 153.
[66] Francis Robinson, "The British Empire and Muslim Identity in South Asia" (1998)
8 Transactions of the Royal Historical Society 271, 272–73.
[67] Robinson, "The British Empire and Muslim Identity" 278.
[68] David Robinson, *Paths of Accommodation: Muslim Societies and French Colonial Authorities
in Senegal and Mauritania, 1880–1920* (Ohio University Press 2000) 76.

seen, for example, in the French destruction of and surveillance of Islamic institutions in comparison with British rule in Northern Nigeria, where Muslim political and religious institutions remained intact. As David Robinson observes,

> The French feared Islam, recalling its long history of opposition to Christendom as well as its "incursions" into southwestern and southeastern Europe. But they had no illusions about rolling back the Muslim identity of most of their subjects. They would have to establish institutions of control. If they were successful in institution building, and in establishing a certain hegemony as a "Muslim power," they might reduce investment in the apparatus of repression.[69]

The French, particularly in Algeria, had several aspirations with regards to the "*mission civilisatrice*" and the idea of an evolutionary progress of civilization in their colonies with religious rituals and gender disparities to be done away with.[70] The French experience in Algeria was brutal, as assimilation was crucial. The impact of colonial rule in Algeria was "more profound and the eventual process of decolonization more violent, than in virtually any other African or Asian country."[71] French authorities made rigorous efforts to impose the rationality of Roman law on a historically qadi (judge)-based Islamic justice system and, in the process, subordinated local courts to the French courts. Initially, they imposed "direct rule" and attempted to remove all vestiges of the previous Ottoman state – they argued this was simply a colonial leftover from Ottoman rule and that there was indeed no "indigenous" Algerian state. They subsequently sought to disband all tribal structures – political units based on the shared kinship; in 1844, they seized religious endowments and, eventually, in the 1880s, there was a major campaign by the French to eliminate Muslim courts and law schools altogether and put Islamic law entirely in the hands of French judges.[72] Unsurprisingly then, "assimilation in Algeria was a highly restrictive and emotion charged process."[73] Paradoxically, it was such colonial expansion into areas considered to be traditionally within the Islamic sphere that ultimately provoked an Islamic revival with the reemergence of the traditional madrasas.[74]

---

[69] Robinson, *Paths of Accommodation* 76.
[70] Motadel, "Islam and the European Empires" 853.
[71] Christelow, *Muslim Courts and the French Colonial State* 9.
[72] Christelow, *Muslim Courts and the French Colonial State* 14.
[73] Christelow, *Muslim Courts and the French Colonial State* 14.
[74] Christelow, *Muslim Courts and the French Colonial State* 245.

Although Algeria was distinct in that the French were exceptionally strong there due to their acquisition of large areas of land and subsequent domination of politics, the general French pattern of subjugating Islam in its colonies was apparent. For example, with regards to Nigeria also, Motadel contrasts the French approach with that of the British:

> The classic example of the accommodation of Islam in the British empire is West Africa. In the Protectorate of Northern Nigeria, established at the turn of the twentieth century in the territories of the former Sokoto Caliphate, Islamic leaders and institutions enjoyed remarkable autonomy. The system of colonial government established by Frederick Lugar, high commissioner of the Protectorate from 1899 to 1906, has often been described as the major example not only of indirect rule, but also of the accommodation of Islam in the colonial state . . . . Under the control of only a few British officials, Muslim authorities of the Caliphate, most notably local judges and the emirs, were employed to govern on a local level.[75]

Indeed, Yadudu writes that the "British colonial administration actually may have helped the advancement of customary laws through the formalization of their institutions, legislative support, state sponsorship and introduction of some measure of certainty to the substantive rules and principles of these legal systems . . . ."[76] He observes that native institutions continued to function in a traditional way and reforms were gradually introduced. As a result, the native courts were progressively anglicized.[77]

> From the time of the colonial conquest of Northern Nigeria in the early years of the twentieth century up to 1960, the British governed . . . through a system known as indirect rule. This system maintained and utilized the region's existing forms of administration from regional emirs to local judges, rather than replacing them with British officers and institutions . . . . Religious beliefs and actions would only become the business of the colonial administration if they threatened peace and "good order" . . . the British sought to legitimize their rule by maintaining a public image of neutrality towards the various Islamic groups found in Nigeria. . .[78]

Christelow also contrasts the behavior of the French with the British in Northern Nigeria, where until the 1940s, "the British intervened little in the affairs of Islamic law at any level, leaving serious criminal cases and property

---

[75] Motadel, "Islam and the European Empires" 836.
[76] Yadudu, "Colonialism and the Transformation" 112.
[77] Yadudu, "Colonialism and the Transformation" 107.
[78] Jonathan Reynolds, "Good and Bad Muslims: Islam and Indirect Rule in Northern Nigeria" (2001) 34 *The International Journal of African Historical Studies* 601.

disputes in the hands of the traditional rulers, the emirs and leaving the appointment of judges up to them as well ... the controlling hand in judicial affairs remained that of the traditional rulers, and Islamic religious education remained outside the orbit of the colonial state, closely tied to traditional political structures and to communities."[79] In Sudan and Nigeria, under the doctrine of indirect rule, the British delegated local powers of jurisdiction to the holders of Islamic legitimacy, while France, for its part, even when it made use of mediation of the Islamic brotherhoods, always refused to invest them with a recognized legal power. This was in contrast of course to the British approach, where "the whole structure of Islamic government was then left virtually intact. The Sharia ... continued to apply as it had before with the exception that so-called inhumane punishments were replaced by supposedly humane alternatives and so on."[80]

Indeed, this "benign" British system of Indirect Rule in Northern Nigeria was in many ways helpful to Islamic structures as it protected them from the tide of social and political change that might have eroded it. In effect, while British administrators were there to guide or "advise" native rulers and they took some care to ensure that they did not disrupt native culture, tradition, and legitimacy, north of the Nigerian border, in Niger, the French practiced a much different policy where, rather than establishing an "advisory" role for the colonial administration, the French constantly asserted their supremacy, were determined to eliminate any conceivable challenge to their own authority, and trod quite harshly upon the indigenous rulers. In contrast to the British, the French were almost cavalier in replacing chiefs. Indeed, appointments to traditional offices, judgeships, and district headships were made not by the British but by the emir; in effect, the British actively attempted to adapt their method of governance to indigenous rule and customs, while the French made no distinctions among the areas under their sovereignty. Their goal was centralization. It is unsurprising then that the relation between the British political officer and the chief was in general that of an adviser who only in extreme circumstances interfered with the chief and the native authority under him, while the French system placed the chief in an entirely subordinate role to the political officer.[81] Traditional norms of legitimacy were much less important than the ability to speak French or prior service to the colonial

[79] Christelow, *Muslim Courts and the French Colonial State* 272.
[80] Julia Clancy Smith, "Islam and the French Empire in North Africa," in David Motadel (ed) *Islam and the European Empires* (Oxford University Press 2014) 115.
[81] Michael Crowder, "Indirect Rule: French and British Style" (1964) 34 Africa: Journal of the International African Institute 198.

regime. Thus, while official British colonial policy was to maintain, guide and improve the chieftaincy; in contrast, for France, it was "crush and destroy."[82] As Martin Klein has commented,

> The British, though remaining more aloof from African society than the French, respected the African community and attached great importance to judicial proceedings. The French thought more in terms of order, obedience and devotion ... as the French ideal was Napoleonic and Cartesian; rationality, centralization and the imposition of equal sized units. The British ideal – reinforced by Britain's experience in India – was the preservation of traditional status roles and institutions.[83]

In contrast to the French, the British strove to train and to employ local staff in the lower and medium echelons of local administration who were able to climb to comparatively high levels of colonial administration and were quite willing to implement British ideas of colonial modernity.[84]

Even the approach to education was distinct, as while "the British made sincere, if artless, efforts to combine traditional Islamic education and secular education in a single syllabus ... the French ... neglected and sometimes positively discouraged traditional Islamic literacy. Instead, they offered an excellent secular, francophone education that made very little concession to Islam. This created largely secularised indigenous, francophone elite in the towns that was increasingly out of touch with the traditional Islam of the countryside."[85] As a result, the French curriculum of out-and-out francophone secularism has meant that in most of the French colonized territories in Africa today, there has been the emergence of a francophone elite, whose Islam is nominal at best and who have widely adopted a European lifestyle.[86]

Based on their experience in India, the British were perhaps more aware than the French that Islam could not simply be discarded and that the political legitimacy of a foreign government in a Muslim region was closely tied to the popular perception of the rulers as respecting Islam and not attacking it. This is not to say that the British accepted Islamic law unconditionally in Nigeria or indeed in India; they disallowed slavery, mutilation, and

---

[82] William FS Miles, "Partitioned Royalty: The Evolution of Hausa Chiefs in Nigeria and Niger" (1987) 25 Journal of Modern African Studies 233, 238.

[83] Martin A Klein, "Islam and Imperialism in Senegal: Sine-Saloum, 1847–1914" (1969) 74 The American Historical Review 285.

[84] Roman Loimeier, *Muslim Societies in African: A Historical Anthropology* (Indiana University Press, 2013) 281.

[85] Mervyn Hiskett, *The Course of Islam in Africa* (Edinburgh University Press, 1994) 117.

[86] Hiskett, *Course of Islam in Africa* 123.

cases involving capital punishment. However, even then, they allowed the shari'a courts to carry out their own sentences and were careful to deny Christian missionaries significant influence in education as a necessary step toward containing Muslim resentment, realizing that introducing Western education through Christian missionaries would inhibit its acceptance. Interestingly, in 1910 the World Missionary Conference at Edinburgh protested the utilizing of Muslim authorities and administrative personnel in systems of indirect rule and sanctioning Islamic education and law. They claimed that such a policy contravened the general goals of colonial rule, namely spreading (Western) civilization.[87]

This distinction between the French and British treatment of Islam was not merely a question of different conceptions of colonial policy but also concerned a particular perception of Islam.[88] Rather. "French culture [had] maintained strong continuity in its negative view and fear of Islam . . .. The hostility to Islam in France also has roots – and this is something that has been recognized less well – in the direct heritage of the French Revolution and the republic; namely in the spirit accompanying the separation between church and state. Both republicans and radical secularists, who had waged an unfettered struggle against the Roman Catholic Church . . . believed that they were encountering the same adversary again . . .. Their struggle against the Islam that dominated life beyond the Mediterranean was thus a direct extension of their confrontation with Catholicism . . . the administrative reports deriving from the colonial period bear witness to the permanent action against Muslim institutions . . .. In contrast to British colonialism, which had other points of reference and other forms of practice, French colonialism always experienced the Muslim presence in the guise of a counterrevolutionary conspiracy."[89]

Of course, French behavior was not linear across all times and regions; for example, in parts of West Africa, French policy was somewhat less interfering.[90] Nevertheless, even in West Africa, relative leniency did not mean

---

[87] Holger Weiss, "Variations in the Colonial Representation of Islam and Muslims in Northern Ghana, ca. 1900–1930," Working Papers on Ghana: Historical and Contemporary Studies 2 (January 2004).

[88] Jean Louis Triand, "Islam in Africa under French Colonial Rule" in Nehemia Levtzion and Randall L Pouwels (eds) *The History of Islam in Africa* (Ohio University Press 2000) 169.

[89] Triand, "Islam in Africa under French Colonial Rule" 170.

[90] Donal Cruise O'Brien, "Towards an 'Islamic Policy' in French West Africa, 1854–1914" (1967) 8 Journal of African History 303, 311. "While the administration desired to know its enemies and repress movements which were considered hostile or potentially hostile, it was also concerned to reward its friends those Muslim notables whose loyalty was valued. Pilgrimages to Mecca were financed and expedited by the administration for its Muslim supporters . . . French decorations were awarded to faithful friends, probably also with the aim of increasing

noninterference.[91] French attitudes were marked by the recurrent patterns of reaction, rhetoric, and quarantine and an ever persistent fear of the Islamic state.[92] Throughout the twentieth century, colonial agents in French West Africa constantly attempted to manipulate religious practices – and intervened actively in spiritual hierarchies – as a matter of policy.[93] Indeed, French policies toward Islam in West Africa at all times relied on the close surveillance of Islamic structures. Today, this means that the role of Islam in political life is comparatively far more circumscribed in these states as compared to former British colonies; so, for example, in Senegal,[94] a country with a 95 percent Muslim population and where Islam has a history spanning around a thousand years, the French colonial legacy has meant that secular and Islamic education are separated and the government does not interfere with or manage internal religious matters, as "Senegal like many other African states, adopted the political system of the former colonial power, France, ... the bureaucratic centralism, the 'laicistic' school, the organization of the trade unions, the legal system based on the Code Napoleon, down to the routes for regulating traffic. Thus, Article 1 of the Senegalese constitution says: 'The Republic of Senegal is laicistic, democratic and social,' a formula that was taken over from the French constitution of 1958."[95]

2.5.3 *Soviet Colonialism in Central Asia*

While French colonization was far less lenient in terms of accommodating and tolerating Islam in its colonies as compared to the British, the Soviets were far more aggressive and determined in subjugating Islam in Central Asia. Of the fifteen states that emerged after the breakup of the Soviet Union in 1991, six have predominantly Muslim populations (Turkmenistan, Tajikistan,

their importance in the eyes of the population ... the administration, with a view to the formation of loyal intermediaries, also tried to secure a certain degree of control over Muslim education."

[91] Andrew F Clark, "Imperialism, Independence, and Islam in Senegal and Mali" (1999) 46 Africa Today 149.

[92] David Robinson, "French 'Islamic' Policy and Practice in Late Nineteenth-Century Senegal" (1988) 29 Journal of African History 415, 416.

[93] Gregory Mann and Baz Lecocq, "Between Empire, Umma and the Muslim Third World: The French Union and African Pilgrims to Mecca" 27 Comparative Studies of South Asia, African and the Middle East 167.

[94] Clark, "Imperialism, Independence, and Islam" 149–50.

[95] Roman Loimeieir, "The Secular State and Islam in Senegal: Islam in Africa under French Colonial Rule" in David Westerlund, Carl F Hallencreutz, and David Westerhund (eds) *Questioning the Secular State: The Worldwide Resurgence of Religion in Politics* (Hurst and Company, 1996) 183.

Uzbekistan, Kazakhstan, Kyrgyzstan, and Azerbaijan). However, none of their constitutions pay any heed to Islam and often proclaim explicitly that the state is secular and that there is no official recognition of religion.[96] As was the case with the Soviet Union, each state has adopted a constitution that provides expressly for the protection of human rights, and all guarantee the fundamental rights for freedom of religion and conscience and prohibit discrimination based on religion.

In Central Asia, Islam is not completely absent from public life though; indeed, it has witnessed a symbolic revival since the collapse of the Soviet Union as mosques sprang up and all regional governments used, to various degrees, symbols of Islam to enhance national identities and strengthen their rule. For example, Uzbekistan adopted, as its flag, a crescent moon and stars symbolizing Islam; the states circulated banknotes with Islamic symbolism.[97] President Karimov of Uzbekistan, the former First Secretary of the Communist Party, took his presidential oath in 1992 on the Qur'an and then went on a pilgrimage to Mecca. The countries have also become members of the OIC.

Nevertheless, secularism remains an entrenched feature of Central Asian constitutions because by the time the Central Asian states declared independence, Islam had already been viciously subjugated for several decades.[98] As a

---

[96] For example, the 1994 Tajik Constitution states that "the Republic of Tajikistan is a sovereign, democratic, law-governed, secular, and unitary state" ([Article 1] 25); the 1995 Kazakh Constitution states that "the Republic of Kazakhstan proclaims itself a democratic, secular, legal and social state whose highest values are an individual, his life, rights and freedoms" ([Article 1] 26), and the 2007 Kyrgyz Constitution states that "Kyrgyzstan is a sovereign, unitary, democratic Republic, constructed on the basis of a legal secular state" (Article 1). Article 61 of the 1992 Uzbek Constitution implicitly declares Uzbekistan as a secular state by stating that "religious organisations and associations shall be separated from the state and are equal before law."

[97] Almost all of Kazakhstan's banknotes feature the portrait of al-Farabi, an Islamic philosopher and scientist. In Kyrgyzstan, the banknote of 50 soms portrays the Ozgon mosque and the banknote of 1,000 soms displays the sacred mountain of Suleyman in Osh. In Tajikistan, the banknote of 5 somani features a mosque. Economically, the post-Communist era of free markets and globalization has not been kind to Central Asia as the states have suffered shocking declines in health and education standards, and all, except oil-rich Kazakhstan, have suffered a disastrous decline in gross domestic product (GDP). In Tajikistan, for example, the GDP today is only 38 percent of what it was in 1990. While a "wave" of democratization swept across many countries, the states of Central Asia remained authoritarian. In fact, these states are unique in that the fundamental political institutions have not been substantially altered from the Communist era. Parliaments and courts are weak and are routinely ignored. Opposition has been circumscribed, co-opted, and/or repressed. Almost all elections have had dubious legitimacy.

[98] Yet there are some differences in the level of tolerance of Islam within these states: Turkmenistan and Uzbekistan are, for example, more restrictive of religious activities (both

result, the meanings attached to Islam in Central Asia remarkably differ from those in other parts of the Muslim world. The Soviets waged a brutal campaign against Islam that far surpassed what French colonies had experienced during French colonialism. In fact, Karimov, Nazarbayev, Akayev, and Rahmonov, the "founding fathers" of the Central Asian states, all received their education during the Soviet period and, as a result, were heavily influenced by the Marxist perception of religion when setting a course for the new states.[99]

Although varying approaches to Islam differentiate the states from each other, their general attitude toward Islam is very similar – that of adopting symbolism while subjugating political practice.[100] Khalid argues that due to the Soviet legacy in the area, "in no other part of the Muslim world is the distance between the state and Islam so great as it is in Central Asia."[101] The emphasis on protecting the population from "extremism" has provided a cover for authoritarian policies. In Uzbekistan, a Soviet-era organization continues to coerce those not toeing the state line with regards to their sanctioned version of Islam. The secular version of Islam that was established following the Soviet legacy is not political. As a result, Islam was not even a part of the discussions culminating in the constitutions of these countries. Thus, although after the fall of the USSR, while Muslim ethnicities have made major efforts to revitalize their Islamic traditions, constitutional debates and political life have not really envisaged a role for Islam; for example, in debates during the drafting of the Constitution of the Republic of Kazakhstan, "there was no serious debate in the constitutional commission on giving special recognition or protection to any religion . . . . The main reasons for the absence of any serious discussion of the matter were the still strong Soviet tradition of secularism and the primary desire to maintain public concord among Muslims and Christians."[102]

Islamic and other religions) than the others. Kyrgyzstan is generally regarded as the most liberal, though it appears to be moving in the direction of its neighbors. Tajikistan is the only state that permits an Islamist party to participate in politics, though this "accommodation" was achieved only after a bloody civil war.

[99] Emmanuel Karagiannis, "Political Islam in Central Asia: The Challenge of Hizb Ut-Tahrir" (2007) 13 Nationalism and Ethnic Politics 297.

[100] T Jeremy Gunn, "Shaping an Islamic Identity: Religion, Islamism, and the State in Central Asia" (2003) 64 Sociology of Religion 389, 402.

[101] Adeeb Khalid, *Islam After Communism: Religion and Politics in Central Asia* (University of California Press, 2014) 190.

[102] Zhenis Kembayev, "The Rise of Presidentialism in Post-Soviet Central Asia" in Rainer Grote and Tilmann J Roder (eds) *Constitutionalism in Islamic Countries: Between Upheaval and Continuity* (Oxford University Press, 2012) 436.

Today, as a legacy of Soviet policy, these states exercise legal controls over Islam through laws (including statutes, provisions of codes, regulations, and decrees) and through state departments tasked with the responsibility of enforcement. The legal regimes generally follow a similar format, where there may be a general law on religion and a committee on religious affairs. Some states, such as Turkmenistan and Uzbekistan, require all religious groups to register with the state, and the failure to do so subjects religious groups to the penalties of criminal law.[103] Central Asian State officials have continued the longstanding practice of manipulating the appointment of the muftiates (chief clerics), whose main duties typically revolve around coordinating the activities of official Islam at the mosque level, as well as supervising religious education at the madrasas. The approved clergy will sometimes be given messages that should be incorporated into sermons, including the unsubtle message of which candidates to support in elections. In Tajikistan and Kazakhstan, the state has exercised an inordinate amount of control over religious institutions and imams, particularly with the requirement of registration, which enabled significant state involvement.[104] Similarly, Islam in Uzbekistan is controlled by a Soviet-era organization that continues to control religion and bans it from any kind of political role while the state coerces all those who will not conform to officially sanctioned forms of Islamic organization and activity.[105] As Khalid writes, the Muslim Board of Uzbekistan (O'zbekiston Musulmonlari Idorasi, or MBU), the state body, "routinely interferes in hiring and firing imams of mosques, controlling what is taught in the madrasas, and vigorously censoring all religious literature. It also requires unwavering loyalty of official ulama and issues fatwas as demanded by the state. In January 1998, for instance, it outlawed the use of loudspeakers in mosques .... Imams are not allowed to compose their own sermons; they must read from texts provided by MBU."[106]

In 1998, following the Law on Freedom of Conscience and Religious Organisations, the government of Uzbekistan launched a renewed crackdown on all Islamist suspects and declared it illegal to preach Islam. All mosques and imams had to be registered. Women were arrested for wearing the hijab, and thousands of men with beards were questioned, many were arrested, and death sentences were awarded.[107] In Kazakhstan similarly, even though the

---

[103] Gunn, "Shaping an Islamic Identity" 404.

[104] Khalid, *Islam After Communism* 171.

[105] Neil Melvin, *Uzbekistan: Transition to Authoritarianism on the Silk Road* (Harwood Academic Publishers 2000) 56.

[106] Khalid, *Islam After Communism* 171.

[107] Rob Johnson, *Oil, Islam and Conflict: Central Asia Since 1945* (University of Chicago Press, 2007) 74.

"Islamic threat" has not been claimed to be as significant as in Uzbekistan, Kazakhstan too has a law, dating from 1993 – On the Freedom of Religion and on Religious Associations – that prohibits the formation of parties or other political formations of a religious character and the participation of religious associations in the activity of political parties or rendering financial assistance to them. It also prohibits proselytism without official permission; in December 2004, the Spiritual Administration for the Muslims of Kazakhstan – a similar body to that existing in Uzbekistan – began testing all imams in questions of belief as a way to assert more control over religion. The testing accompanied a requirement that all mosques and religious associations register with the government or be closed down.[108]

All of this present-day aversion to Islam and fidelity to an aggressive form of secularism has historical context rooted in Soviet colonialism. It was recognized by the Soviets that religion could potentially threaten the regime. Consequently, the Soviets endeavored to repress any religious expression beyond that which was state sanctioned. They also sponsored an "official" Islam and exercised an extremely high level of control over the dwindling number of schools and madrasas in the region as they simultaneously manipulated the appointment of imams and muftis and attacked religion through propaganda. This attack on Islamic expression and all physical manifestations of the religion completely drove Islam out of public spaces.[109] Mosques were closed, the hijab was banned, religious rituals were forbidden,[110] Ramadan was opposed, and shari'a law was banned,[111] and Muslim intellectuals in Central Asia were isolated from their peers abroad.[112] The Soviets created an "official" version of Islam that was approved by the state and could be used as a tool to quell unrest.[113]

In comparison to the French, Soviet policies were far more ambitious in their aim to strongly repress any ideologies – in this case Islam - that were not in accordance with the Communist or Soviet party line. Islam was regarded as a bourgeois decadence, reactionary and "backward." It was also, the Russians knew, a potent mobilizing ideology that threatened the regime with civil unrest; hence, religious observance and ritual were generally restricted in Central Asia. By the 1930s, there were fewer than a hundred mosques and

---

[108] Khalid, *Islam After Communism* 185–86.
[109] Khalid, *Islam After Communism* 2.
[110] Johnson, *Oil, Islam and Conflict* 26.
[111] Martha Brill Olcott, *Roots of Radical Islam in Central Asia* (Carnegie Endowment for International Peace 2007) 8.
[112] Khalid, *Islam After Communism* 82.
[113] Johnson, *Oil, Islam and Conflict* 63.

no madrasas left in the region. The goal was to distance the Central Asians from "reactionary" Islam and convert them into urbanized proletarians.[114] During seventy years of Soviet rule, the Islamic mosques and madrasas that had previously thrived in Central Asia were closed, destroyed, or converted into museums or factories;[115] ulama were arrested and qadi courts abolished. Religious activity was only allowed where it was registered with authorities.[116] Uzbekistan bore the brunt of this assault as it was the most "Islamic."[117] In Tajikistan, in the 1920s and 1930s, Soviet anti-Islam campaigns led to a curtailment of religious observance as policy makers attempted to eradicate Islamic traditions. Ulama were cast as counterrevolutionaries who had to be decimated, as thousands of ulama had been arrested and sent off to forced-labor camps or killed. With old-method schools and madrasas destroyed, waqf property confiscated and redistributed, and qadi courts and the religious boards abolished, the patterns through which Islam had been transmitted in Central Asia were largely destroyed. Religious activity could only take place in officially recognized societies or groups of "believers," who had to register with local authorities.

Additionally, Central Asian Islam was cut off from developments in the rest of the Muslim world so the migration of religious ideas – including those to do with political/constitutional life were impeded. The lack of religious texts and abolishment of educational institutions that could spread Islamic knowledge meant that Islam was only continued due to familial transmission.[118] At the same time, because no new religious texts could be published and oral chains of transmission were often destroyed, the available religious knowledge was vastly circumscribed. Thus, what remained of Islam was rendered synonymous with tradition, and religious knowledge was being pushed into the private sphere. Accordingly, Central Asia remained beyond the reach of much of mid-century Muslim religious thought, including the entire phenomenon of political Islam.[119]

All in all, the eradication of Islam from political life was quite successful.[120] Despite some liberalization under Khrushchev between 1955 and 1958, the

---

[114] Johnson, *Oil, Islam and Conflict* 63.
[115] Gunn, "Shaping an Islamic Identity" 390.
[116] Khalid, *Islam After Communism* 73.
[117] Khalid, *Islam After Communism* 71.
[118] Khalid, *Islam After Communism* 82.
[119] Adeeb Khalid, "A Secular Islam: Nation, State, and Religion in Uzbekistan" (2003) 35 International Journal of Middle East Studies 573, 577.
[120] Khalid, *Islam After Communism* 71–85.

Soviet regime continued to suppress Islam. It is accurate to argue then that "the Soviet regime was largely successful in the attempt to deprive Islam of its traditional holder over and influence upon society and ... in the course of time, this population became basically secularized from conviction, education and/or force of habit . . .. Their knowledge of Islam was reduced to a very few practices."[121] Unsurprisingly then, Olcott notes, in the context of Kazakhstan but applicable to the region generally, that after independence, most Muslims had only basic knowledge of Islam.[122]

In practice then, all Central Asian states continue to view public activities associated with Islam with suspicion as they regulate religious life through formal bureaucratic channels and show no hesitation in interfering in religious affairs and curtailing religious activity they deem undesirable. Islam is then viewed as the expression of private beliefs, and there are institutions and policies in place to suppress any political opposition that may manifest itself in Islamic terms.[123] Khalid observes,

> In the official rhetoric of the regimes, the task for the present is to achieve a better tomorrow. This task is conceived in entirely worldly terms: achieving economic progress, improving educational and health indicators, and so forth. Public discourse remains entirely secular, with no attempt to use Islam to legitimize the authority of the state. The new constitutions written in the aftermath of the Soviet collapse all retain Soviet-era provisions for the separation of religion from the state and from education. State schools remain resolutely secular, with no religious education whatsoever, not even in the guise of lessons in ethics or morality, which feature prominently in the curricula of most Muslim (and non Muslim) states. In a fundamental sense,

---

[121] Olcott, *Roots of Radical Islam in Central Asia* 15–16.

[122] Gunn, "Shaping an Islamic Identity" 390.

[123] Islamic inclinations were curbed in Tajikistan due to the civil war in the 1990s in which Islam played a part. The secularism versus Islamism debate was ignored in the eventual UN-sponsored resolution to the conflict, which meant that this issue continued to plague the nation in the long term. Kazakhstan and Uzbekistan turned towards the Sufi order of Islam, and in Uzbekistan in particular, Sufi masters are celebrated in a way that is not within Islamic tradition. This resurgence of Islam could be seen as a way to decolonize and dissociate their Soviet past from their independent present. The Hanafi school of thought propagated in Central Asia is traditional and philosophical and emphasizes practicality as opposed to strict adherence. Observance of Islam in the region therefore remains traditional and has been used as an ideology to fill the lacuna left by Communist/Soviet departure rather than as a religion to be understood. Defining the religion in a way that could be accommodated with their culture was deemed a suitable way to reconcile people's various identities, as opposed to a stricter approach that may alienate those not willing to submit themselves to more demanding rituals.

then, the de-Islamization of public life characteristic of the Soviet period is still solidly in place.[124]

In this way, post-Soviet-era constitutional and political life is completely devoid of Islam.[125] Indeed, even in Tajikistan, which is the only state in the region where an Islamic movement participated in politics legally, the Tajik Islamic Revival Party stated that "they had no intention of establishing a theocratic fundamentalist state in Tajikistan."[126]

The strong secularist tendencies of the Soviet tradition continue to permeate the countries of Central Asia and the propagation of an atheistic education had far-reaching effects. Olcott argues that in time, Muslims accepted the secular norms that were imposed on them.[127] Thus, the exclusion of the religion from the public space was seen as appropriate among people themselves. Islam is only mildly used to legitimize the state or those in power; religious life is regulated, and public Islamic activity is treated with suspicion.[128] Indeed, political Islam has been portrayed in a negative light as a means to gain power that is not in line with the religion.[129] Ulama have to pass a political literacy test which involves expressing support for the current constitutional system before being appointed. The Muslim Board of Uzbekistan is state-controlled and advocated a traditional Hanafi view in its religious publications that allowed the state to define and propagate its own version of Islam.[130] Even in Tashkent Islamic University, students are taught a secular, state-defined version of the religion.[131]

Yet, during the course of seven decades of political control, Soviet policy makers were unable to eradicate Islam completely. Although they succeeded largely in destroying Islamic learning and the knowledge of Islamic teachings, they did not eliminate the majority of the population's self-perception of having an Islamic identity. Being a "Muslim" is widely understood as constituting an integral part of the identity of the majority of Central Asia's population, though many are unsure of what it means. Most Central Asians believe that being Muslim distinguishes them from those of other faiths; as such, they think of Islam as being a part of their social identity, similar to how they

---

[124] Khalid, *Islam After Communism* 131.
[125] Khalid, *Islam After Communism* 132–33.
[126] Khalid, *Islam After Communism* 149.
[127] Olcott, *Roots of Radical Islam in Central Asia* 15.
[128] Khalid, *Islam After Communism* 132.
[129] Khalid, *Islam After Communism* 133
[130] Khalid, *Islam After Communism* 171.
[131] Eric McGlinchey, *Chaos, Violence, Dynasty: Politics and Islam in Central Asia* (University of Pittsburgh Press, 2011) 118.

conceive of their ethnicity, family, and mother tongue.[132] As such, it "shows little sign of affecting everyday life. There is little concern about observing the basic prohibitions of Islam against alcohol and even pork. The rhythms of everyday life remain secular in a way that is inconceivable even in other secular Muslim countries. Pride in Islam as national heritage can coexist with complete lack of observance or indeed any belief at all, let alone a desire to live in an Islamic state."[133] Indeed, wide segments of the population share a suspicion of Islam in political life. The school system remains secular, with no religious instruction whatsoever and although Islam has been rekindled, it is notably absent from public discourse.

Of course, as with other Muslim countries, factors other than Soviet colonialism would have also played a part in determining the negligible role of Islam in political life. It has been argued that Islam is not as important a player in Kazakhstan, Kyrgyzstan, and Turkmenistan as it is in Tajikistan and Uzbekistan *because* of its relatively late arrival and subsequent lack of deep penetration into the nomadic life of the tribal people who have largely retained their mobile lifestyle.[134] Also, pluralism has historically characterized the religious landscape of Asian Muslim societies as Islam coexisted with other religions, including Zoroastrianism, Buddhism, and Shamanism. Further, isolation from Arab centers of Islam contributed to the development of syncretic variants of Islam that were less orthodox.[135] Yet it would be correct to argue that constant and authoritarian suppression of Islam has paved the

---

[132] Johnson, *Oil, Islam and Conflict* 391.

[133] Khalid, *Islam After Communism* 121. It was only a familial, indigenous culture that enabled Islam to remain a part of people's lives. While Islam was displaced publicly in Central Asia, observance of Islamic rituals continued, and religion became an ethnic marker of identity. Religious adherence also rapidly grew after local Communist elites stopped persecuting religious activities in 1988 with new mosques, more prayer, and many making the pilgrimage to Mecca. Today, for most people, Islam is cultural – in that it implies a "return" to tradition, the rediscovery of a cultural heritage that was much maligned during the Soviet era.

[134] Zhenis Kembayev, *Regime Transition in Central Asia: Stateness, Nationalism and Political Change in Tajikistan and Uzbekistan* (Routledge 2013) 181.

[135] "Islam's roots in Uzbekistan and in Kyrgyzstan's Fergana Valley span a thousand years. In contrast, it was not until the eighteenth and nineteenth centuries that Islam saw wide adoption in what to-day is northern Kyrgyzstan and Kazakhstan. The ethnic and cultural reach of the Russian state was less pronounced in Uzbekistan than it was in Kazakhstan and Kyrgyzstan . . .. Given these societal endowments, we would anticipate that Islamic identification in the immediate post-Soviet years would be most pronounced in Uzbekistan and least prevalent in Kazakhstan. We would also expect that Islamic identification within Kyrgyz society would lie somewhere in between the high of Uzbekistan and the low of Kazakhstan. Indeed, this is what we find. In surveys that the International Foundation for Electoral Systems (IFES) conducted in 1996, fewer than 20 percent of Kazakh respondents reported they were Muslim, whereas approximately half of Kyrgyz and 90 percent of Uzbek respondents identified as Muslim."

way for the intense secularization we see in Central Asian constitutional life today, in contrast to other Muslim countries.

This section has sought to expand the debate on the origins of constitutional Islamization by setting out the empirical landscape of Islamic constitutions and exploring whether colonial history could partially explain the variation between the Islamic content of constitutions of various Muslim-majority countries. The preliminary analysis showed that generally higher levels of Islamic content are found in the constitutions of Muslim-majority countries that were colonized by the British vis-à-vis the French (and in some cases for French colonies, the constitution is explicitly secular, e.g., in the case of Mali). Further, there are no Islamic clauses in the constitutions of the Central Asian countries that were under Soviet influence. Indeed, Islamic repugnancy clauses and Islamic supremacy clauses, which arguably are the strongest form of Islamic clauses, are most likely to occur in countries that have in the past been associated with a British colonial legacy.

By analyzing select colonies, we suggest that this divergence may be explained by the colonial treatment and tolerance of Islam: the British, unlike the French and Soviets, adopted a relatively neutral stance toward Islam and attempted not to subjugate it. In contrast, the French were far less accommodating to Islam. That is, while the British interfered in or modified Islamic institutions and norms, they did not generally seek to eradicate it. The French, in West Africa and Algeria, in contrast, saw Islam as something to be done away with. Outdoing the French, we saw in Central Asia that the Soviets exercised an extremely high level of control over Islamic schools and restricted Islamic expression and all physical manifestations of the religion with a view to eradicating Islam from the public space; mosques were closed, the hijab was banned, religious rituals were forbidden, observance of Ramadan was opposed, and shari'a law was disbanded. In comparison to the French, Soviet policies were therefore far more repressive.

Thus, we make the novel argument that colonial history is a key variable in explaining the variation of Islamic content observed across the constitutions of Muslim-majority countries. The colonial powers brought not only their own legal systems but also adopted particular approaches in how they dealt with, tolerated, and treated established Islamic norms, institutions, and laws in the colonies; this had significant practical consequences on the space and scope for Islam to operate in the public and political life of these countries, and this would, in turn, impact the potential for Islamic content within these

Dobrosława Wiktor-Mach, "On Secularization, Modernity and Islamic Revival in the Post-Soviet Context" (2011) 175 Polish Sociological Review 393, 405.

countries' constitutions. As such, the identity of the colonizer could in some senses be a predictor of postcolonial constitutional incorporation of Islam.

Of course, further work needs to be done to explain and explore variations in constitutional Islamization, and, admittedly, there will be unique factors specific to each state that would have influenced the role and scope of Islam in public and constitutional life in that state (including but not limited to geography, economic factors, the entrenchment of Islam, the proximity and exchange of ideas with other Muslim states, the religiosity of the population, and so forth). Nevertheless, the finding that colonial origins may influence the potential for prospective constitutional Islamization and shape the political space for Islam within a state is a key finding and has several implications.

At the broadest level, it suggests that those involved in constitution-making in Muslim-majority countries should bear in mind colonial history and its legacy when engaging in democratization projects and appreciate that events and policies imposed by a colonizer several decades earlier may continue to impact the public landscape, influence, and demand for Islam in constitutional and legislative life. Also, the finding may be relevant to modernization and/or secularization attempts in some Muslim-majority countries; that is, it could be argued that "secularization" or political programs to make the state less Islam-focused may be more difficult to achieve or meet significantly more resistance in Muslim-majority countries that have been part of the British colonial tradition, simply due to the greater sway, tolerance of, and historical influence of Islam in political life within these countries. On the other hand, the Soviet and French legacy of secularism in their colonies and parallel erosion and intolerance of Islam may make states colonized by these powers more receptive to secular ideas. This is not to imply that countries (colonized by the British) where Islam has been allowed to flourish in public life are not susceptible to secular inclinations, only that the path of secularization might be more difficult to realize or require an altogether different strategy.

Part II

3

Constitutional Islamization and Islamic Supremacy Clauses

Constitutions of many Muslim countries contain several religion-related clauses, including clauses declaring Islam to be the state religion, the requirement that the president should be a Muslim, and so forth. The insertion of such clauses is not surprising; the Islamic world has continually wrestled with a rather nuanced relationship between integrating the norms of religion, managing colonial influences, and progressing the core ideas of modern constitutionalism. Islam and its relation to law has always played a critical role when reformers strove to develop a constitutional system that accommodates Islam.

To balance and achieve these ostensibly competing goals, modern practices were carefully framed and cast in Islamic idiom.[1] Since then, the status of Islamic law, and specifically, its relationship with man-made law, has tended to remain a central issue of constitutional design in the Muslim world. That is, modern constitutions establish lawmaking processes, but where does Islam stand in relation to these processes? More specifically, what is to be done with legislation that contravenes Islamic law? There have been several different solutions as constitution makers in Muslim countries sought to maintain fidelity to religion while embracing modern constitutionalism. This chapter, to illustrate the dynamics of constitutional Islamization, focuses on one popular and potent solution to resolving this tension, that is, the adoption of Islamic "source of law" clauses, which declare Islam to be "a" or "the" source

---

Credit for the empirical findings and analysis in this chapter largely goes to Tom Ginsburg, with whom Dawood Ahmed has already published work on this topic. Much of this work is included, with edits, in this chapter.

[1] Nathan J Brown and Abel Omar Sherif, "Inscribing the Islamic Shari'a in Arab Constitutional Law" in Yvonne Yazbeck Haddad and Barbara Freyer Stowasser (eds), *Islamic Law and the Challenges of Modernity* (Altamira Press 2004) (using the examples of Tunisia and the Ottoman constitutions to illustrate the reframing of Islamic vocabulary to fit constitutional practices).

of law. The repugnancy clauses declare that any laws contrary to Islam will be void. Constitutional language that refers to Islamic law as "a" or "the" source of law was first introduced in Syria in 1950 and has been found in some thirty-eight constitutions.[2] The "repugnancy clauses" were first introduced in Iran in 1907 and have been utilized in over a dozen constitutions since then. In this chapter, we collectively refer to the Islamic "source of law" clauses and Islamic "repugnancy clauses" as "Islamic supremacy" clauses.

What the source of law and repugnancy clauses have in common is that both seek to articulate the normative superiority of Islamic law or norms over "mere" man-made laws. The source of law clause is important not only because of its ubiquity but also for its effect; that is, the effect of such provisions then, according to Nathan Brown and Abel Omar Sherif, is "to imply a very different basis for the legal order [where] rather than the constitution sanctioning Islam ... the Shariah itself stands prior to the positive legal order – including, potentially and by implication, the constitution itself."[3] Islam, in this constitutional order, then seeks to provide an additional source of limitations on earthly authority. This set of higher law limitations has obvious similarities with the core motivating idea of modern constitutionalism and judicial review.[4]

Despite its importance, there is relatively little literature available that explains the origins and spread of the Islamic source of law and repugnancy clauses.[5] Despite the stereotypical and popular perception of the supposed incompatibility of a constitution that incorporates both Islam and human

---

[2]   Clark Lombardi, "Constitutional Provisions Making Sharia 'A' of 'The' Chief Source of Legislation: Where Did They Come From? What Do They Mean? Do They Matter?" (2013) 28(1) American University International Law Review 733, 743–46.

[3]   Brown and Sherif, "Inscribing the Islamic Shari'a" 63.

[4]   Tom Ginsburg and others, "When to Overthrow Your Government: The Right to Resist in the World's Constitutions" (2013) 60(1) UCLA Law Review 1,184, 1,184–1,260. Although the focus is not on Islam, the article notes that similar clauses do exist in in other contexts. Article 9 in chapter 2 of the current Sri Lankan constitution, entitled "Buddhism," states, "The Republic of Sri Lanka shall give to Buddhism the foremost place and accordingly it shall be the duty of the State to protect and foster the Buddha Sansa, while assuring to all religions the rights [to freedom of belief and worship] granted by Articles 10 and 14(1)(e)." Nevertheless, the idea of normative superiority of religion over positive law seems to be associated almost exclusively with Muslim-majority countries.

[5]   Lombardi, "Constitutional Provisions" 733; Brown and Sherif, "Inscribing the Islamic Shari'a" 107–10, 161–93 (tracing the historiography of the idea that the origin of Western constitutionalism lies in Christianity and the history of the role of shari'a in Middle Eastern governance); Noah Feldman, *The Fall and Rise of the Islamic State* (Princeton University Press 2008) 103–40 (exploring the emergence of modern Islamism and its constitutional proposals); Jan-Michel van Otto, "Sharia and Law in a Bird's-Eye View: Reform, Moderation and Ambiguity" in Jan Michiel Otto and Hannah Mason (eds), *Delicate Debates on Islam:*

rights, there has been little empirical investigation of how the incidence of Islamic supremacy clauses actually correlates with the provision of rights, if at all, in constitutions across Muslim-majority countries. Even constitutions written under substantial foreign influence, such as the Afghan and Iraqi constitutions, contain Islamic supremacy clauses, as does the current constitution of Egypt, produced by a military regime that has violently suppressed Islamists. In our view, it remains crucial to understand the historical origin and spread of constitutional Islamization. Since constitution writing is as much a political as a legal process, we must carefully understand the sociopolitical dynamics behind these clauses. In the words of John Burgess, "the formation of a constitution seldom proceeds according to the existing forms of law. Historical and revolutionary forces are the more prominent and important factors in the work .... These cannot be dealt with through juristic methods."[6]

This chapter seeks to fill this gap in the existing scholarship. Relying on a unique data set based on the coding of all national constitutions since 1789 and case studies of constitution writing from four countries, it traces the development of Islamic supremacy clauses within the constitutions of Muslim-majority countries since their first appearance in Iran in 1907. By tracing *when* constitutions first incorporated Islam or shari'a as a constraint on lawmaking or as a source of law, we aim to explain *why* constitutions did so. The focus of this chapter is *not* how the clauses operate in practice, nor their effects, but rather how they came about.[7]

The chapter makes three major, counterintuitive claims. First, it shows, that the repugnancy clause – the most robust form of Islamic supremacy clause – has its origins in British colonial law and that all forms of Islamic supremacy clauses are more prevalent in former British colonies than in other states. This provides further color to the findings of the last chapter, which argued that the identity of the colonizer played a part in determining the extent of constitutional Islamization in a country. As this chapter demonstrates, the birth and subsequent proliferation of the Islamic repugnancy clause, in particular, owes much to a historic British tolerance of Islam in its colonies that allowed such accommodations to evolve and flourish. Second, we illustrate that in some cases, the states introduced Islamic supremacy clauses into their respective

Policymakers and Academics Speaking with Each Other (Leiden University Press 2012) 73 (examining the changing role of shari'a over time in twelve Muslim countries).
6   John William Burgess, *Political Science and Comparative Constitutional Law* (University of Michigan Library 1896) 90.
7   We shall explore the impact of these clauses in the two case studies of Egypt and Pakistan in the next chapters.

constitutions to legitimize their regimes or co-opt and pacify opposition to modernization and liberalization reforms. Thus, contrary to popular assumption, these clauses are not generally the outcome of "impositions of theocracy" but carefully negotiated and bargained provisions, adopted in a spirit of compromise, that may help legitimize the road to political modernization. Indeed, arguments in this chapter suggest that, adopting a hasty detour to marginalize the role of Islam in the constitutional sphere, as is often the case, may lower the legitimacy, and thus potentially undermine the success, of progressive constitutional reform in some Muslim countries.[8] Third, and most importantly, contrary to the claims of those who skeptically see the incorporation of Islam in political frameworks as completely antithetical to rights, we empirically show that constitutions that incorporated Islamic supremacy clauses were accompanied by *more* human rights and are indeed even *more* rights-heavy as compared to constitutions of other comparable jurisdictions that did not incorporate these clauses. Further, constitutions that adopt Islamic supremacy clauses are more rights-intensive than their immediate predecessors.[9] Thus, instead of being antithetical to the constitutional entrenchment of rights, this chapter demonstrates that constitutional Islamization accompanies formal rights. In this sense, constitutional Islamization is "as modern as the internal combustion engine," to paraphrase an important description of rights.[10]

---

[8] Michael MJ Fischer, "Islam and the Revolt of the Petit Bourgeoisie" (1982) 111(1) Daedalus 101, 105 (discussing the struggle over Islam in formulas of legitimacy in major Muslim countries). Binnaz Toprak, *Islam and Political Development in Turkey* (Brill 1981) 25–38 (discussing how, under Mustafa Kemal Atatürk, Turkey underwent one of the most comprehensive programs of reform and secularization ever seen in the Muslim world. Yet its 1924 constitution initially declared Islam as the state religion. The goal was similar: it was believed that the immediate adoption of a secular, modern constitution may be too ambitious; the provision allowed for an accommodated and gradual compromise so that people and elite could be gradually "socialized" to alternative modes of governance. The state religion provision was removed from the constitution in 1924.)

[9] We acknowledge that in order to make a more determinative claim about how the clauses effect the realization of democracy in practice, we will need to critically observe and analyze their effects and how the rights and Islam provisions interact. Certainly, it may be that the rights provisions may be under-enforced in practice, which may cut against the claim that they are compatible with the basic principles of liberal democracy. However, the same could be assumed of the Islamic supremacy clauses and, in fact, for other clauses in a constitution. Nevertheless, all we argue is that the co-occurrence of rights in a constitution, alongside Islamic supremacy clauses, is a starting point in terms of empowering downstream decision makers to interpret and enforce the constitution in a way that may be compatible with liberal democracy.

[10] Kenneth Minogue, "The History of the Idea of Human Rights" in Walter Laqueur and Barry Rubin (eds), *The Human Rights Reader* (Plume 1979) 3.

In order to comprehensively trace the historical origins and adoption of Islamic supremacy clauses, the analysis also draws on case studies of constitutional Islamization in constitutions from Afghanistan, Egypt, Iran, and Iraq in the next chapter. In these case studies, we find that constitutions that are drafted in more democratic settings or in response to democratic sentiment (e.g., after a popular revolution or where the existing regime needs to obtain popular support) tend to undergo constitutional Islamization to a greater degree. Similarly, most constitutions that are the first to "Islamize" in any given country also contain many liberal features, in that they grant more rights and impose more constraints on government. We can, therefore, predict that in many cases, greater democracy in the Muslim world may lead to greater constitutional enactment of rights, but it will also most likely lead to greater constitutional Islamization – the two will often go hand in hand and indeed may be linked. As Professors Esposito and Voll observe, "the processes of democratization and Islamic resurgence have become complementary forces in many countries."[11]

We explain the incidence of this surprising relationship using the logic of coalitional politics. Many situations of Islamization occur when the existing political regime is under pressure to expand the base of input into governance. In Muslim-majority countries, these impulses – even if they do not lead to full democracy as conventionally defined – will tend to produce Islamization. At the same time, there are often other political forces at work, sometimes operating in opposition, that seek modernization, either in the form of liberal democracy, secularism, or in terms of limited constitutional government.[12] Sometimes these interest groups overlap, as both rights and Islamization may be seen as complementary tools to constrain rulers. But even if these two groups do not overlap, they often form a coalition that spurs political reform. Once reform begins, the two groups have to negotiate the terms of future governance, which in turn may lead to a new consensus memorialized in a constitutional text. In this bargaining process, each side may wish to constrain the other by demanding that the interests most dear to it are protected.[13] Liberals may want rights, and religiously inclined groups

---

[11] John L Esposito and John O Voll, *Islam and Democracy* (Oxford University Press 1996) 16.

[12] The definition of "liberal democracy" is of course contested and subject to debate. For our purposes, we take the basic principles of liberal democracy as being constitutional recognition of the basic features of constitutionalism – limits on governments, separation of powers, and the provision of basic rights and civil liberties.

[13] Barry Weingast, "The Political Foundations of Democracy and the Rule of Law" (1997) 91(2) American Political Science Review 245 (describing this logic as the "rationality of fear").

may want Islam. If each group gets what it wants, the new constitution contains both – rights and an Islamic supremacy clause.

The analysis is consistent with the views of those who have suggested that Muslim-majority nations are unlikely to modernize in a Western direction. According to Huntington, for example, a reaffirmation of Islam in contemporary times should not be perceived as a rejection of modernity; rather, it steers and sets course for a modernization that is more aligned to the cultural appetite: that is, it becomes a case of "Islamizing modernity" rather than "modernizing Islam."[14] In his view, an emphasis on Islam can be understood as a rejection of the "secular, relativistic" values that people in the Muslim world associate with the West, a means of declaring cultural independence and saying "we will be modern but we won't be like you."[15] It is true that poll results that show "liberty and freedom of speech" as among some of the values that Muslims admire most about the West also suggest that Muslims disapprove of the perceived "promiscuity and moral decay" of the West.[16] An emphasis on Islam in constitutions could then also be interpreted as an assertion of indigenous cultural and nationalist authenticity in a postcolonial order.[17] Indeed, to paraphrase Haddad and Stowasser's argument in their book on Islam and modernity, "globalization pushing societies towards … legal norms … based largely on Western notions [has resulted in] local populations asserting their rights to determine their own laws and to maintain their own traditions."[18] Amid the tumult of regime change, it then seems to be true that constitution makers would selectively borrow tools from the West, but their borrowing would be refracted through their own beliefs and would follow their own trajectory.[19] Of course, it would be naive and simplistic to assume that Islam would be all that determines the scope for constitutionalism for Muslim masses; social, political, and economic factors play a critical part too. Nevertheless, that does not negate the reality that some Muslims may view political ideas, including constitutionalism, as

[14] Samuel P Huntington, *The Clash of Civilizations and the Remaking of World Order* (Simon and Schuster 2011) 96.

[15] Huntington, *Clash of Civilizations* 101.

[16] Dalia Mogahed, *Islam and Democracy* (Gallup 2006) 3.

[17] Sami Zubaida, *Law and Power in the Islamic World* (I.B. Tauris 2005) 175 (arguing that shari'a is advocated for because of cultural nationalism and the quest for authenticity).

[18] Yvonne Yazbeck Haddad and Barbara Freyer Stowasser, *Islamic Law and the Challenge of Modernity* (Almitra Press 2004) 1.

[19] David Brooks, "Huntington's Clash Revisited" The New York Times (March 3, 2011) <www.nytimes.com/2011/03/04/opinion/04brooks.html> accessed March 25, 2021.

somewhat lacking in legitimacy if such ideas are perceived as incompatible with the normative values of Islam.[20]

3.1 ISLAMIC SUPREMACY CLAUSES IN NATIONAL CONSTITUTIONS

Many Muslim countries, including Saudi Arabia, Kuwait, Bahrain, Yemen, and the United Arab Emirates adopted constitutions that entrenched Islam or Islamic law (shari'a) as "a" source, "a primary" source, or "the primary" source for legislation. For example, the Egyptian Constitution has since 1980 provided that "principles of Islamic law are the principal source of legislation."[21] Similarly, the Iraqi constitution states that "Islam . . . is a fundamental source of legislation."[22] Some of these constitutions went a step further and also provided for "repugnancy clauses." In Pakistan, Afghanistan, Egypt, Iran, and Iraq, for example, it is constitutionally prohibited to enact legislation that is antithetical to Islam. The Constitution of Pakistan of 1973 requires that "no law shall be enacted which is repugnant to the Injunctions of Islam."[23] The Afghan Constitution of 2004 similarly demands that "no law can be contrary to the beliefs and provisions of the sacred religion of Islam."[24] Other Muslim countries require that the head of the state or the government must be Muslim, while others simply refer to their Islamic identity in their preamble.[25]

While the Iranian/Persian constitution introduced the repugnancy clause in 1907, the "source of law" clause introduced by the Syrian constitution in 1950 can serve as a functional equivalent. It, too, like the repugnancy clause, may allow courts to undertake an "Islamic judicial review," as Noah Feldman labels it, the purpose of which will be "not merely to ensure [legislation's] compliance with the constitution but rather, to *guarantee* that it does not violate Islamic laws or values" and thus be fully consistent with it.[26] That is, both types of clauses imply the supremacy of or – at the very least – create a privileged space for Islam and Islamic law within the normative constitutional-

---

[20] Abdullahi Ahmed An-Na'im, *African Constitutionalism and the Role of Islam* (University of Pennsylvania Press 2006) 9 (discussing factors influencing Muslim views of constitutionalism, including whether the constitution is consistent with shari'a).

[21] Provisional Constitution of the Arab Republic of Egypt 2011, art. 2; Constitution of the Arab Republic of Egypt 1971, art. 2.

[22] The Constitution of Republic of Iraq 2005, art. 2.

[23] The Constitution of Islamic Republic of Pakistan 1973, art. 227.

[24] The Constitution of Islamic Republic of Pakistan 1973, art. 3.

[25] Morocco Constitution 2011.

[26] Feldman, *Fall and Rise of the Islamic State* 122.

legal order.[27] That is, while formulating a supremacy clause in the form of a repugnancy clause would arguably imply a more robust ability to challenge legislation on the basis of violation of a "superior" normative order grounded in Islam, the source of law clause, depending on the degree to which it entrenches Islam, that is, as "a" or "the" source, could also potentially serve this function.[28] Indeed, as Brown and Sherif opine, even simply privileging Islam as "a" source of law – the weakest formulation of a supremacy clause – in the constitution means that it becomes possible for many to argue that Islam authoritatively forms part of the "fundamental legal framework."[29] And this can be observed through a comparison of constitutional jurisprudence in Egypt, Kuwait, and Pakistan, each of which have different constitutional formulations of an Islamic supremacy clause.

In Egypt, after President Sadat amended Article 2 of the constitution in 1980 to make shari'a "the" principal source of legislation, dozens of constitutional petitions were launched that challenged the "Islamic" constitutionality of a variety of laws, including stipulations in the Egyptian civil code that required payment of interest on delinquent payments;[30] laws governing personal status issues of divorce, child custody, and alimony; and those regulating alcohol and gambling.[31] Conversely, in Kuwait, where Islam is only "a" major source of legislation, the constitutional provision has been invoked to defend laws that bar women from government positions[32] and to block the induction into parliament of female lawmakers who do not wear headscarves.[33] In Pakistan, a country where the constitution does not provide that Islam will be a source of legislation, but rather makes all legislation repugnant to Islam invalid, we see almost identical lawsuits, challenging laws to be declared

[27] Brown and Sherif, "Inscribing the Islamic Shari'a" 63 (citing examples of Arab constitutional texts which cite shari'a as a source of law, and the effect of these provisions).
[28] Brown and Sherif, "Inscribing the Islamic Shari'a" 63.
[29] Brown and Sherif, "Inscribing the Islamic Shari'a" 63.
[30] Tamir Moustafa, *The Struggle for Constitutional Power: Law, Politics, and Economic Development in Egypt* (Cambridge University Press 2009) 107–10 (chronicling cases brought to the Supreme Constitutional Court by moderate Islamists to challenge the secular foundations of the state, especially after the assassination of President Sadat).
[31] Tamir Moustafa, "The Islamist Trend in Egyptian Law" (2010) 3(1) Politics and Religion 610, 620.
[32] Human Rights Watch, "Kuwait: Court Victory for Women's Rights" (May 6, 2012) <www.hrw .org/news/2012/05/06/kuwait-court-victory-women-s-rights> accessed January 12, 2022.
[33] Ran Hirschl, *Constitutional Theocracy* (Harvard University Press 2010) 116 (describing the debate over the dress of female elected representatives that eventually made its way to Kuwait's Constitutional Court, which ruled against the edict ordering female parliamentary representatives to wear a hijab on the basis that shari'a law is not adequately unified in its approach to headscarves).

invalid for their incompatibility with shari'a.[34] Therefore, while repugnancy and source of law clauses may vary in form or substance, they empower the same kind of challenges to the state that allow for laws and regulations to be enforced.[35]

3.1.1 *The Colonial Origins of the Repugnancy Clause*

At the turn of the twentieth century, Iran adopted its first constitution in 1906, which was soon followed by a supplementary constitution in 1907. Article 2 declared that "laws passed by [the National Assembly] must never to all ages be contrary to the sacred precepts of Islam and the laws laid down by the Prophet."[36] This was the first repugnancy clause in the constitutional history of Muslim countries. It bears credit for introducing the very language of repugnancy that would migrate transnationally into future constitutions. An earlier episode of constitution making, that of Tunisia in 1861, mentioned Islam but had no language purporting to limit lawmaking. The idea that laws "repugnant to Islam" would be void and that a council of clergy would review laws to see whether and which laws should thus be void is, on its face, an Iranian innovation.[37]

But where did the idea for Article 2 come from? While constitutional drafters in Iran borrowed much from the Belgian, French, and Ottoman constitutions, none of these constitutions contained a clause in any way

---

[34] Hirschl, *Constitutional Theocracy* 125–26 (discussing the Pakistani Supreme Court's debate over shari'a-related jurisprudence and the supremacy of federal legislation over provincial legislation and providing an example of the Court's block on attempted laws to enforce Islamic morality in the North-West Frontier Province).

[35] To be sure, the argument here is not that the different formulations of supremacy clauses found in constitutions are identical in their jurisprudential effects; this will almost certainly not be the case. A clause stating that the principles of Islamic law will be "a" primary source of legislation among other sources (as in Egypt 1971) will most likely lead to fewer successful challenges to legislation than a constitutional clause making the principles of Islamic law "the" source of legislation (Egypt 1980); similarly a clause making Islam "one of the basis of all the laws" (Maldives 2008, art. 10.a) will most likely have a milder impact than a clause declaring that "no law contrary to any tenet of Islam shall be enacted" (art. 10.b). Clearly, depending on the formulation, these clauses will have differential impacts in terms of their effects. Accordingly, our definition of Islamic supremacy clauses only includes repugnancy clauses and those source of law clauses which make clear that Islam will, at the very least, be a major or basic source of law; it does not include clauses simply making Islam "a" source of law among other sources.

[36] The Constitution of the Islamic Republic of Iran 1907, art. 2.

[37] Nathan J Brown, *Constitutions in a Nonconstitutional World: Arab Basic Laws and the Prospects for Accountable Government* (State University of New York Press 2001) 30. (This council of clerics provision was effectively ignored throughout most of the history of the Iranian constitution.)

similar to Article 2. Noah Feldman has opined that it is likely that the idea of repugnancy came from colonial India, where the British had implemented a similar repugnancy doctrine to constrain the application of domestic and customary laws that they deemed to be repugnant to British law or moral sentiment.[38] Interestingly, while Iran was not a British colony, this implies a narrative of constitutional ideas migrating across borders. The context here was that people in a number of British colonies applied customary and indigenous laws in some of their affairs. In India, for example, Hindus and Muslims were permitted to apply their respective personal laws in family matters such as marriage, divorce, and inheritance. Both Hindu and Muslim judges assisted in the interpretation of their customary laws, which were applied alongside British statutory laws. Similarly, in Nigeria, positive state law coexisted with about 350 types of customary laws. The 1886 Charter of the Royal Niger Company provided that the customs and laws of the people in Nigeria must be respected and upheld.[39] However, colonial respect for local customs and legislation created a paradox for the colonial powers when these norms either clashed with the laws of England or, for one reason or another, were considered "morally" repugnant in their view. To reconcile this tension, and establish a colonial order, a hierarchy of laws also needed to be established. Thus, the British implemented two types of repugnancy doctrines. First, the imperial government reserved the ability to disallow legislation in the colonies that were "repugnant to the laws of England." That is, legislation could be declared invalid if it was inconsistent with the laws of England.[40] This was the case, for example, in Australia, Canada, and New Zealand. Second, and more importantly, for present purposes, in other colonies and certainly throughout Africa, magistrates had the power to refuse the application of customary laws if, essentially, they offended "civilized standards." This doctrine was justified on the basis that it would eradicate unjust customs.[41]

Although the specific wording of the clause varied between colonies,[42] the gist was that customary laws were acceptable to the colonial administrators

---

[38] Feldman, *Fall and Rise of the Islamic State* 83.

[39] Colin Walter Newbury, *British Policy Towards West Africa: Select Documents 1875–1914; with Statistical Appendices, 1800–1914* (Clarendon Press 1971) 254.

[40] Damen Ward, "Legislation, Repugnancy and the Disallowance of Colonial Laws: The Legal Structure of Empire and Lloyd's Case (1844)" (2010) 41(1) Victoria University of Wellington Law Review 381, 382; Claire Natoli, "Legal Independence in Australia" (2011) 7(1) Bruce Hall Academy Journal 65, 66.

[41] Bonny Ibhawoh, *Imperialism and Human Rights: Colonial Discourses of Rights and Liberties in African History* (State University of New York 2007) 60.

[42] Gerald Caplan, "The Making of 'Natural Justice' in British Africa: An Exercise in Comparative Law" (1964) 13(1) Journal of Public Law 120.

only if they were "not repugnant to natural justice, equity and good conscience or incompatible either directly or by implication with any law for the
time being in force."[43] This clause essentially implied that customary law
would not be applied if it was contrary to natural justice or public policy – as
interpreted by the imperial government. It was thus a supreme normative
constraint on the substantive norms and laws of the colonial subjects, leaving
the British with wide discretion to decide "what should or should not be
woven into the fabric of the law of the land."[44] This general repugnancy
proviso was common in all African colonies.[45] While most colonies repealed
the doctrine after gaining independence, Nigeria still maintains it.[46] British
colonial administrators viewed a number of laws – including Islamic law –
followed by colonial peoples as "backward with the tendency to be
repugnant."[47]

Some have even argued that the repugnancy clause served an important
function since it eliminated gross injustices that were inherent in the application of customary law.[48] Accordingly, by invoking this repugnancy clause,
customary rules related to slavery, trial by ordeal, and human sacrifice were
subjugated.[49] In this sense, the repugnancy doctrine motivated the creation of
the supremacy clause. It is fair to say then that, as Leon Sheleff argues, this
clause was not presented "merely, or even mainly, as being some sort of

---

[43] Bethel Chuks Uweru, "Repugnancy Doctrine and Customary Law in Nigeria: A Positive
Aspect of British Colonialism" (2008) 2 *African Research Review* 286, 292. (The repugnancy
doctrine in Nigeria emerged from the decision in the case of *Eshugbaye Eleko v Government of
Nigeria* [1931]. In that case, Lord Atkin held, "The court cannot itself transform a barbarous
custom into a milder one. If it stands in its barbarous character it must be rejected as repugnant
to natural justice, equity and good conscience.")
[44] Caplan, "The Making of 'Natural Justice'" 120.
[45] Pieter Bakker, "Indigenous Family Law in South Africa: From Colonial Repugnancy to
Constitutional Repugnancy," paper delivered at Law and Society Association Annual
Meetings, Denver, CO (May 25–29, 2009).
[46] EA Taiwo, "Repugnancy Clause and Its Impact on Customary Law: Comparing the South
African and Nigerian Positions – Some Lessons for Nigeria" (2009) 34(1) Journal for Juridical
Science 89. ("There is no known repugnancy case that has been decided on the basis of
conflict with any other law. Rather, all repugnancy cases were decided by reference to the
universal standard of morality which in human transactions is founded on what is 'good, just
and fair.'").
[47] Abdulkadir Hashim, "Coping with Conflicts: Colonial Policy Towards Muslim Personal Law
in Kenya and Post-Colonial Court Practice" in Shamil Jeppie, Ebrahim Moosa, and Richard
Roberts (eds), *Muslim Family Law in Colonial and Postcolonial Sub-Saharan Africa*
(Amsterdam University Press 2010) 224.
[48] T Olawale Elias, *The Nature of African Customary Law* (Manchester University Press 1956)
128. (For example, ordinances banning witchcraft.)
[49] Ibhawoh, *Imperialism and Human Rights* 61.

compromise between conflicting value-systems and their normative rulings, but as being an expression of minimum standards being applied as a qualification to the toleration being accorded – by recognition – to the basically unacceptable norms of 'backward' communities."[50] Of course, subjecting customary law to some imported moral standard mostly unknown and certainly alien to colonial people would presumably often have led to a state of uncertainty as to whether certain laws deemed to be valid previously would now conform to colonial notions of justice and fairness.[51] Indeed, "in applying the repugnancy clause, the British reviewing judges ... tended to smuggle in common law concepts under the cloak of natural justice."[52] Thus, in pointing out that repugnancy was applied in an unpredictable, ad hoc fashion, Mahmood Mamdani argues that the purpose of the doctrine was primarily to reinforce colonial power.[53] The haphazard, selective application of native laws meant that rather than sustain a local past, the project of empire was assisted.[54]

Considering the significant procedural similarities between Islamic repugnancy and the British colonial imposition of the repugnancy doctrine, it is likely that the repugnancy clause migrated from neighboring British India to Iran. Indeed, the concept of repugnancy in British colonies mirrored the idea of Islamic repugnancy. Both the British and Islamic repugnancy clauses attempt to subject all laws to some higher normative standard rooted in a higher law, or in the case of the "moral" repugnancy clauses, to a "fair and just" type test. The difference, of course, is that while the colonial repugnancy clauses looked for morality in European standards of natural law and good conscience, the Iranian repugnancy clauses held Islam to be the source of morality. That is, while the British sought to make customary norms more "British" in Muslim countries, it was modern constitutionalism that was to become more "Islamic." Also, in Iran in particular, the intention was that it would be Muslim jurists, rather than civil judges as in the case of the British, who would assess the compatibility or incompatibility of laws with the repugnancy doctrine.[55]

---

[50] Leon Sheleff, *The Future of Tradition: Customary Law, Common Law and Legal Pluralism* (Routledge 2000) 123.

[51] Ibhawoh, *Imperialism and Human Rights* 61.

[52] Caplan, "The Making of 'Natural Justice'" 120, 132.

[53] Mahmood Mamdani, *Citizen and Subject: Contemporary Africa and the Legacy of Late Colonialism* (Princeton University Press 1996) 117.

[54] Ravit Reichman, "Undignified Details: The Colonial Subject of Law" in Harold Bloom, *Bloom's Modern Critical Interpretations: Chinua Achebe's Things Fall Apart* (Chelsea House Publisher 2001) 51, 56.

[55] But see Amirhassan Boozari, *Shi'i Jurisprudence and Constitution: Revolution in Iran* (Palgrave Macmillan 2011) 159 (explaining that the Council idea never really took off until 1979).

3.1.2 *The Spread of Islamic Supremacy Clauses*

Earlier we introduced the data set that illustrates which countries have Islamic supremacy clauses in their constitutions. To supplement this data, time-series data from the Comparative Constitutions Projects (CCP) was drawn upon to further illustrate the origins and timing of these clauses. Analysis of the data shows that Islamic supremacy clauses have spread rapidly to become a common feature in the constitutions of Muslim countries. Almost half of the constitutions of Muslim countries contain "source of law" or "repugnancy clauses." From 1907 to 1950, only two constitutions (Iran/Persia and Afghanistan) contained such clauses.[56] The newly drafted Syrian Constitution of 1950 contained a clause specifying that "Islamic jurisprudence is a main source of legislation."[57] Almost four decades later, after a hiatus of constitutional Islamization, in the years between 1990 and 2012, we see a five-fold increase in the number of countries where the constitutions contain such clauses. This is a result of both the proliferation of new Muslim-majority countries and constitutional systems generally. In absolute terms, the number of Muslim countries with such constitutional provisions has continued to grow and today it stands at nineteen. In the second part of the twentieth century, constitutional Islamization clauses spread much more widely and are a staple feature of the constitutions of about 40 percent of Muslim countries today.[58] In 2008, the Maldives became the latest nation to adopt constitutional Islamization in its constitution. Egypt's newly drafted 2012 constitution also essentially reproduced the Islamic supremacy clause from its 1980 constitution, which made the principles of Islamic law (shari'a) the principal source of legislation.

3.2 AN EMPIRICAL ANALYSIS OF ISLAMIC SUPREMACY CLAUSES

In assessing the relationship between Islamic supremacy clauses and rights in constitutions, we rather counterintuitively find a surprising co-occurrence between the two – that is, the incorporation of Islam in constitutions is accompanied by an increase in the number of rights in the constitution,

---

[56] The Constitution of Afghanistan 1931, art. 65. ("Measures passed by the Council should not contravene the canons of the religion of Islam or the policy of the country.")

[57] Lombardi, "Constitutional Provisions" 733, 735.

[58] Benjamin Wormald, "Beliefs About Sharia" (Pew Research Center, April 30, 2013) <www .pewforum.org/2013/04/30/the-worlds-muslims-religion-politics-society-beliefs-about-sharia> accessed June 20, 2020 (saying that there are 49 countries with more than 50 percent Muslim population).

and the incidence of both are rising. This correlation results from the constitutional bargain rooted in coalitional politics whereby different parties enter into a compromise reflecting a kind of "insurance swap" where one side desires protection for Islam and the other the provision of rights. The net effect of these potentially contradicting clauses is to delegate balancing between the two to downstream decision makers – courts and legislators.

3.2.1 *The Determinants of Constitutional Islamization*

What determines the decision to adopt an Islamic supremacy clause? Our account of the origins of the clauses suggest that a British colonial legacy may be helpful. Colonial structures have enduring legacies on legal systems, long after the colonial power has packed up and moved home.[59] To test this proposition, we conduct a statistical analysis of factors predicting the adoption of supremacy clauses. Our dependent variable is Islamic supremacy; we include in separate analyses the narrower category of repugnancy clauses and the broader set that includes source of law clauses.

We are concerned with factors that predict the onset of these clauses, that is, the time at which a country adopts a clause for the first time. The unit of analysis is the country-year. Looking at onset makes sense because there is a good deal of stickiness in these clauses; once adopted, countries tend not to eliminate them.[60] We estimate a probit model where the dependent variable is a binary variable that captures whether or not a country has adopted a repugnancy or Islamic source of law clause in any given year. The variable takes a value of 1 for the first year a country's constitution contains an Islamic supremacy clause and 0 for every year before. Every year after adoption falls out of the data.[61]

As explanatory variables, we include a dummy variable that takes value 1 if the British were the last colonial power to colonize a country, and 0 otherwise.[62] We also experimented with a similar variable for French colonialism.

---

[59] Daniel M Klerman and others, "Legal Origin or Colonial History?" 3 Journal of Legal Analysis 379, 380 (2011).

[60] Although they occasionally do. See Interim National Constitution of Republic of Sudan July 6, 2005 (no repugnancy clause).

[61] We also ran a similar analysis with the constitution as the unit of analysis, in which we are predicting which constitutions have the clauses relative to those that do not. These results are substantially similar.

[62] This is taken from the CEPII Database, GeoDist Database. Thierry Mayer and Soledad Zignago, "Notes on CEPIH's Distance Measures: The GeoDist Database" 8 (2011) <www.cepii.fr/PDF_PUB/wp/2011/wp2011-25.pdf> accessed January 15, 2022. The dummy variable takes value 1 if CEPII variable Colonizer 1 is coded GBR.

Variables	(1) Repugnancy	(2) Islamicity
Year	0.093	0.09
	(0.12)	(0.01)
GDP	−.00007	.00005
	(.00006)	(.00002)
Democracy (UDS)	−0.06	−0.03
	(0.29)	(0.29)
British colony	1.84***	0.59
	(0.40)	(0.36)
Percent Muslims	4.73***	6.32**
	(1.79)	(3.15)
Global total percent	74.74***	168.37***
	(27.88)	(45.64)
Constant	−27.17	−27.26
	(23.94)	(24.15)
Observations	1,351	1,136

Standard errors in parentheses
*** p<0.01, ** p<0.05, * p<0.1

FIGURE 3.1. Determinants of the adoption of Islamic supremacy clauses (Muslim-majority countries only)

However, we find that no country in the French colonial tradition has ever adopted Islamic repugnancy clauses, so it was not useful in the statistical analysis of that dependent variable. To examine the effects of time, we include a variable for year, as well as wealth and level of democracy.[63] We also include a variable that captures the total number of countries with clauses in force in each year. This captures whether or not there is a trend associated with the large literature on policy and institutional diffusion.[64] We restrict the analysis to countries with more than 50 percent Muslim population (Figure 3.1).

The results are consistent with our expectations. Controlling for level of democracy, wealth, and time, British colonial heritage is a predictor of

---

[63] We use the Unified Democracy Score (UDS) measure, which aggregates other measures of democracy. See Daniel Pemstein and others, "Democratic Compromise: A Latent Variable Analysis of Ten Measures of Regime Type" (2010) 18 Political Analysis 426, 428 (establishing the UDS measure).

[64] Z Elkins and Beth Simmons, "On Waves, Clusters, and Diffusion: A Conceptual Framework" (2005) 33 The ANNALS of the American Academy of Political and Social Science 598; David S Law and Mila Versteeg, "The Evolution and Ideology of Global Constitutionalism" (2011) 99 California Law Review 1,163.

repugnancy clauses; it is also associated with greater likelihood of superiority clauses more generally, though the result is just shy of statistical significance. In unreported analysis, we find that replacing British colonial heritage with that of French produces a statistically significant negative coefficient: French colonies are associated with less supremacy. In addition, and perhaps unsurprisingly, the higher the percentage of Muslims in the country's population, the more likely it is that a country will adopt a supremacy clause. This suggests that the clauses may be popularly demanded. We do not, however, find an effect for democracy. That is, more democratic countries are neither more nor less likely to adopt supremacy. This is a significant finding: contrary to popular assertions about the incompatibility of Islam with democracy, nondemocratic countries are not more likely to adopt Islamic supremacy clauses. We also find a result for global trends; the more countries that have repugnancy clauses or supremacy clauses, the more likely other countries are to adopt them.

3.2.2 *The Co-occurrence of Rights and Islamic Superiority*

We also observe, counterintuitively, that constitutions that undergo constitutional Islamization also contain many rights. That is, constitutions that incorporate Islamic supremacy clauses also seem to contain, relative to a predecessor constitution and to the constitutions of other Muslim countries without Islamic supremacy clauses, a larger number of constraints on government.

Why would Islam go together with rights? There are three possibilities. One is that the same political forces that are pushing for Islamization are also pushing for more rights. In some cases, the parties perceiving both rights and Islam as indivisible are part of the constitution-making process. Drawing upon Egypt's experience of constitution making in 1971, Kristen Stilt observed that those who desired to see Islam institutionalized associated it as linked with more rights.[65] Rights to freedom of association and expression, for example, can help protect religious movements. We also know from polls that the majority of Muslims desire Islam to be a source of legislation because they associate many positive rights with Islam that also overlap with modern-day human rights norms. For example, a majority believed that incorporating Islam as a source of law would mean the provision of justice for women,

---

[65] Kristen A Stilt, "Constitution in Authoritarian Regimes: The Case of Egypt" in Tom Ginsberg and Alberto Simpser (eds), *Constitutions in Authoritarian Regimes* (Cambridge University Press 2013) 111–40.

constraining government, a reduction in corruption, the protection of minorities, and a fair judicial system. Even in secular Turkey, less than a third of Muslims who want Islamic law to be a source of legislation perceive it to limit personal freedom. Thus, it could very well be that the demands for rights and Islam are motivated by the same forces.[66]

Alternatively, a second possibility is that of an extremely polarized political sphere where completely different groups with comparable popularity advocate for their respective positions. On one hand, there may be groups who push for an Islamic supremacy clause in the constitution, while on the other, completely unrelated liberal groups assert for inclusion of rights. Alongside these contrasting positions, their interests may also overlap. For example, both groups might want more democracy and constraints on government as protection against an incumbent authoritarian regime, even if they view the path to achieving this in ideologically different terms. One group might feel, as the Muslim Brotherhood in Egypt that "Islam is the solution," while another group, composed of non-Muslims or secularists, might favor a more rights-based approach. The parallel inclusion of both Islam and rights in the constitution may thus owe itself to the compromise between different political forces, even with the same ultimate political agenda, operating concurrently.

A third possibility is that Islam and human rights are adopted together in a kind of coalition process, in a spirit of compromise. Suppose in the context of Islam that you have a constitutional bargain between secular liberals, an Islamist party, and the military. Any two of these groups can get together to adopt a constitution and impose it on the third group. The Islamic party insists on the supremacy of Islam. The military prefers to control its own budget. The liberals want to have an extensive set of rights. None of them particularly trust each other. If the constitutional bargain is between the military and the Islamic party, there will be no rights but a supremacy clause. If the bargain is concluded between the military and the liberals, there will be rights but no supremacy. And if it is between the Islamists and the liberals, there will be both. In this way, coalitional politics explain the co-occurrence of rights and Islam.

Beyond this simple coalitional story, there might be a need for what could be called "coalitional insurance." The basic dynamic has been laid out in the context of South Africa, in which the particular set of rights adopted in the constitution reflected a kind of "insurance swap" between two sides to a

---

[66] Magali Rheault and Dalia Mogahed, "Many Turks, Iranians, Egyptians Link Sharia and Justice" (Gallup, July 25, 2008) <www.gallup.com/poll/109072/many-turks-iranians-egyptians-link-sharia-justice.aspx> last accessed date May 2, 2022.

political bargain.[67] In that negotiation, left-wing and right-wing factions both valued different rights: the left valued socioeconomic rights, like those of housing, while the right insisted on strong property protections. Since neither was sure it would control subsequent politics, both insisted on their preferred rights as a way of protecting their future interests. The net effect is to delegate policies to decision makers down the road, but in a way whereby those decision makers are constrained by a set of competing priorities. In this way, each faction in constitution making has some protections for its core interests. In Muslim countries, such an insurance swap provides Islamists or religious clerics with an assurance that future progressive legislation that violates Islamic principles will be constitutionally invalidated. In exchange, they agree to the inclusion of certain rights in the constitution. In effect, the insurance swap allows parties that may potentially have competing or conflicting aims to bargain in a more efficient way that provides more space for reaching a compromise. That is, while during constitutional negotiations, the Islamists may not be inclined to agree to the inclusion of certain controversial rights, such as absolute freedom of speech without limits to prevent, for example, blasphemy, and the secular liberals may similarly not be willing to agree to the *noninclusion* of such a right, the Islamic supremacy clause, swapped against certain rights, then provides a means for both to reach an agreeable outcome. That is, liberals can have, for example, a right to freedom of speech in the constitution as long as that right is subjugated to an Islamic supremacy clause that provides "insurance" that the right may not be used, for example, to insult Islamic beliefs. In the absence of such "insurance," the Islamic parties may not agree to a free speech clause. In this sense, the insurance swap delegates the interpretation and reconciliation of the potentially contradictory right in relation to the Islamic supremacy clause to future legislators and perhaps, more importantly, to the courts and resolves political deadlock. The clause then satisfies the Islamists because it guarantees that rights and laws would not violate Islam and the provision of the desired right in the constitution then in parallel satisfies secular liberals. Eventually, courts will need to maintain a balance between rights that may potentially conflict with Islam. And, as scholarship by Nathan Brown, Ran Hirschl, and Clark Lombardi shows, it seems that courts in many Muslim countries have been doing precisely that – adopting progressive interpretations of rights while attempting to ensure fidelity to Islamic values. We will return to this theory in the case studies in the

---

[67] Rosalind Dixon and Tom Ginsburg, "The South African Constitutional Court and Socio-Economic Rights as 'Insurance Swaps'" (2011) 4(1) Constitutional Court Review 1, 4.

next chapter, but for now, let us examine the relationship between rights and Islamic supremacy in modern constitutions.

Table 3.1 provides such an analysis. It lists the major constitutional events in countries that have adopted Islamic supremacy at some point, along with the number of rights in each national constitution. To comprehend Islamic supremacy clauses, we use two variables as constitutional Islamization takes two forms – repugnancy and source of law clauses. The table also indicates a good deal of "stickiness" in constitutional Islamization clauses. Once adopted, they tend to endure through subsequent constitutions. This is a general feature of constitutional design.[68] In the case of Islamization clauses, only two countries failed to sustain such clauses in subsequent constitutions: Afghanistan, after the Soviet invasion in 1979, and the Comoros, which briefly had a consultative role for religious scholars (ulama) on legislation from 1996–2001.[69] The number of rights is taken from the CCP, which has generated a list of 117 rights found in national constitutions since 1789.[70] The table indicates the number from this list; we note that it is possible that there may be other rights not tracked by the CCP that are of idiosyncratic importance. In Table 3.1, * indicates a repugnancy clause; + indicates a clause that stipulates that Islam is "a" or "the" basic, main, or supreme source of law.

Notably, constitutions that introduce some form of Islamic supremacy clause also contain more rights. For countries that *had* a previous constitution and then introduced an Islamic supremacy clause, all but two (Mauritania 1985 and Afghanistan 1931) featured more rights *after* adopting supremacy clauses.[71] The average increase was 20.5 rights out of our list of 117 rights. The average constitution with some form of supremacy had 35.8 rights (n = 37), relative to 31.9 for those without (n = 668). Islamic supremacy is thus, quite surprisingly, associated with *more* constitutional rights.

---

[68] Zachary Elkins, Tom Ginsburg, and James Melton, *The Endurance of National Constitutions* (Cambridge University Press 2009) 59.

[69] Constitution of the Federal Islamic Republic of the Comoros 1996, art. 57. ("The Council of the Ulemas may, at its own initiative, in the form of recommendations, direct the attention of the Federal Assembly, the Government and the governors to reforms that appear to it as conforming [to] or contrary to the principles of Islam.")

[70] These are available in an online appendix.

[71] The case of Comoros in 1978 is consistent as well. That constitution introduced language to the effect that the country would "draw from Islam, the religion of the state, the permanent inspiration of the principles and rules that govern the Union." This language is not strong enough to count as a supremacy clause in our coding, but it still represented a shift in Comoros law toward Islamization. It was accompanied by an increase of sixteen rights over the earlier 1975 document.

TABLE 3.1. *Number of rights in constitutions for Muslim countries that adopt Islamic supremacy clauses*

Country	Year	Number of rights
Afghanistan	1923	15
	1931[*]	11
	1933[*] (amendment)	13
	1964[*]	28
	1977[*]	26
	1980	36
	1987[*]	50
	1990[*]	60
	2004[*]	37
Bahrain	1973+	45
	2002+	45
Comoros	1975	8
	1978	24
	1980	28
	1987	23
	1992+	30
	1996+[a]	28
	2001+	23
Egypt	1923	28
	1930	24
	1953	3
	1956	33
	1964	31
	1971+	43
	1980+	43
	2011+	46
Iran	1906	1
	1907[*]	48
	1979[*] +	45
Iraq	1925	23
	1964	28
	1970	34
	1990	33
	2004[*] +	44
	2005[*] +	52

Country	Year	Number of rights
Kuwait	1962+	39
Libya	1951	41
	1969	15
	2011+	24
Maldives	1968	15
	1998	18
	2008*	72
Mauritania	1961	9
	1978	19
	1985+	0
	1991+	28
Oman	1996+	40
Pakistan	1956*	26
	1962*b	29
	1973*	41
	2002*	37
	2010* (amendment)	45
Qatar	1970+	0
	2003+	33
Saudi Arabia	1992+	13
Somalia	1960+	43
	1979	39
	2004+	43
Sudan	1955	N/A
	1964	N/A
	1971	N/A
	1973+	46
	1985+	29
	1998* +	41
	2005+	49
Syria	1950+	38
	1953+	41
	1964+	24
	1973+	29
	2012+	29

(*continued*)

TABLE 3.1. (*continued*)

Country	Year	Number of rights
UAE	1971+	29
Yemen	1962+	22
	1970+	31
	1991+	33

* Repugnancy clause
+ Islamic supremacy clause
a The Comoros in 1996 introduced an Ulama Council that could make legislative recommendations if it felt that law was violating Islam. We do not count this as supremacy or repugnancy because the role is only advisory, but we nevertheless include it in the table.
b Pakistan's 1962 constitution is an ambiguous case. Although it contains a clear statement that no law should be repugnant to Islam, it also states that the "validity of a law shall not be called in question on the ground that the law disregards, violates or is otherwise not in accordance" with this clause. Constitution of the Islamic Republic of Pakistan, art. 6(2). As in the Comoros in 1996, Pakistan's 1962 constitution established the Advisory Council of Islamic Ideology, to render "advice" to the legislature regarding the repugnancy of laws.

3.2.3 *Multivariate Analysis*

Of course, it is possible that the correlation between rights and Islamization in the constitution is caused by something else, a "missing variable" that is independently affecting both types of provision. One possibility is time. We know that, as a general matter, the number of rights found in national constitutions has increased over time.[72] Constitutions adopted later tend to have more rights, if only because the total number of rights has continued to expand, from "first-generation" civil and political rights to second, third, and even fourth-generation rights.[73] We also note that the era after the adoption of the Universal Declaration of Human Rights in 1948 has corresponded with a rapid increase in national constitutional rights. Because, as we noted in Part I, the adoption of Islamic clauses tends to be a modern phenomenon, it is

[72] Zachary Elkins and others, "Getting to Rights: Treaty Ratification, Constitutional Convergence, and Human Rights Practice" (2013) 54 Harvard International Law Journal 61, 76–77 ("As one indicator, the nine constitutions written in 1947 contain an average of 17.6 rights, while the six written in 1949 contain at average of 31.0 rights.") David S Law and Mila Versteeg, "The Evolution and Ideology of Global Constitutionalism" (2011) 99 California Law Review 1,163.

[73] Philip Alston, "A Third Generation of Solidarity Rights: Progressive Development or Obfuscation of International Human Rights Law?" (1982) 29 Netherlands International Law Review 307 (third-generation rights); Louis Henkin and others, *Human Rights* (2nd ed., Foundation Press 2009) 369 (fourth-ageneration rights); Beth A Simmons, *Mobilizing for Human Rights: International Law in Domestic Politics* (Harvard University Press 2009).

possible that the co-occurrence of the two phenomena is simply the result of time trends and not the result of any direct relationship.

Another potential missing variable is British colonialism. Recall our earlier argument that British colonialism had an influence on the adoption of Islamic superiority clauses. But what if British colonialism also leads countries to adopt more rights in constitutions? If so, if we see a co-occurrence of rights and Islam, we may be simply observing two independent effects of British colonialism.[74]

To test for such possibilities requires a multivariate analysis, in which we can control for various factors to determine the independent contribution of each one. We analyze a data set in which the unit of analysis is the constitution; the data set contains 983 total documents, of which 161 are from Muslim-majority countries. Our dependent variable in the following analyses is the number of rights found in any particular constitution from our list of 117. It ranges from zero to eighty-eight in our data. Our independent variables of interest are "repugnancy," which captures whether or not the constitution has a repugnancy clause, and "Islamicity," which includes constitutions both with repugnancy clauses and other forms of normative superiority as described in Part I. We also include as control variables the year the constitution was adopted, the level of democracy as measured by the Unified Democracy Score (UDS),[75] whether the country is a former British colony, and, as a proxy for wealth, energy consumption, etc.[76] (Note that the number of observations in each regression is smaller than the entire data set because not all of these control variables are available for each constitution.)

Because our dependent variable is "count data," in which the variable ranges from zero upward in integers, a Poisson regression is the appropriate statistical method. The table reports the results in "incident rate ratios," which can be interpreted as the shift in the odds that a constitution will contain an additional right. Any value greater than 1 indicates an increased probability associated with the factor in question, while a value less than 1 indicates a decreased probability. The values can be read as the increased probability

---

[74] Jerg Guttman and Stefan Voigt, "The Rule of Law and Constitutionalism in Muslim Countries" (2015) 162 Public Choice 351–80 (arguing that colonial history plays an important role in explaining variation in civil liberties across countries).

[75] James Melton and others, "Democracy Scores" (*Unified Democracy Scores*, May 12, 2014) <www.unified-democracy-scores.org/uds.html> accessed January 15, 2022.

[76] This is a standard variable used in empirical analyses that extend before 1945, when GDP data began to be systematically collected. Zachary Elkins and others, "Getting to Rights: Treaty Ratification, Constitutional Convergence, and Human Rights Practice" (2013) 54 Harvard International Law Journal 61, 95.

Variable	All countries		Muslim majority	
	(1)	(2)	(3)	(4)
Year	1.04***	1.01***	1.01***	1.02***
	(0.0006)	(0.0006)	(0.001)	(0.001)
Democracy (UDS)	1.18***	1.17***	1.13***	1.13***
	(0.016)	(0.016)	(0.047)	(0.047)
GDP	1.00	1.00	1.00	1.00
	(1.64e-06)	(1.69e-06)	(2.63e-06)	(2.64e-06)
Former British colony	.94***	.95***	1.18***	1.19***
	(.018)	(0.19)	(.05)	(.05)
Repugnancy	.99		1.12**	
	(0.05)		(0.06)	
Islamicity		0.90		1.02
		(0.032)		(0.05)
Constant	3.57e-11***	2.65e-11***	5.16e-12***	2.21e-12***
	(4.50e-11)	(1.55e-08)	(1.45e-12)	(6.21e-12)
Observations	337	337	78	78

Standard errors in parentheses
*** $p<0.01$, ** $p<0.05$, * $p<0.1$

FIGURE 3.2. Poisson regression predicting number of rights (odds ratios reported)

associated with the particular variable in question. For example, for Muslim-majority countries, a constitution with a repugnancy clause (column 3 in Figure 3.2) is predicted to have 12 percent more rights than one without. Each additional year is predicted to add 1 percent more rights.

As one can see, time *does* have an effect on the probability of the adoption of additional rights. Each additional year is predicted to increase the number of rights by roughly 1 percent. Democracy, too, has a positive effect, unsurprisingly, both within Muslim-majority countries and the broader set of countries. An additional unit in the UDS is associated with between 13 percent and 18 percent more rights. The findings on British colonial heritage are interesting in light of our concern that it might be driving both rights and Islamic provisions. British colonial heritage is associated with 5 to 6 percent fewer rights in the full set of constitutions, but 18 to 19 percent *more* rights in Muslim-majority countries. These results are statistically significant.[77]

---

[77] In unreported analysis, we included a variable for whether or not the constitutional system has some form of judicial review, on the theory that judicial review might be driving these constitutional choices. Although the judicial review variable is associated with more rights in all specifications, the results for our key variables were not substantially different from the analysis reported here.

Our central variables of interest – the inclusion of Islamic repugnancy and supremacy clauses – are not associated with increases in the number of rights when we look at the full sample of countries worldwide. However, a better and more meaningful comparison is with other countries that have a Muslim-majority population. A country with few or no Muslims, after all, cannot be expected to have a constitutional provision stating that law contrary to Islam is void or that Islam will be a superior source of law. Nor are any other religions associated with constitutional clauses about religious superiority. Accordingly, when we restrict the analysis to constitutions adopted in countries with a Muslim population of more than 50 percent, we see that repugnancy clauses are in fact associated with more rights, *even* controlling for the effects of time, democracy, and British colonialism. We do not find the same effect for the broader category of Islamic supremacy clauses. But a constitution with a repugnancy clause can be expected to have 12 percent more rights. This is a significant and important finding: Islamic repugnancy clauses and rights are not only compatible, they are also connected in constitutional design.

4

Case Studies

To better understand the historical origins and cultural motivations for the adoption of Islamic supremacy clauses in national constitutions, it is important to trace the incidence of the initial adoption of Islamic supremacy clauses in the constitutions of Muslim-majority states. For this purpose, we engaged in case studies of four countries: Iran, Afghanistan, Egypt, and Iraq. These countries were selected because each adds something unique to our knowledge and understanding of the genesis of constitutional Islamization: Afghanistan and Iran were two of the earliest constitutions in the Muslim world to adopt repugnancy clauses. While Egypt was not the first country in the Arab world to incorporate a strong supremacy clause in the form of a source of law clause in its constitution (it was Syria that did so in 1950), the history of the adoption of supremacy clauses in the Egyptian constitution is well-documented. Iraq, on the other hand, provides a relatively recent account of the insertion of an Islamic supremacy clause during constitution making. The Iraqi experience of Islamic supremacy clauses is peculiar in the sense that an Islamic supremacy clause was introduced in 2004 for the first time, and that too under foreign occupation. This phenomenon is also instructive as to how Islamic supremacy clauses can operate as a bargaining chip for the foreign occupying power as well. Importantly, it also tells us how the dynamics of the insertion of an Islamic supremacy clause played out in a constitutional setting of foreign occupation. As compared to Afghanistan, which was also under foreign occupation at the time of the adoption of its 2004 constitution, Iraq is a more relevant case study because 2005 was the first time an Islamic supremacy clause was adopted in its constitution; Afghanistan, on the other hand, has had such a clause since 1931.

These case studies, when read together, imply that the incorporation of Islamic supremacy clauses can be in response to popular, democratic sentiment and that they are often adopted in a spirit of compromise, during moments of political liberalization. These case studies demonstrate that, depending on the context, the motives of constitution makers in incorporating Islamic supremacy clauses range from legitimizing progressive rights and reform to co-opting political opposition or simply legitimizing the incumbent regime.

4.1 IRAN

Iran has experimented with two constitutions, both of which were adopted in the aftermath of popular revolutions in 1906 and 1979 and both of which contain strong Islamic supremacy clauses. Iran's first constitution, adopted in the aftermath of the "Constitutional Revolution" in 1906, was the first constitution in the world to contain the most robust form of Islamic supremacy clause, that is, the repugnancy clause.[1]

In August 1906, the Iranian monarch, Mozaffar al-Din Shah signed a proclamation for constitutional government. This declaration marked Iran's transition from absolutist monarchy to a parliamentary form of government. The transition was not easily won; rather, it came after months of incessant agitation by a cross section of Iranian society consisting of clergy, traders, peasants, and merchants. These events culminated in what came to be popularly known as the "Constitutional Revolution." One important outcome of that revolution was the promulgation of a constitution that recognized the people as the source of political power, codified numerous rights, and established separation of powers within the government.[2]

4.1.1 *The Prelude to the Revolution*

During the course of the nineteenth century, Iran was deteriorating economically and militarily, much to the resentment of the country's inhabitants. Reliance on cash crops, the increasing export of raw materials, and the growing rate of unemployment had contributed to this economic situation and also raised questions of modernization in parallel with debates about how to curb the impact of European commerce on Iran's economy. Afary cites these transformations as the root causes of the Constitutional Revolution.[3]

---

[1] Constitution of Islamic Republic of Iran 1907, art. 2.

[2] Asghar Schirazi, *The Constitution of Iran: Politics and the State in the Islamic Republic* (I. B. Tauris 1998) 19 (discussing the Constitutional Revolution that produced the first Iranian constitution that separated judicial, executive, and legislative branches of government).

[3] Janet Afary, *The Iranian Constitutional Revolution, 1906–11: Grassroots Democracy, Social Democracy and the Origins of Feminism* (Columbia University Press 1996) 17 (detailing the

Externally, too, Iran, had become significantly dependent on European powers – namely Britain and Russia. Rather than resisting foreign domination, the monarchs of the Qajar dynasty had clearly succumbed to British and Russian pressure, ultimately turning Iran into "a prisoner of imperial interests" by the late nineteenth century.[4]

In pursuit of economic interests, Britain and Russia imposed humiliating economic "concessions" upon Iran in the form of asymmetric commercial agreements.[5] While such concessions in the short term brought in much needed revenue to the ailing economy, they were often raised to finance ostentatious foreign trips for the Qajar monarchs and damaged local interests. When the Shah first made public news of a concession granted to the British for the tobacco industry in February 1891, an alliance of secular reformers and religious dissidents, merchants and Shiite clerics, jointly opposed it. In December 1891, people stopped using tobacco when a prominent cleric issued a religious opinion (fatwa) that the consumption of tobacco was un-Islamic.[6] Eventually, left with no option and facing such strong cleric-led resistance, in January 1892, the Shah terminated the concession and paid a hefty termination penalty. This event demonstrates quite vividly the weakness of the incumbent Qajar regime to resist both foreign domination and domestic unrest.

4.1.2 *The Constitutional Revolution*

In the next decade, resentment against the Qajar regime only intensified. In 1905, protests initiated by a coalition of forces that included radical members of secret societies, secular and religious reformers, orthodox clerics, merchants, shopkeepers, and members of trade guilds erupted against the

---

origin of the Constitutional Revolution of 1906 in the structural and ideological transformations at the turn of the century, resulting from decades of economic change and damaging European influence).

4   Ali Geissari, "Constitutional Rights and the Development of Civil Law in Iran, 1907–41" in HE Chehabi and Vanessa Martin (eds), *Iran's Constitutional Revolution: Popular Politics, Cultural Transformations and Transnational Connections* (I. B. Tauris 2010) 69, 71.

5   Nikki R Keddie, "Iranian Revolutions in Comparative Perspective" (1983) 88(3) The American Historical Review 579, 580 (discussing the British tobacco concession in 1890 and the subsequent mass rebellion).

6   Sami Zubaida, *Law and Power in the Islamic World* (I. B. Tauris 2005) 185 (exploring the events of the tobacco concession to a British company and subsequent successful boycott of the tobacco monopoly because Mirza Hassan Shirazi, senior mujtahid, issued a fatwa banning the use of tobacco on pain of "eternal damnation").

Shah.[7] Opposition had galvanized against a government which was "not only tyrannical but was also engaged in selling the country to foreign imperialists"[8] as "the country had become a semi-colony [of the Europeans]."[9] External events, such as the Russian Revolution and the victory of Japan in the Russo-Japanese War 1904–5 also played a part in catalyzing opposition. While the Russian Revolution demonstrated that it would be possible to have "another and better form of government," the Japanese victory symbolized the victory of a non-white nation armed with a constitution over a major European power without a constitution.[10]

While some commentators ascribe the making of the paradoxical coalition – of clerics and revolutionaries – to the leadership of the clerics and a strong sense of justice in Shi'ite theological doctrines, others focus on various ideological and economic factors, such as contact with Western ideas of liberalism and democracy, that created a consensus among all segments of society that government authority must be controlled by a constitution and parliament.[11] Some reformers simply felt that an expression of constitutional ideas guised in religious rhetoric would be more effective or perhaps necessary in achieving revolutionary objectives.[12] Certainly, Iranian clerics have been

---

[7] Afary, *Iranian Constitutional Revolution* 22 (explaining the origins of the coalition despite the long history of animosity between religious and secular reformers by examining the literature on diversity, economic factors, and ideological changes).

[8] Said Amir Arjomand, *The Turban for the Crown: The Islamic Revolution in Iran* (Oxford University Press 1989) 79.

[9] Shahrough Akhavi, "Iran: Implementation of an Islamic State in Islam" in John L. Esposito (ed), *Islam in Asia: Religion, Politics and Society* (Oxford University Press 1987) 27, 29.

[10] Afary, *Iranian Constitutional Revolution* 14 (noting that the only Asian constitutional government defeated the only major Western nonconstitutional government). Nikki Keddie, *Modern Iran: Roots and Results of Revolution* (Yale University Press 2006) 66 (discussing the revolutionary plans in Iran strengthened by the Russo-Japanese War and the Russian Revolution. The Japanese victory has been perceived to have inspired a number of revolutions across Asian countries). Nikki R Keddie, *Iran and the Muslim World: Resistance and Revolution* (Palgrave Macmillan 1995) 14 (discussing the mass movements in Asian Countries between 1905–12, sparked by the Japanese victory in the Russo-Japanese War.)

[11] Afary, *Iranian Constitutional Revolution* 23 (examining several interpretations of the link between secular and religious reformers, the earlier emphasis on the implicit sense of justice in Shi'ite doctrine, and the more recent focus on economic and ideological factors). Vanessa Martin, *Islam and Modernism: The Iranian Revolution of 1906* (Syracuse University Press 1989) 35 (arguing that ulama were responding to the government's economic difficulties and the subsequent question of the legitimacy of ulama).

[12] Afary, *Iranian Constitutional Revolution* 23 (discussing the religious dissidents' strategy to guise constitutionalism in religious rhetoric). Mansoor Moaddel, "The Shi'i Ulama and the State in Iran" (1986) 15(4) Theory and Society 519 as quoted in Afary, *Iranian Constitutional Revolution* 31 (arguing that the merchants called upon the ulama as a clever use of religion for secular and anti-imperialist ends).

described as the "prime movers" in the various opposition movements formed against the Shah in this period.[13] As one scholar notes, "one remarkable feature of this revolution here ... is that the priesthood have found themselves on the side of progress and reform."[14] In fact, alliances between the religious leadership in Iran and modernizing political activists have been a recurring feature of Iranian history.[15] Historians argue that the clerics' religion-based anti-tyrannical discourse greatly legitimized the cause of the revolution. For example, one well-known jurist, Muhammad Husain Na'ini, invoked Islamic doctrine in support of the concept of liberty and equality, declaring that "liberty meant people's freedom from any type of capricious rule, unaccountability and coercion by any powerful individual, even the king."[16] Another reformist cleric who came to prominence in the constitutionalist movement, Sayyid Muhammad Tabatabai, argued that the monarchical system of government was not sufficient for defending religion or ensuring just government. Such arguments no doubt facilitated the popularity of the revolutionary cause. Also, over the years, clerics in Iran had accumulated significant financial resources derived from the religious foundations and canonical taxes, which provided them with a financial base independent from the state.[17] Further, the state had been adopting policies that were increasingly encroaching upon their interests; thus, their leadership and contribution to the cause should be viewed as at least partly born out of strategic considerations.[18]

The central demand of this diverse group of protestors in the Constitutional Revolution was for the rule of law and establishment of representative government. Since 1860, there had been a recurring demand among many Iranians for a House of Justice (*adalatkhana*) that would dispense justice in contrast to

---

[13] Martin, *Islam and Modernism* 1 (discussing the role of the ulama during the Constitutional Revolution, as "prime movers").

[14] Martin, *Islam and Modernism* 199; Keddie, *Iran and the Muslim World* 68 ("unique case of a traditional religious leadership supporting and even leading a modernizing constitutional revolution").

[15] Keddie, *Iran and the Muslim World* 5 (discussing recurring alliances and coalitions between religious leadership and liberal or radical nationalist activists in Iranian history from 1890 to the present).

[16] Amirhassan Boozari, *Shi'i Jurisprudence and Constitution: Revolution in Iran* (Palgrave Macmillan 2011) 58

[17] Martin, *Islam and Modernism* 35 (discussing how the ulama relied on the lack of centralization in the Qajar political system to gain enough financial wealth so as to be independent of the state.)

[18] Willem F Floor, "The Revolutionary Character of the Iranian Ulama" (1980) 12(4) International Journal of Middle East Studies 501, 502.

the arbitrary justice delivered by the Qajars.[19] This is not surprising as the Shah was an "absolute monarch" in whose "person were fused the three-fold functions of government, legislative, executive, and judicial. He was the pivot upon which turned the entire machinery of public life." Vanessa Martin argues that the absence of a written law in Iran meant that government was often "arbitrary and unsystematic. Many of the complaints of the merchants ... [were] related to arbitrary taxation and to maladministration of the revenues .... One of the themes of the Constitutional Revolution [was] that government be regulated by law .... [T]he cry for justice and law ... illustrates [how much less developed the Iranian system was]."[20] These demands became more pronounced as some clerics openly pleaded for a House of Justice.[21] This limited demand soon morphed into calls for a parliament – a majlis that would facilitate representative government.[22] Nevertheless, the ideological foundations of the idea for a parliament had its initial origins in the demand for a House of Justice.[23] In parallel, a constitution, or *mashrutiyat*, also emerged as a demand.[24] One commentator writes that, in light of the demands being made, the "anti-despotic revolution [was] aimed at restricting the ruler's power" and "unbridled tyranny of the Qajar dynasty's monarchs."[25]

Ultimately, the protestors sought to place limits on the monarchy and were concerned with ideas of popular sovereignty and justice, in accordance with

---

[19] Martin, *Islam and Modernism* 76 (discussing the 1860 reorganization of the Ministry of Justice and ulama's request for *adalatkhana*, or courts of justice); Afary, *Iranian Constitutional Revolution* 57 (examining the public cry for a majlis that was "national" not "Islamic").

[20] Martin, *Islam and Modernism* 10.

[21] Martin, *Islam and Modernism* 10. Clerics would preach to large congregations demanding a House of Justice, *adalatkhana*. These actions were part of mounting agitation against the government.

[22] Afary, *Iranian Constitutional Revolution* 57 (examining the rhetoric involved in the creation of *majalis* and the debates between nationalists and the religious government who wanted "Islamic *majalis*" versus "national *majalis*"); Mansour Bonakdarian, *Britain and the Iranian Constitutional Revolution of 1906–1911: Foreign Policy, Imperialism, and Dissent* (Syracuse University Press 2006) 56; Martin, *Islam and Modernism* 97 (discussing the ulama's request for a majlis, probably resulting from disagreements among the ulama about constitutionalism).

[23] Stephanie Cronin, "The Constitutional Revolution, Popular Politics, and State-Building in Iran" in HE Chehabi and Vanessa Martin (eds), *Iran's Constitutional Revolution: Popular Politics, Cultural Transformations and Transnational Connections* (I. B. Tauris 2010) (describing the roots of the parliamentary idea of a majlis in the early demands for a "House of Justice").

[24] Nikki Keddie and Mehrdad Amanat, "Iran under the Late Qajars 1848–1922" in P Avery, GRG Hambly, and C Melviller (eds), *The Cambridge History*, vol 7 (Cambridge University Press 1991) 174, 203.

[25] Boozari, *Shi'i Jurisprudence and Constitution* 45.

religious norms, and were not really focused on secularism of personal liberties.[26] Indeed, this was not novel: Islamic law had been frequently used as a language of protest and contestation against injustice and to demand accountability; hence it was not expected even during this popular revolution that a constitution would replace Islamic law – to the contrary, it would reinforce Islamic law.[27]

4.1.3 *Iran's First Constitution*

On August 5, 1906, the monarch, Mozaffar al-Din Shah, finally capitulated and issued a proclamation for the formation of a majlis, or parliament, and the drafting of a new constitution. Subsequently, elections were held and members of the majlis were elected. Majlis members drafted a constitution, which was ratified on December 30, 1906.[28] The constitution, influenced by the French 1791 and the Belgian 1831 constitutions,[29] significantly reduced the monarch's absolute powers and made him duty bound to uphold the constitution. Government ministers were responsible to the majlis. Equality before the law and personal freedoms were guaranteed, subject to some limitations, even for non-Muslims. The press was to be freer than ever before and the majlis could, in contradistinction to the shah, propose measures it considered to be conducive to the well-being of the government and the people.[30] Compulsory public education was also guaranteed. Essentially, the "intent of the constitution was to setup a true constitutional monarchy."[31]

---

[26] Geissari, "Constitutional Rights and the Development of Civil Law" 69, 73.

[27] Geissari, "Constitutional Rights and the Development of Civil Law" 69, 73.

[28] Afary, *Iranian Constitutional Revolution* 65.

[29] Afary, *Iranian Constitutional Revolution* 67, 108 (concerning the Belgian constitution as the model for the law and the Supplementary Law); Keddie, *Modern Iran* 68 (arguing the Fundamental Law and the Supplementary Fundamental Law were largely based on the Belgian Constitution. This was a reasonable choice for the new constitutional movement in Iran, which had little experience with democratic politics. In their choice of the Belgian Constitution, we should also note that there appears to have been no substantial borrowing from the constitutions of the two great powers, Russia and Great Britain, or the United States. The choice of the Belgian Constitution as a model was evidently not accidental, nor was it simply dictated by existing circumstances. Rather, the decision seems to have been the product of a discerning and critical analysis of Western constitutions in order to uncover aspects that would work in a predominantly Muslim society).

[30] Constitution of Iran 1906, art. 15.

[31] Keddie, *Modern Iran* 68.

4.1.4 *Coalitional Cracks*

Soon after the constitution was ratified, shifting combinations of self-interest, idealism, and group attachments in the amorphous alliance that had enabled the revolution became visible.[32] The progressive direction that the country followed through the majlis created unease in the elite segments of society. Delegates of the landowning class were unsympathetic to the social and economic reform programs and did not favor efforts to collect funds from affluent members of the community.[33] The provisions of rights in the constitution began to cause much anguish, especially among the clerics and other conservatives.[34] In particular, the scope of the majlis's constitutional authority to enact all kinds of laws without any limitations was novel and thus troubling. Even the constitutionalist clerics in the majlis firmly believed that the majlis should incorporate the rules of Islamic law in all its work.[35] It soon became clear to the clerics that their initial assumption that personal and religious laws would remain within their prerogative even after the enactment of the constitution and that the majlis would deal solely with commercial and political aspects was misguided. If this was the case, the enactment of bold new rights and freedoms and women's educational provisions would not have been possible. One prominent cleric, Shaikh Fazlollah Nuri, Tehran's "most learned" cleric,[36] who had previously supported the constitutionalist movement, began to emerge as a strong opponent to the majlis and the country's first constitution.[37] He based his opposition to the constitutional movement upon Islamic law,[38] arguing that constitutionalism was an innovation against

---

[32] Joanna de Groot, "Whose Revolution? Stakeholders and Stories of the 'Constitutional Movement' in Iran, 1905–1911" in HE Chehabi and Vanessa Martin (eds), *Iran's Constitutional Revolution: Popular Politics, Cultural Transformations and Transnational Connections* (I. B. Tauris 2010) 23 (discussing the instabilities and complexities of the alliances formed for the Constitutional Revolution).

[33] Afary, *Iranian Constitutional Revolution* 70 (exploring how the reforms affected the landowning class, namely that the abolition of the fief system and tax reform increased their share of taxes and the effort to collect more money from the landowning class to avoid foreign debt.)

[34] Martin, *Islam and Modernism* 115 (discussing the clashes between the clerics and the landed interest with the local constitutionally protected councils, as well as the debate in the majlis about whether to abolish the fief system in order to save money).

[35] Boozari, *Shi'i Jurisprudence and Constitution* 119.

[36] Martin, *Islam and Modernism* 58.

[37] Afary, *Iranian Constitutional Revolution* 71 (concerning Nuri and the struggle between pro-constitutionalists and anti-constitutionalists).

[38] Martin, *Islam and Modernism* 3 (discussing Shaikh Fazlollah Nuri's campaign against constitutionalism based on fundamental points of Islamic law).

Islam.[39] A number of other clerics agreed[40] and began to undermine the constitution by invoking religious rhetoric.[41] They claimed that the new constitution violated Islam and that only a legal code based on the shari'a would be acceptable to them. Their view remained that "Man is not to make laws." Rather, this was the prerogative of God, not that of a parliament composed of mere mortals.[42]

However, there were a number of clerics who also invoked Islamic arguments in *favor* of the constitution and led protests against the conservative clerical opposition to constitutionalism. For example, leaflets were published that challenged the authority of the clerics to pronounce on seemingly "secular" matters such as constitutional laws.[43] In Tehran, protests took place against the anti-constitutionalist clerics, and delegates of an urban council vowed to camp outside a main square until the supplementary constitution was ratified.[44] Shaikh Fazlollah Nuri was at one point even driven out of town.[45] Nevertheless, the argument that the constitutionalists wished to replace Islamic law with a law of foreign origin had become very powerful in popular imagination.[46] Indeed, the most powerful argument employed by the anti-constitution clerics was that the majlis was an institution that had no legitimate basis in Islamic law and that it was introducing laws of Europe which had no place in Islamic law. Nuri's chief objection to the constitution – and a popular one – was that the majlis would enact the "customs and practices of the realms of infidelity" and that it would thus violate the laws of Islam.[47] The constitution was, in this view, a form of cultural imperialism that would weaken Islam.[48]

[39] Masoud Kamali, *Revolutionary Iran: Civil Society and State in the Modernization Process* (Ashgate Pub Ltd 1998) 119.
[40] Martin, *Islam and Modernism* 165 (discussing general disillusionment with constitutionalism among previously supportive clerics.)
[41] Kamali, *Revolutionary Iran* 113.
[42] Mehrangis Kar, "Shari'a Law in Iran" in Paul Marshall (ed), *Radical Islam's Rules: The Worldwide Spread of Extreme: Shari'a Law* (Rowman and Littlefield Publishers 2005) 31, 43 (fierce opposition to constitutionalists' modernist tendencies by fundamentalists).
[43] Afary, *Iranian Constitutional Revolution* 89.
[44] Afary, *Iranian Constitutional Revolution* 89.
[45] Afary, *Iranian Constitutional Revolution* 115.
[46] Martin, *Islam and Modernism* 138 (discussing difficulty on the part of constitutionalists to refute Shaikh Fazlollah's points).
[47] Said Amir Arjomand, "The Ulama's Traditionalist Opposition to Parliamentarianism: 1907–1909" (1981) 17(2) Journal of Middle Eastern Studies 174, 179.
[48] Arjomand, "Ulama's Traditionalist Opposition to Parliamentarianism" 185. Arjomand also argues that while there were indeed such divisions between constitutionalist clerics who supported the constitution and anti-constitutionalist clerics who opposed it, ultimately, they acted as a unified body when their interests were at stake.

As conservative opposition to the constitution was building up, the idea of constitutionalism was itself waning in popularity as the financial situation of the country deteriorated even further since the election of the majlis.[49] Further, the ailing monarch, Mozaffar al-Din Shah, had died and his son, Muhammad Ali Shah, was intent on dismantling the constitution. Certain conservative clerics who had already grown dismayed with constitutionalism – such as Shaikh Fazlollah Nuri, the leading cleric of the Imam Riza Shrine in Mashhad, and those in charge of the rapidly proliferating urban councils – pledged their allegiance to the new monarch.[50] The Shah, desiring to capitalize on these circumstances, recognized that the most effective way to undermine the constitution was to assert that it was incompatible with Islamic law.[51] He thus actively encouraged the clerical opposition and also began to demand that the constitution and its civil rights not violate Islamic law. This was a clever strategy that had the effect of developing an "Islamic opposition" to constitutionalism.[52]

4.1.5 *The Supplementary Constitution of 1907 and Islamic Supremacy Clauses*

It had become clear that not only was the Constitution of 1906 causing much consternation among various elements of Iranian society, but it was also textually incomplete. There was no bill of rights, nor were limits to the authority of the executive, legislature, and judiciary clearly defined. Thus, work immediately began on a supplementary constitution which would solidify the gains of the Constitutional Revolution and fill gaps in the earlier constitution. Deliberations over this supplementary constitution were marked by great acrimony. The committee that was drafting this supplement was constituted by constitutionalists and prominent left-wing delegates.[53] Many clerics became particularly concerned about the work of this committee. From their perspective, the initial constitution did not contain enough Islamic provisions or an adequate role for the clerics and, in fact, contained

---

[49] Arjomand, "Ulama's Traditionalist Opposition to Parliamentarianism" 185.

[50] Afary, *Iranian Constitutional Revolution* 77.

[51] Afary, *Iranian Constitutional Revolution* 115.

[52] Martin, *Islam and Modernism* 139 (discussing how emerging constitutional law threatened the ulama's privilege and authority, causing a growing opposition).

[53] Janet Afary, "Social Democracy and the Iranian Constitutional Revolution of 1906–11" in John Foran (ed), *A Century of Revolution: Social Movements in Iran* (University of Minnesota Press 1982) 21, 27 (discussing the proposed supplements to the constitution, which were essentially a bill of rights, and the makeup of the committee).

many provisions that were deemed to be un-Islamic. The supplementary constitution provided a means to remedy these defects. Therefore, conservative clerics began to attend meetings of the committee to ensure the conformity of the constitution with Islamic law.[54]

Perhaps with the hope of placating clerical opposition, majlis parliamentarians eventually agreed to the formation of an additional committee, composed of ranking clerics and headed by Shaikh Fazlollah Nuri; their role would be to "review" amendments to decide what was or was not compatible with the shari'a. In these meetings, debates occurred about the place of the Qur'an in the constitution with some arguing that it was the very foundation of the constitution itself while others argued that it was only the foundation of religion, and not the constitution.[55] Conservative clerics and deputies initially rejected many of the proposed civil liberties on the grounds that they were incompatible with Islam and unacceptable to the majority Shi'a population. The anti-constitutionalist clerics led by Shaikh Fazlollah Nuri strongly opposed compulsory public education and freedom of the press. The measure that most antagonized the clerics was equal treatment of all males, since, in their view, Muslims and non-Muslims could not have the same rights.[56] The conservative clerics were of the view that the very doctrine behind constitutional equality disregarded the rules of Islam.[57] They perceived equality to be a clever way to circumvent the dictates of Islamic law under the guise of constitutionalism. An argument was also made that members of the majlis may not have the required competence to ascertain what was or was not Islamic.[58] On this issue, pro and anti-constitutionalist clerics debated extensively.[59] Ultimately, to guard against the provision of non-Islamic rights and legislation, the anti-constitutionalist clerics wanted a Council of Clerics with veto power over all laws of the majlis.[60]

---

[54] Martin, *Islam and Modernism* 117. (Shaikh Fazlollah attended meetings to ensure law conformed to shari'a.)

[55] Kamali, *Revolutionary Iran* 113.

[56] Martin, *Islam and Modernism* 129 (discussing the differing treatment of Muslims and others under shari'a and the argument that equal rights and mandated education were simply imported European ideas).

[57] Boozari, *Shi'i Jurisprudence and Constitution* 119; Martin, *Islam and Modernism* 119 (discussing the argument that "infidels and Muslims" could not receive equal rights under shari'a); Keddie, *Iran and the Muslim World* 61 (discussing the ulama's opposition to the parliament's draft of the constitution, which proposed equality of all religious communities, which the ulama claimed as "un-Islamic").

[58] Boozari, *Shi'i Jurisprudence and Constitution* 120.

[59] Afary, *Iranian Constitutional Revolution* 105.

[60] Afary, "Social Democracy and the Iranian Constitutional Revolution" 21, 27 (discussing the debate over a proposal for a Council of Ulama with veto power over all laws).

As a result of these debates and disagreements, compromises had to be made which were explicitly reflected in the 1907 Supplementary Constitution. A comparison of the first draft of the 1907 law and the final version clearly demonstrates that major concessions were made to clerical sentiment.[61] The Supplementary Constitution contained an extensive bill of rights, providing protection to property, life, domicile, privacy regarding letters and telegrams, and the right to a fair trial. The state, rather than the clergy, was placed at the head of the public educational system (Article 19). An additional civil rights provision (Article 14) even stated that no Iranian citizen could be exiled from the country or prevented from living there. Yet many rights were subject to Islamic law. The study of science, art, and crafts was permitted "save in the case of such as may be forbidden by the [*sharia*]" (Article 18). Freedom of the press was granted except for "heretical books and matters hurtful to the lucid religion" (Article 20). Freedom of organization was granted throughout the nation, provided the associations were "not productive of mischief to religion or the state" (Article 21). Most importantly, this constitution, unlike its predecessor, included a very strong-form Islamic supremacy clause. The majlis delegates had agreed that a committee of leading clerics would review and rewrite articles of the constitution that were in conflict with Islamic law.[62] Article 2 of the 1907 Supplementary Constitution thus called for the establishment of a Council of Clerics – an Islamic review mechanism – and also stated that laws ratified by the majlis could not be at variance with the shari'a. In exchange for the Islamic supremacy clause, Shaikh Fazlollah Nuri specifically campaigned for the most controversial article of the constitution, that is, Article 8, which provided that citizens would enjoy equal rights before the law, regardless of religion. The anti-constitutionalist clerics perceived it to be in clear contradiction with Islamic law.[63] The majlis could also enact customary laws as long as these laws did not conflict with Islamic law.[64] Other

---

[61] Janet Afary, "Civil Liberties and the Making of Iran's First Constitution" (2005) 25(2) Comparative Studies of South Asia, Africa and the Middle East 341, 341–59.

[62] Afary, *Iranian Constitutional Revolution* 89. Afary argues that the concept of "freedom" was generally ignored in the 1907 Constitution. This is not surprising "since many members of the ulama continued to oppose the notion of freedom, and the word soon adopted a highly pejorative connotation. Freedom, including the right to be different and to act differently from other people, was equated with non-religiosity, immorality, lack of chastity, and licentious behavior. With regard to gender, words such as freedom and liberation had come to have a doubly negative connotation. For example, a "free woman" meant "a vulgar, immoral, and sexually promiscuous one." Afary, *Iranian Constitutional Revolution* 220.

[63] Martin, *Islam and Modernism* 117 (discussing the contention around Article 8); Afary, *Iranian Constitutional Revolution* 108.

[64] Kamali, *Revolutionary Iran* 113.

provisions, such as Article 27, concerning who should decide in which court a case was to be tried, and Article 71, dealing with the powers of the tribunal of justice, were deliberately left ambiguous so as to facilitate a compromise.[65]

In effect then, the Supplementary Constitution's Islamic supremacy clauses became a medium through which clerics safeguarded their institutional and ideological concerns in return for acceding to progressive provisions in the constitution.[66] Alarmed by the secular implications of imported, foreign models and potential negative connotations this may have on the country, the clerical establishment pushed for a concept of constitutionalism compatible with Shi'ite Islam.[67] The inclusion of Islamic supremacy clauses in Iran's Constitution (the first Islamic supremacy clause in history) can, therefore, be understood as essentially the outcome of bargaining – or, as we discussed earlier, an "insurance swap" – between constitutionalists and conservative clerics. In light of the fact that many among the elite and certainly the Shah were vehemently opposed to constitutionalism, the constitutionalists had no option but to compromise with the clerics if the constitution was to survive with its progressive rights. Rights and constitutionalism necessarily invoked negative reactions from the clergy and even from many members of a conservative, religiously inclined society. The constitutionalist project, if it was not to be derailed, required that such reactions be tamed. The idea that non-Muslims or women would have the same rights as Muslims or that the press would be free to publish anything, even texts that went against Islamic principles, was surely an anathema and revolutionary in a society in which most people identified deeply with religion. Thus, Iran's Constitution was certainly progressive in that it contained many civil rights and freedoms, yet this was precisely the reason *why* it also needed to contain Islamic supremacy clauses. A willingness on the part of constitutionalists – borne out of necessity – to balance the constitutional provision of rights with a strong Islamic supremacy clause arguably played a significant part in the endurance of the Constitution of 1906. As Keddie writes, "from 1905 ... an ideology has been worked out associating liberal constitutionalism with Islam."[68] Considering the traditional nature of Iranian society, the approval of the clerics – as

---

[65] Martin, *Islam and Modernism* 140 (discussing the intentional vagueness in Articles 27 and 71 so as to facilitate a compromise between the ulama and the constitutionalists.)

[66] Afary, *Iranian Constitutional Revolution* 89.

[67] Rainer Grote and Tilmann J Roder (eds), *Constitutionalism in Islamic Countries: Between Upheaval and Continuity* (Oxford University Press 2012) 5 (describing how the idea of constitutionalism compatible with shari'a first gained ground in Iran in 1906 as a response to foreign models and the belief in the uniqueness of Iranian constitutionalism).

[68] Keddie, *Iran and the Muslim World* 77.

gatekeepers of Islam – was needed to legitimize the majlis and the constitution.[69] Islamic idiom wrapped in the language of constitutional Islamic supremacy clauses thus provided insurance that limited government and rights did not mean a subjugation of Islam. As we will see in the other case studies in the following sections of this book, this assurance – provided through Islamic supremacy clauses – would also be repeated elsewhere.

4.2 AFGHANISTAN

Similar to Iran, Afghanistan's constitutions have almost always been written after some major political upheaval.[70] The first two constitutions, in 1923 and 1931, were established after the final battle for independence from Great Britain and after the revolt of 1929 that deposed King Amanullah, respectively.

Like the Iranian Constitution, Afghanistan's first constitution also contained many rights, but it contained only symbolic references to Islam and did not contain any Islamic clauses. It was this failure to incorporate strong Islamic clauses that initially led to its amendment and eventually its demise and replacement with a constitution that provided robust Islamic clauses. Unlike the Constitution of Iran, the first Afghan constitution failed to balance the "novel" provision of rights with Islam. In other words, it failed to provide adequate constitutional insurance that Islamic law and Islam would not be trumped by an enactment of rights and other liberal features. This proved to be fatal to its existence.

4.2.1 *The Prelude to Afghanistan's 1923 Constitution*

At the turn of the twentieth century, Afghanistan was a hereditary monarchy and had no written constitution like many other countries. It would be fair to describe Afghanistan as a tribal society composed of different ethnicities that, for centuries, had regulated much of its affairs through Islamic law and customary law, including *Pashtunwali*, the tribal code of honor of Pashtuns.[71] Since Pashtun tribes also constituted the bulk of the military, they were the most influential as far as governance was concerned. It was

---

[69] Martin, *Islam and Modernism* 142 (discussing the idea that "the will of the people" meant the approval of the ulama by Iran's people who were profoundly influenced by tradition).

[70] Mohammad Hamid Saboory, "The Progress of Constitutionalism in Afghanistan" in Nadjma Yassari (ed), *The Sharia in the Constitutions of Afghanistan, Iran and Egypt* (Mohr Siebeck 2005) 5–6.

[71] Tom Ginsburg, "An Economic Interpretation of the Pashtunwali" (2011) University of Chicago Legal Forum 89, 89.

understood that the ruler would primarily comply with the precepts of Islamic law, as well as with the principles of *Pashtunwali*. Although the legitimacy of a ruler was determined by Islamic law, it was partly negotiated with tribal leaders.[72] This meant that the monarch, while not *constitutionally* constrained, was constrained by the consent of the important tribes in the country.[73] In this system in which de facto state power was shared between the monarch and the tribes, the clerics occupied a vital third role in the running and dispensation of the judicial system. Since rulers often needed favorable fatwas (religious opinions) from clerics on important issues, such as fighting foreign invaders or persuading people to fight against "infidels," Afghan clerics gained significant prominence and thus became an important part of the governance structure.[74] The central government granted large allowances and privileges to the clerics, and they were free to administer justice in accordance with their interpretation of Islamic principles.[75]

4.2.2 *The 1923 Constitution*

Afghanistan, like Iran, was also subject to significant foreign influences due to a strategic rivalry between Britain and Russia known as the Great Game. Successive British governments viewed Afghanistan as a buffer state that could be used to guard India against Russian expansionary forces. The British feared that Afghanistan would become a staging post for a Russian invasion of India.[76] It was such suspicion that led the British to rather unsuccessfully launch various wars against Afghanistan, known as the Anglo-Afghan Wars. In the aftermath of one of these wars, Amanullah Khan acceded to the Afghan throne in 1919. He defeated the British, led Afghanistan to victory, and, more importantly, gained sovereignty in the Third Anglo-Afghan War, fought in

---

[72] Senzil K Nawid, *Religious Response to Social Change in Afghanistan, 1919–29: King Aman-Allah and the Afghan Ulama* (Mazda Pub 2000) 6.

[73] Ramin Moschtaghi, *Max Planck Manual on Afghan Constitutional Law* (vol 1, Max Planck Institute for Comparative Public Law and International Law, Heidelberg 2009) 13.

[74] Ramin Moschtaghi, *Max Planck Manual on Afghan Constitutional Law* 13. Rulers would engage ulama to declare fatwas, inciting the public against "infidels" and declaring jihad. Amir Abdul Rahman, who reigned from 1880–1901, successfully reduced the power of the ulama by centralizing religious authority into the state, requiring qadis to pass state-controlled examinations and giving them salaries.

[75] Mohammad Hashim Kamali, *Law in Afghanistan: A Study of the Constitutions, Matrimonial Law and the Judiciary* (Brill Academic Pub 1985) 7 (discussing the power of the ulama in the nineteenth century, in regard to most aspects of political and cultural life).

[76] Konstantin Penzev, "When Will the Great Game End?" (November 15, 2010) Oriental Review <http://orientalreview.org/2010/11/15/when-will-the-great-game-end/>accessed January 15, 2022.

1919. This certainly helped boost his credibility among his countrypeople and facilitated his rise.[77] Riding on this wave of popularity, cognizant of modernization efforts being undertaken in the Ottoman Empire,[78] and armed with a desire to see his country similarly modernized, Amanullah Kahn began adopting a series of very ambitious legal reforms, soon after taking power. These reforms included the adoption of Afghanistan's first constitution in 1923, which transformed the country from an absolute monarchy to a constitutional one.[79]

The Constitution of 1923, which was based on the 1906 Iranian constitution and the constitution of Turkey during Ataturk's rule,[80] was drafted with the help of French and Turkish advisors who drew heavily on the Napoleonic Code.[81] Amanullah hoped that by making reforms inspired by Turkey, the reforms would be seen as legitimate and acceptable to clerics.[82] The constitution contained a bill of rights and guaranteed that all Afghan subjects would have "equal rights and duties to the country in accordance with sharia and the laws of the state."[83] The constitution also promised greater rights to religious minorities. It abolished torture, slavery, and forced labor; created a legislature; and, in a rather bold move, decreed that followers of religions other than Islam, such as Hinduism and Judaism, were entitled to the protection of the state. Elementary education was made compulsory for boys and girls. Personal freedom, freedom of the press, freedom of association, and freedom of property were guaranteed. The constitution declared "all courts of justice are free from all types of interference and intervention."[84] The principle of legality in criminal law was also adopted. The homes and personal dwellings of all

---

[77] Leon B Poullada, *Reform and Rebellion in Afghanistan, 1919–1929; King Amanullah's Failure to Modernize a Tribal Society* (Cornell University Press 1973) 66 (discussing Amanullah's reputation as an anti-British nationalist, which helped his popularity).

[78] Bruce Etling, *Legal Authorities in the Afghan Legal System (1964–1979)* Afghan Legal History Project at Harvard Law School 11 (2013) <www.law.harvard.edu/programs/ilsp/research/etling .pdf> last accessed September 3, 2013.

[79] Senzil Nawid, "The Khost Rebellion: The Reaction of Afghan Clerical and Tribal Forces to Social Change" (1996) 56 Review of Department of Asian Studies and Department of Study and Research on African and Arab Countries 311–19 <http://opar.unior.it/1317/1/Annali_1996_ 56_%28f3%29_S.Nawid.pdf> accessed January 15, 2022.

[80] Fausto Biloslavo, "The Afghanistan Constitution between Hope and Fear" (2004) 2(1) CeMiSS Quarterly 61.

[81] Nighat Mehroze Chishti, *Constitutional Development in Afghanistan* (Royal Book Co 1998) 21.

[82] Nawid, *Religious Response to Social Change in Afghanistan* 78. Interestingly, neither Turkey's recent move toward secularism, nor Iran's Shi'ite character seemed to have deterred Amanullah from seeking constitutional inspiration from those countries.

[83] The Constitution of Afghanistan 1923, art. 16.

[84] The Constitution of Afghanistan 1923, art. 53.

Afghan subjects were inviolable. The constitution also contained provisions for a State Council consisting of elected and appointed members (Article 39), though it had only advisory functions. The king was also authorized to appoint the ministers, including the prime minister, without consulting with the State Council. One particularly controversial reform was that Hindus and Jews were no longer required to wear distinctive dress marking their status. Apart from the adoption of a constitution, the King also introduced progressive legislative reforms: he passed laws outlawing child marriage, marriages between close relatives, polygamy, excessive dowries, and the exchange of women as "blood money" in payment of interfamilial disputes. He also opened girls' schools and sent women students abroad for higher education.

The 1923 Constitution also contained many references to Islam. Islam was the religion of the state and the king was the "servant and the protector of the true religion of Islam."[85] Article 72 provided that legislators had to give "careful consideration" to the "requirements of the laws of Sharia."[86] Yet, moderating the effects of this provision, Article 72 also stated that in the process of legislation, the actual living conditions of the people and require-ments of the time would be given serious consideration, *in addition* to rules of the sharia. The constitution also provided that "all disputes and cases will be decided in accordance with the principles of Sharia and of general civil and criminal laws."[87]

While the constitution was not overtly democratic by modern standards, it was impressive by the standards of that time, and certainly outside the realm of Europe. As one commentator notes, "the Constitution of 1923 constituted great progress for the country and changed the legal system of Afghanistan to one of the most modern ones throughout the region."[88] It is pertinent to note that it was written without any meaningful political participation on the part of those outside of government[89] but still brought remarkable and significant social and political changes to Afghanistan.

4.2.3 *Revolt against Reform and Rights*

Ultimately, despite the fact that Amanullah Khan was a deeply religious man who often invoked Islamic principles in support of his reforms and even

---

[85] The Constitution of Afghanistan 1923, art. 5.
[86] The Constitution of Afghanistan 1923, art. 72.
[87] The Constitution of Afghanistan 1923, art. 21.
[88] Moschtaghi, *Max Planck Manual on Afghan Constitutional Law* 16.
[89] J Alexander Thier, "The Making of a Constitution in Afghanistan" (2006) 51(4) New York Law School Law Review 557, 569.

though the constitution contained symbolic references to Islam,[90] the constitutional reforms were seen as having a Western taint.[91] This proved to be precisely the problem – the reforms were too ambitious for Afghan society. The constitutional provision of rights was seen by the religious and tribal elite as an innovative attack on traditional values, culture, and religion. Conservatives had much to object to in these reforms: the compulsory education for girls, the failure of the constitution to identify the Hanafi school as the brand of Islam to be followed in the state, the abolition of the requirement for Hindus and Jews to wear symbols that distinguished their identity, the free press, and the restriction on polygamy the child marriages. These were too much to accept.[92]

Some clerics attacked the new code and the constitution as contrary to Islamic law with others brandishing "in one hand the Qur'an and in the other the new laws, inviting true Muslims to choose between them."[93] In response, a revolt broke out in 1924 that "shook the Afghan government to the core."[94] The rebellion has been cited as the "reaction of indigenous religious and tribal groups to ... rapidly modernize Afghanistan."[95] Ultimately, it was religious leaders who were in the forefront of the opposition, with many influential tribal leaders staying neutral and senior clerics only voicing opposition later on.[96] The clerics saw the efforts of Amanullah to codify Islamic law as a means to "secularize" the law – which was unacceptable.[97] Even among the religious groups, it was the village clerics who interpreted the reforms as diluting the social force of Islam and encroaching upon their prerogatives in areas such as education, where the constitution provided for compulsory education and Amanullah, rather courageously, set about opening schools for girls.[98] To be sure, the rebellion was also partly caused by the introduction of universal conscription and tax reforms. Efforts at centralization and state-building – which adversely affected tribal autonomy but nevertheless introduced the innovative rights contained in the legal code and the constitution – were

---

[90] Poullada, *Reform and Rebellion in Afghanistan* 59 (discussing the use of propagandistic assertions that Amanullah was anti-Muslim when in fact he was a well-read and pious Muslim who would often argue the finer points of Islam in his lectures in Egypt).

[91] Nawid, *Religious Response to Social Change in Afghanistan* 78.

[92] Kamali, *Law in Afghanistan* 28 (discussing reservations in response to Amanullah's ambitious and somewhat culturally foreign reforms).

[93] Poullada, *Reform and Rebellion in Afghanistan* 85.

[94] Nawid, "The Khost Rebellion" 311.

[95] Nawid, "The Khost Rebellion" 311.

[96] Nawid, *Religious Response to Social Change in Afghanistan* 92.

[97] Nawid, *Religious Response to Social Change in Afghanistan* 99.

[98] Nawid, *Religious Response to Social Change in Afghanistan* 96.

major reasons for the rebellion. Among the rebellious groups, the low-ranking clergy were particularly suspicious of the constitution.[99] In fact, the earliest calls to rise up in protest came from such clerics in rural areas.[100] Soon, the oppositional protests in the country turned into a full-scale rebellion in Khost, when some religious clerics condemned the reforms as antithetical to the shari'a.[101] A reactionary call to Islam thus energized the revolt immensely and a delegation Amanullah sent to placate the rebels returned with a message asking the government to make certain amendments to the constitution and other laws if it desired the revolt to end.[102]

4.2.4 *Compromise and Islamic Entrenchment*

Afghanistan's modern history is replete with frequent tensions between modernizing elements and conservative ones, and the revolt to Amanullah's reforms is one such example.[103] In the midst of the rebellion and facing regime collapse, in the autumn of 1924, King Amanullah called the *Loya Jirga* to review and possibly reconsider certain provisions of the constitution and laws that were objectionable.[104] Despite the fact that the King's constitution, as described earlier, paid symbolic respect to Islam, it became apparent that the constitutional provisions contained were too weak to placate the storm of opposition. Ultimately, the *Loya Jirga* decided that major concessions had to be made. In addition to demands concerning the repeal of some of the reformed laws, the clerics at the *Loya Jirga* urged that Article 2 of the Constitution be amended to declare the Hanafi school the official school of religious jurisprudence in Afghanistan – just as the Iranian Constitution had earlier adopted Shi'ism as the official state religion.[105] They also demanded that restrictions on non-Muslims, which were removed from the 1923

---

[99] Nawid, "The Khost Rebellion" 311, 312.

[100] Nawid, "The Khost Rebellion" 313.

[101] Nawid, "The Khost Rebellion" 314.

[102] Kamali, *Law in Afghanistan* 28 (discussing how Amanullah's delegation to the rebels returned with recommendations for amendments to the constitution).

[103] Paul Fishstein, "Afghanistan's Arc of Modernization: 1880 to 1978" (*The Globalist*, September 1, 2010) <www.theglobalist.com/afghanistans-arc-of-modernization-1880-to-1978/> accessed January 15, 2022.

[104] Poullada, *Reform and Rebellion in Afghanistan* 94 (stating that Amanullah assembled the *Loya Jirgah* for a second time to reconsider legislation that the rebellion objected to and consequently amended several of the constitutional laws).

[105] Saboory, "Progress of Constitutionalism in Afghanistan" 5, 6–7 (discussing reassembling the *Loya Jirga* to reconsider the religious issue).

Constitution, be reinstated.[106] Indeed, constitutional measures of tolerance shown to non-Muslims were particularly offensive for the clerics.[107] Rights granted to women also had to be diluted, torture was reintroduced when "in accordance with the rules of the *sharia*," the prior abolition of child marriage and polygamy was rescinded, and Hindus and Jews were to pay a special poll tax and wear distinctive signs that would mark out their identity. Furthermore, similar to the case of Iran, an Islamic supremacy clause was inserted: a Council of Islamic Scholars were to "decide whether new laws were in accordance with Islamic law."[108] Article 9 was also amended to read that "Afghan subjects were bound by the religious rite and political institutions of Afghanistan."[109] The clerics also demanded a redefinition of the word "freedom" used in Article 9 of the constitution, as it could be construed to mean religious freedom or freedom to engage in activities contrary to Islam and thus needed to be changed.[110] In return for these concessions, the constitution was unanimously approved by all the members of the *Loya Jirga*.[111]

While the crisis may have been resolved for the time being, unfortunately for Amanullah, problems would arise again. Amanullah's visit to Russia and Turkey in 1928 demonstrated his visible leaning toward both those countries – one communist and the other secular – which continued to generate much suspicion in Afghanistan, and not just among the religious elite.[112] Further, the King's rash commencement of a new set of reforms – including the removal of the veil, the mandated education of women, the adoption of Western clothing, and the changing of the weekly holiday from Friday to Thursday – soon after his old reforms had just been grudgingly accepted and moderated to be "Islamic" alienated many Afghans. Such sweeping changes, along with Western influence, ignited deep resentment among the people and rekindled memories of a long struggle for independence against Westerners.[113] This time, even the clergy who had supported the government during the previous revolt were alienated.[114] In response, in January 1929, another larger revolt

[106] Kamali, *Law in Afghanistan* 29 (discussing the pre-1923 constitution custom that required Hindus and Jews to wear distinctive clothing and headdress and pay extra taxes).

[107] Nawid, *Religious Response to Social Change in Afghanistan* 99.

[108] Poullada, *Reform and Rebellion in Afghanistan* 122.

[109] Kamali, *Law in Afghanistan* 30.

[110] Nawid, *Religious Response to Social Change in Afghanistan* 109.

[111] Nawid, *Religious Response to Social Change in Afghanistan* 112.

[112] Nawid, *Religious Response to Social Change in Afghanistan* 154.

[113] Nawid, *Religious Response to Social Change in Afghanistan*, 158–59; Said Amir Arjomand, "Constitutional Developments in Afghanistan: A Comparative and Historical Perspective" (2005) 53 Drake Law Review 943, 947.

[114] Nawid, *Religious Response to Social Change in Afghanistan* 161.

broke out,[115] ending with Kabul falling to rebel forces led by a bandit, Bacha-i-Saqao. In October 1929, Nadir Khan defeated this bandit to become the new King of Afghanistan and promulgated a new constitution in 1931.[116]

4.2.5 The 1931 Constitution and Islamic Supremacy

Although Nadir Shah allied himself with traditionalists, he was a modernist personally.[117] The constitution he promulgated in 1931 to replace King Amanullah's 1923 Constitution, in the words of Louise Dupree, "embodied a hotchpotch of unworkable elements, extracted from the Turkish, Iranian and French constitutions including the 1923 Constitution of Amanullah plus many aspects of Hanafi *sharia* of Sunni Islam and local customs (*adat*), several of them in fact contradicting the *sharia*."[118] Said Arjomand argues that Nadir Shah's constitution was in many respects more liberal than the earlier constitution of 1923.[119] Indeed, invoking a curious mix of principles of Islamic supremacy and rights, Article 91 even provided that "every person may plead in court *any* provision of Shariat law to protect his rights."[120] Free compulsory education was to be continued, slavery and torture were prohibited, press freedom was guaranteed, and, rather liberally, it was stated that "all the subjects of Afghanistan have equal rights and duties."[121] The constitution also created a national parliament with legislative power, a royally appointed upper House of Nobles, and a consultative council in each province, and ministers were held accountable to parliament. The constitution also granted the right to vote to Afghan women. Even outside the constitutional context, some of Amanullah's more controversial reforms concerning marriage were retained, albeit in a weakened form.[122]

At the same time, the 1931 Constitution also contained more frequent references to Islam. The king was "to carry on the administration in accordance with the dictates of the expounders of the sacred Shariat of the Holy Prophet (peace be upon him!) and the Hanafi religion and the fundamental

[115] Biloslavo, "Afghanistan Constitution between Hope and Fear" 61, 62.
[116] Arjomand, "Constitutional Developments in Afghanistan" 943, 948.
[117] Asta Olesen, *Islam and Politics in Afghanistan* (Routledge 1995) 176 (discussing the modernist, rather than traditionalist, Nadir Shah and how this reflected on the constitution).
[118] Louise Dupree, *Afghanistan* (Princeton 1980) 464.
[119] Arjomand, "Constitutional Developments in Afghanistan" 943, 948.
[120] The Constitution of Afghanistan 1931, art. 91.
[121] The Constitution of Afghanistan 1931, art. 91.
[122] Olesen, *Islam and Politics in Afghanistan* 181 (discussing the Marriage Law of 1934 which kept, albeit weakened, the same ideas as the Marriage Laws of 1921 and 1924).

principles of the country."[123] Religious courts were required to base their decisions on Hanafi jurisprudence. Most importantly for our purposes, the constitution contained two strong-form Islamic supremacy clauses. It also added an explicit repugnancy clause, similar to Iran, requiring that "measures passed by the National Council should not contravene the canons of the religion of Islam or the policy of the country."[124] Further, all laws and regulations were to be submitted to a Council of Clerics to ascertain their conformity with the shari'a.[125] Even equality and press freedom were subject to "Shariat law and the law of the state." Similarly, whereas the 1923 Constitution gave precedence to state law to direct state activity, the 1931 Constitution proclaimed shari'a as *the* law of the state.[126]

With minor amendments made in 1933, Nadir Shah's constitution survived thirty-three years[127] and its "enabling liberal features ... produced a democratic interlude with the free municipal and national elections after World War II."[128] King Amanullah's constitution lasted a mere eight years and that was with great difficulty. Despite being more liberal and modern, the 1931 Constitution lasted much longer than the previous one. One explanation for this may be that the pace of modernization Amanullah sought to achieve was unacceptable and perhaps too much for a conservative society to tolerate. As Olesen writes, Amanullah's reforms of "symbolic secularization" were greatly responsible for alienating the population, and ultimately then, the failure of his reform efforts.[129]

Yet, the explanation we advance in addition to this is that the reforms had not been accompanied by sufficient constitutional Islamization. That is, had Amanullah incorporated strong-form Islamic supremacy clauses in his constitution to provide "insurance" against novel and perceivably "un-Islamic" rights, he might have succeeded in placating the opposition to his constitutional reforms. Even if this insurance was only symbolic, it would have denied his opponents a powerful tool for mobilization. This lesson was not neglected by Nadir Shah, who distanced himself from Amanullah's model of aggressive and hasty secularization without providing adequate constitutional insurance for Islam – a recipe which necessarily alienated traditionalist

---

[123] The Constitution of Afghanistan 1931, art. 5.
[124] The Constitution of Afghanistan 1931, art. 65.
[125] Arjomand, "Constitutional Developments in Afghanistan" 943, 950.
[126] Kamali, *Law in Afghanistan* 21.
[127] Saboory, "Progress of Constitutionalism in Afghanistan" 5, 7–8 (considering the endurance of the 1931 Constitution).
[128] Arjomand, "Constitutional Developments in Afghanistan" 943, 950.
[129] Olesen, *Islam and Politics in Afghanistan* 180.

elements in Afghan society and symbolized "godlessness."[130] Nadir Shah was no traditionalist – he and his brothers were modernizers[131] – yet he understood the utility of employing religious symbolism and constitutionally co-opting religious sentiments and clerical interests. In contrast, Amanullah's fall from power and the demise of his constitution demonstrates how a leader in a Muslim-majority country, initially well respected by the religious elite and even considered to be a defender of Islam, soon had his constitutional reform thwarted as anti-Islamic and therefore illegitimate.[132] Although future constitutions of Afghanistan drew upon the 1923 Constitution, Amanullah's reforms were not only publicly rejected by the elite but also by much of the largely rural, traditional Afghan population.[133] Despite the compromise that resulted in a constitutional amendment in 1924, a stubbornness to implement the reform program without providing further constitutional insurance upset the delicate status quo achieved in the first amendments after the Khost Rebellion. Nadir Shah, in contrast to his predecessor, deliberately kept a low ideological profile and was not seen as someone who publicly imposed an alien worldview upon Afghan society, even as he sought to promulgate a constitution that was in practice no less liberal.[134] Like Iran, in Afghanistan, constitutional rights could be acceptable and secure legitimacy, as long as these rights did not impinge upon Islam. Had Nadir Shah tried to impose upon Afghan society a constitution that was too liberal but did not contain Islamic supremacy clauses to balance those liberal provisions – that is, without adequate and strong constitutional safeguards for Islamic law and the clerics, such as a repugnancy clause – his constitution too may have died a quick death as did his predecessor's.

As Saboory notes, considering Afghanistan's deeply traditional nature, implementing constitutionalism was inevitably going to present a significant challenge.[135] Thus, in a country where the population is not only overwhelmingly Muslim but where "Islam [remained] the common cultural

---

[130] Olesen, *Islam and Politics in Afghanistan* 180 (discussing Nadir Shah's strategy of distancing from Amanullah's "godlessness" by repeatedly stressing conformity to Islam in his constitution).

[131] Olesen, *Islam and Politics in Afghanistan* 180, 181 (discussing Nadir Shah's "modernizing," which by no means returned to the status quo but did not include liberalization in his definition of modernizing).

[132] Nawid, *Religious Response to Social Change in Afghanistan* 71.

[133] Etling, *Legal Authorities in the Afghan Legal System* 7–8.

[134] Olesen, *Islam and Politics in Afghanistan* 182 (discussing how Nadir Shah used religious concepts rather than the alien worldview as Amanullah did, with words like "progress" and "interests of the nation").

[135] Saboory, "Progress of Constitutionalism in Afghanistan" 5 (discussing Islamic and traditional society as factors for the difficult implementation of constitutionalism).

denominator,"[136] strong-form Islamic supremacy clauses were a requirement of constitutional design. Weak-form Islamic supremacy clauses and symbolic references to Islam, as provided in the 1923 Constitution, were certainly not enough to reach sustainable compromise between clerics and constitutionalists. A constitutional emphasis on Islam and strong Islamic supremacy clauses may thus, paradoxically, have helped rather than defeated Nadir Shah's liberalization efforts.

4.3 EGYPT

4.3.1 *Constitutional History before 1971*

Unlike Afghanistan and Iran, Egypt has had a number of constitutions that incorporated an Islamic supremacy clause.[137] The first Egyptian constitution, in 1882, was promulgated in the midst of a financial crisis when Egypt was a part of the Ottoman Empire but had significant political autonomy.[138] It was fairly brief and drafted with British assistance, and it contained few rights provisions.[139] It was soon terminated due to British occupation of the country. Egypt's next constitution was promulgated in 1923, after Egypt became independent.[140] It was modeled after the Belgian Constitution of 1830–31. It was a very liberal document despite the fact that it was written by a commission indirectly appointed by the monarch.[141] The 1923 Constitution laid the foundation for the emerging Egyptian nation-state. In this constitution, references to Islam and rights coincided. The 1923 Constitution declared Egypt a sovereign, free, and independent state, with Islam as its religion and Arabic its official language (Article 149). The constitution guaranteed freedom of thought and gave freedom of expression "according to the limits of the law"

---

[136] Nawid, *Religious Response to Social Change in Afghanistan* 1.

[137] Clark Lombardi, "Constitutional Provisions Making Sharia 'A' of 'The' Chief Source of Legislation: Where Did They Come From? What Do They Mean? Do They Matter?" (2013) 28(1) American University International Law Review 733, 754–58.

[138] Nathan J. Brown, *Constitutions in a Nonconstitutional World: Arab Basic Laws and the Prospects for Accountable Government* (State University of New York Press 2001) 26; Maurice Sheldon Amos, *Constitutional History of Egypt for the Last Forty Years* (1928) 14 Transactions Grotius Society 131.

[139] Brown, *Constitutions in a Nonconstitutional World* 62.

[140] Nathan J Brown and Roni Amit, "Constitutionalism in Egypt" in Daniel P Frankling and Michael J Baun (eds), *Political Culture and Constitutionalism: A Comparative Approach* (Routledge 1995) 184.

[141] Abdeslam M Maghaoui, *Liberalism without Democracy: Nationhood and Citizenship in Egypt, 1922–1936* (Duke University Press 2006) 130.

(Article 14). It gave freedom of assembly, also subject to the law (Articles 20 and 21). The constitution ensured the equality of all citizens before the law regardless of origin (*asl*) or language. It stipulated the equality of all Egyptians before the law regardless of religion (Article 3) and granted absolute freedom of belief (Article 12). It stipulated that "the state protects freedom to practice religious rites and creeds according to prevailing customs in Egypt within the bounds of public order (*al-niẓām al-ʿāmm*) and decency (*adab*)" (Article 13).[142]

In 1930, this constitution was suspended and replaced with a more restrictive one, only to be reestablished again in 1936.[143] In 1952, a revolution – known as the July 23 Revolution – overthrew the monarchy, abrogated the 1923 Constitution, and enacted a 1953 Interim Constitution that remained intact until a new constitution was drafted in 1956. After Egypt's short-lived merger with Syria, a new constitution was promulgated in 1958. In 1964, Gamal Abdel Nasser enacted yet another constitution.

It is important to note that none of these short-lived constitutions contained more than symbolic references to Islam, such as making Islam the religion of the state. This would change, however. In 1971, an Islamic supremacy clause would be added to Egypt's most enduring constitution – a constitution that lasted forty years and longer than any of its predecessors.[144]

4.3.2 The 1971 Constitution

Anwar Sadat assumed the presidency in Egypt after Nasser's sudden death in 1970. Nasser was a popular leader, and Sadat did not possess the public charisma of his predecessor. In fact, he came to power based upon an explicit understanding within the executive committee of the Arab Socialist Union that he would engage in a form of "collective leadership," in which there would be no individual rule – as had occurred under Nasser. Rather, the party elite would be consulted on all important decisions.[145] Accordingly, some party members saw Sadat as a "yes-man" who could be easily manipulated.[146]

---

[142] Rachel M Scott, *Recasting Islamic Law: Religion and the Nation State in Egyptian Constitution Making* (Cornell University Press 2021) 65.

[143] Scott, *Recasting Islamic Law* 66.

[144] Nathan J Brown, "Islam in Egypt's Cacophonous Constitutional Order" in Nathan J Brown and Said Amir Arjomand (eds), *The Rule of Law, Islam and Constitutional Politics in Egypt and Iran* (State University of New York Press 2013) 233–48.

[145] Kirk J Beattie, *Egypt During the Sadat Years* (Palgrave 2000) 44.

[146] Beattie, *Egypt During the Sadat Years* 43 (discussing Sadat's reputation as Nasser's poodle and a "yes-man").

It was on the basis of this agreement that he was unanimously voted into power by the executive committee members of the Arab Socialist Union.[147] While Sadat certainly respected the collective leadership principle for a short period from September 1970 to January 1971,[148] he soon pushed aside his opponents, purged them from senior posts, and imprisoned them.[149]

It was clear that Sadat wanted to signal a break from Nasser's regime and enhance his legitimacy. As one commentator notes, "Nasser left a void that few men could have filled. Tellingly, in the early days of his rule, Sadat's picture was routinely seen alongside that of Nasser."[150] Sadat distanced himself from the legacy of his predecessor by claiming that his was a new "era of legality."[151] He released many political prisoners, including members of the Muslim Brotherhood, who had been imprisoned under Nasser, and also began to court the religious right and students.[152] Detention camps were closed[153] and 119 "reactionary" judges who were removed in 1969 were reinstated.[154] Lawyers who had been jailed under Nasser due to their affiliation with banned political organizations were freed. He also significantly cut back on the powers of the hated secret police.[155] As a parallel to these liberal political gestures, Sadat also sought to enhance his Islamic credentials. Apart from the release of the leaders of the Muslim Brotherhood, he concurrently cultivated the image of the "believing president"[156] – one committed to Islamic values and encouraged the use of "Muhammad" as a prefix to his name.[157] While Nasser had no interest in mixing Islam with politics,[158] Sadat

---

[147] Beattie, *Egypt During the Sadat Years* 44 (discussing Nasser's preference for collective leadership in contrast to Nasser's more authoritarian style).

[148] Beattie, *Egypt During the Sadat Years* 44 (discussing Sadat's short period of commitment to collective leadership).

[149] Beattie, *Egypt During the Sadat Years* 76 (discussing Sadat's purge of several hundred individuals, mostly Centrists, from his government).

[150] Raymond William Baker, *Sadat and After: Struggles for Egypt's Political Soul* (Harvard University Press 1990) 58.

[151] Baker, *Sadat and After* 58.

[152] Beattie, *Egypt During the Sadat Years* 81–83 (discussing Sadat's sympathies with the religious right and students as part of a new governmental strategy).

[153] Baker, *Sadat and After* 58 (describing the steps taken to liberalize the political climate and the popularity of Sadat's "de-Nasserization").

[154] Beattie, *Egypt During the Sadat Years* 83.

[155] Beattie, *Egypt During the Sadat Years* 83.

[156] R Hrair Dekmejian, *Islam in Revolution: Fundamentalism in the Arab World* (Syracuse University Press 1995) 82.

[157] Glenn E Perry, *The History of Egypt* (Greenwood 2004) 121 (arguing that Sadat's growing religiosity was characterized by the return of his unused first name Muhammad).

[158] Fareed Zakaria, "Islam, Democracy and Constitutional Liberalism" (2004) 119 Political Science Quarterly 1, 13 (describing Nasser's vicious crackdown on the Muslim Brotherhood).

deliberately sought to demonstrate that his regime was strengthening religion's role in politics and did not shy away from using Islam as a political instrument.[159]

In 1971, Sadat sparked liberal hopes when he announced that he would promulgate a new constitution. This constitution was to mark a "considerable step forward" from the 1956 Constitution, although the latter was to serve as its foundation.[160] It contained a number of liberal measures. It expressly obligated the government to ensure the rule of law; prohibited torture; guaranteed freedom of speech, assembly, artistic freedom, and religious belief; and prohibited unauthorized searches and seizures. It also strengthened parliamentary autonomy and the independence of the judiciary.[161] Sadat's constitution also had many illiberal features and centralized power in the presidency. For example, Article 108 authorized the president to issue decrees having force of law in situations of emergency.[162] The president was also made the chair of the Supreme Judicial Council. There was, however, a two-term limit on presidential power. In Egypt's constitution, the juxtaposition of liberal provisions on rights alongside contradictory illiberal provisions that concentrate extensive powers in the president could be attributed partly to the diverse committee that was drafting it, which had "liberal law professors and presidential legal advisors who each worked to tailor the constitution to their own vision."[163] Most importantly, the 1971 Constitution, for the first time in the history of Egypt, introduced an Islamic supremacy clause contained under Article 2, which decreed that the shari'a would be "a primary source of legislation."[164]

4.3.3 *Legitimating Presidential Rule through Islamic Supremacy*

One significant difference between early twentieth century Iran and Afghanistan and 1971 Egypt was that clerics or religious figures were not a significant political force in Egypt. By this time, owing to the changes brought

---

[159] Beattie, *Egypt During the Sadat Years* 102.
[160] James Feuille, "Reforming Egypt's Constitution: Hope for Egyptian Democracy?" (2011) 47(1) *Texas International Law Journal* 237. See generally Kristen A Stilt, "Constitution in Authoritarian Regimes: The Case of Egypt" in Tom Ginsberg and Alberto Simpser (eds), *Constitutions in Authoritarian Regimes* (Cambridge University Press 2013).
[161] Beattie, *Egypt During the Sadat Years* 83 (describing the constitutional inclusion of liberal clauses).
[162] Constitution of the Arab Republic of Egypt 1971, art. 108.
[163] Bruce K Rutherford, *The Struggle for Constitutionalism in Egypt: Understanding the Obstacles to Democratic Transition in the Arab World* (PhD thesis, Yale University 1999) 221–49.
[164] Constitution of the Arab Republic of Egypt 1971, art. 2.

about by Muhammad Ali's modernization efforts in the nineteenth century and the general dismantling of clerical institutions, the religious establishment was generally subsumed within, or stood in subjugation to, the state. In fact, in Egypt, as in much of the rest of the Sunni world, clerics and the religious establishment generally drew authority from the state. Contrarily, in Iran and to a lesser extent in Afghanistan, the religious establishment operated independently of the state. Thus, religious opposition or pressure on any matter in Egypt in 1971 would have come from "Islamist" political organizations, the most prominent of which was the Muslim Brotherhood. While the Muslim Brotherhood was certainly a rising political force in Egypt at the time, there is no suggestion that they were strong enough to challenge the incumbent regime of Sadat politically. In fact, Nasser cracked down intensely on the Muslim Brotherhood, imprisoning over 30,000 members and executing several of its leaders.[165] By the mid-1960s, the Muslim Brotherhood "was in a state of disarray as its key leaders were arrested or dead, its branches were dissolved and its wealth was confiscated."[166] Thus, rather than being forced to concede to the demands of the Muslim Brotherhood or some other Islamist opposition group during the early era of his regime, it was Sadat who *chose* to be lenient with them. And as part of a general amnesty designed to demonstrate the openness of his regime, Sadat released many of their leaders and allowed them to organize on university campuses and later allowed them to undertake social and religious activities.[167] Apparently, Sadat did not face disconcerted coalitions as Iran did during its constitution-making process in 1906–7. To the contrary, Sadat boasted that "as the father of the Egyptian people," he had written the constitution in one evening and with the help of a single legal specialist, as a gift to the Egyptian people.[168] This was certainly a far cry from how the Iranian constitution was written. While this may be an exaggeration, it is certainly true that members of the committee that drafted the constitution were handpicked by Sadat.[169]

---

[165] Bruce K Rutherford, *Egypt after Mubarak: Liberalism, Islam, and Democracy in the Arab World* (Princeton University Press 2013) 81 (chronicling the tensions between Nasser and the Muslim Brothers from 1954 to 1966).

[166] Rutherford, *Egypt after Mubarak* 81–82.

[167] Rutherford, *Egypt after Mubarak* 82–83 (arguing that the revival of the Muslim Brotherhood in the 1970s was due to Sadat's leniency in an effort to counter the influence of leftist and Nasserist groups).

[168] Baker, *Sadat and After* 59 (describing the relationship between Sadat and the Egyptian liberals, who viewed Sadat's official liberalization as paternalistic and "cavalier").

[169] Mona El-Ghobashy, "Unsettling the Authorities: Constitutional Reform in Egypt" in Jeannie Sowers and Toesnsing (eds), *The Journey to Tahrir: Revolution, Protest, and Social Change in Egypt* (Verso 2012) 121, 126.

We believe Sadat's motivation in including an Islamic supremacy clause then lay in using it as a political device that would legitimate the extensive presidential authority contained in his constitution. After Sadat engaged in his "corrective revolution" and having "barely won an internecine battle with the Nasserist old guard ... [Sadat] was keen to fuse as many powers as possible in the person of the president [himself]."[170] The constitution was no exception, as Sadat himself acknowledged before his assassination that he had deliberately packed it with presidential prerogatives.[171] This is in line with Sadat's other overtures after he assumed the presidency, such as bolstering his reputation as the "believing president" – certainly a marked change from the secularizing legacy of his predecessor. Furthermore, Sadat claimed that his era would represent a new dawn of legality. Nasser was a hugely popular and charismatic leader, while Sadat did not yet possess that standing among his countrypeople. Therefore, the inclusion of rights and an Islamic supremacy clause would surely signal the sincerity of his claims of legality and respect for Islam and hence bolster Sadat's legitimacy.

While the Iranian Constitution of 1906–7 was a genuine attempt to contain executive power, the Egyptian 1971 Constitution, in contrast, seemed to be an attempt to enhance executive power. This is perhaps true for much of the Arab world where constitutions are more accurately defined as instruments of rule rather than instruments of constraint on the arbitrary exercise of power.[172] For example, in the case of Iran, an Islamic supremacy clause represented a compromise or exchange, in return for obtaining the support of the religious establishment for a constitution that innovatively limited the monarch's power and contained a bill of rights. Contrarily, the Egyptian constitution contained an Islamic supremacy clause, not as an "Islamic" concession in exchange for rights between political groups seeking modernization, but as a tool for legitimating Sadat's regime and facilitating the concentration of greater power in the executive. As such, the Islamic supremacy clause could be seen as a form of concession in one sense, that is, to secure the regime and its constitution's legitimacy despite its "non-constitutionalist" features. Even the rights in the constitution – as we argue is the case with the Islamic supremacy clause – seem to have been inserted as concessionary gestures for the expansion of presidential power. In fact, there is evidence that the "liberalizing" articles in the Egyptian constitution were included in response to Prime

---

[170] El-Ghobashy, "Unsettling the Authorities" 121, 126.
[171] El-Ghobashy, "Unsettling the Authorities" 121, 126.
[172] El-Ghobashy, "Unsettling the Authorities" 125–26; Brown, *Constitutions in a Nonconstitutional World* 67.

Minister Mahmud Fawzi's strong objections against unconstrained presidential powers. Certainly, as Stilt has pointed out, public consultations in Egypt at the time made it clear that people understood Islam and rights to be linked in constitutional design, in that they both served the cause of just governance.[173] Nevertheless, unlike the Iranian Constitution, since the 1971 Constitution in Egypt was written mainly not to limit but to expand executive power, the Islamic supremacy clause served as simply one tool – and the provision of rights, another – to legitimate a concentration of power in the ruler.[174] It was a legitimacy-boosting device for a president who wished to cultivate his image as the religious "believing president." An Islamic supremacy clause could work to boost Sadat's legitimacy precisely because there had been an Islamic revival in Egypt and the broader Arab world in the aftermath of the Egyptian defeat to Israel in the 1967 war – a defeat which exposed the weakness of Nasser's ideology of secular nationalism.[175] Sadat must have realized that the Islamic supremacy clause would appeal to this heightened sense of religious awareness in Egyptian society and mark a break from the socialist and secular decades of the past that had delivered little for Egypt.[176] Further, the Islamic supremacy clause would also legitimate Sadat's "Islamic" credentials in the eyes of Islamic movements, previously suppressed under Nasser – people that Sadat came to rely upon to dampen the threat he faced from Nasserites and

---

[173] Stilt, "Constitution in Authoritarian Regimes" 110.

[174] Maye Kassem, *Egyptian Politics: The Dynamics of Authoritarian Rule* (Lynne Rienner Publishers 2004) 26. However, we do not argue that the rights and Islamic supremacy clauses in the constitution both served the *same* legitimating function. The provision of rights may have not only legitimated Sadat's regime but also served as a signal that the regime will not abuse its extensive powers. It is conceivable that a promise that all enacted laws or rights will not be repugnant to Islamic law can insure against the enactment of provisions that may be contradictory to Islamic law; similarly, it is understandable how provisions guaranteeing that the state will not torture or detain arbitrarily can theoretically be a bulwark or insurance against extensive state power and certainly arbitrary exercises of it. Constitutional rights certainly impede the exercise of state power. On the other hand, it is slightly harder to argue that a clause stating that shari'a will be "a primary source of legislation" was also inserted to signal such a bulwark against presidential power, since it targeted the legislature. This is especially so since per the wording in the constitution, the ruler was not constrained by Islamic law, as may be the case with rights which were more specifically detailed. Rather Islam was to be a source of legislation, and it would be more difficult to use such a provision to prevent misbehavior by the executive.

[175] Perry, *History of Egypt* 120–21 (discussing the Islamic revival in Egypt after the war in 1967, involving a trend away from Nasser's secularism).

[176] Murits Berger and Nadia Sonneveld, "Sharia and National Law in Egypt" in Jan Michiel Otto (ed), *Sharia Incorporated: A Comparative Overview of the Legal Systems of Twelve Countries in Past and Present* (Leiden University Press 2011) 51, 62.

Marxists, and therefore people that he needed to appeal to in turn.[177] For example, to build up alternative bases of political support, Sadat actively sought to call upon the Muslim Brotherhood's leaders who had fled abroad[178] and deliberately courted the religious right.[179] As Tamir Moustafa argues,

> Article 2 was almost certainly intended to bolster the religious credentials of the regime at a time when Sadat was using the Islamist trend to counterbalance Nasserist power centers within the state and society. Just as Sadat gave free rein to the Islamist trend to organize on university campuses for tactical purposes, so too was religion used to build a new base of legitimacy in contradistinction to the failures of the Nasser era in achieving economic growth and pan-Arab unity.[180]

Article 2 was precisely the goodwill gesture that signaled a desire for rapprochement with the Islamic groups.[181] Indeed, by the mid-1970s, Islamists had become the dominant political force in Egypt's universities.[182] The Islamic supremacy clause served two purposes: first, it appealed to religious clerics, satisfied them, and enhanced Sadat's legitimacy; second, it spoke to liberals by including rights to insure people against excessive presidential power. This seemingly contradictory method of appealing to two audiences – at home and abroad – would come to be a hallmark of Sadat's regime.[183]

4.3.4 *The Amendment of 1980: Further Constitutional Islamization*

As compared to Nasser, Sadat sought to politically liberalize Egypt.[184] However, his close advisors were mistaken in their assumption that they would be able to control the pace of liberalization without opening up a Pandora's

---

[177] Perry, *History of Egypt* 122 (discussing Sadat's techniques to portray religiosity to the growing Islamic political movement).

[178] Beattie, *Egypt During the Sadat Years* 82.

[179] Beattie, *Egypt During the Sadat Years* 83.

[180] Tamir Moustafa, *The Struggle for Constitutional Power* (Cambridge University Press 2009) 617.

[181] Mohamed Abdelaal, "Religious Constitutionalism in Egypt: A Case Study" (2013) 37 Fletcher Forum of World Affairs 35, 36. Dekmejian, *Islam in Revolution* 80. "Internally, Sadat faced a legitimacy crisis because he lacked the charisma of his predecessor; nor did he possess a secure base in the Egyptian power structure dominated by his Nasserist rivals. To counterbalance the latter, he progressively liberated the Brothers from jail and encouraged their entrenchment in the student unions and elsewhere in society . . . . Sadat's question for legitimacy also involved increasing reliance on Islamic themes as a partial substitute for the ideological vacuum that he had created by progressively jettisoning Nasserism."

[182] Beattie, *Egypt During the Sadat Years* 252.

[183] Berger and Sonneveld, "Sharia and National Law in Egypt" 51–64.

[184] Beattie, *Egypt During the Sadat Years* 180.

box of political forces.[185] Liberalizing the press and allowing political formations, albeit limited, was not always possible without undermining the legitimacy of the liberal ideas on which Sadat claimed his state was situated.[186]
Different political interests vehemently opposed many of Sadat's policies and
Egyptian society, and, as a result, became increasingly polarized during the
1970s.[187]

Sadat's measures to "let the Islamist 'genie' out of Egypt's political bottle"[188]
had visible effects. Initiatives such as releasing Muslim Brotherhood leaders
and encouraging Islamic activist groups to flourish on university campuses was
part of Sadat's strategy to counter the leftist opposition and enhance his
appeal. The Muslim Brotherhood, in particular, realized that Sadat would
continue to seek a tactical alliance with them to contain the Nasserite and
Marxist threat.[189] Although leftist students remained active on campus, they
were rapidly outpaced by the Islamist groups that flourished under Sadat.
Once the regime allowed them to operate, it became difficult to oppose them
since opposition to them could be dismissed as anti-religious.[190] Through the
Islamic press, the Muslim Brotherhood's leadership appealed to its members
to fully utilize the peaceful means that were now available to them as a result
of Sadat's liberalization.[191] Amid this relatively open domestic political environment, Sadat signed a peace treaty with Israel. This event, along with the
Iranian revolution that had been steadily building up momentum since 1978,
"represented a watershed in regime-Islamist relations ... [as] nearly all
Islamists were enervated and energized by that development."[192] The peace
process led the Islamic press to launch a marked critique of the regime.[193]
Beattie writes that by the time the peace treaty was signed, religious consciousness was intensifying in Egyptian society. In this environment, student union
elections in 1978–79 were overwhelmingly won by Islamist candidates, who

---

[185] Beattie, *Egypt During the Sadat Years* 199.
[186] Beattie, *Egypt During the Sadat Years* 199.
[187] Beattie, *Egypt During the Sadat Years* 211.
[188] Beattie, *Egypt During the Sadat Years* 257.
[189] Beattie, *Egypt During the Sadat Years* 248 (explaining the reasons for Sadat and the Muslim
   Brotherhood to act in conjunction against the Nasserist left in the 1970s).
[190] Beattie, *Egypt During the Sadat Years* 203–4.
[191] Beattie, *Egypt During the Sadat Years* 246 (describing the Brothers' strategic approach in the
   1970s, particularly through the Islamic press, to realize their goal of a new Islamic order in
   Egypt in the 1980s).
[192] Beattie, *Egypt During the Sadat Years* 252.
[193] Baker, *Sadat and After* 244 (relating the escalating differences between Sadat and the
   Brotherhood after Sadat's 1977 trip to Jerusalem, including growing domestic criticism
   countered by warnings against treason).

opposed peace with Israel, praised the new Iranian Constitution, and called for the full application of shari'a law.[194] While the joint project to subjugate the Nasserists initially proved to be a common ground of collaboration for the Muslim Brothers and Sadat, the peace treaty would soon unravel that relationship.[195]

In January 1977, major food riots shook the regime and set off a protracted crisis for Sadat.[196] Sadat's reforms failed to encourage economic growth, and his popularity had now begun to wane. In response, Sadat became increasingly dictatorial, and among other measures, took over the post of prime minister, passed a "law of shame" that would punish anyone who undermined the "dignity of the state," and frequently resorted to referenda that produced "yes" votes from over 99 percent of the population.[197] On May 22, 1980, facing increasing domestic opposition for his economic and foreign policies, Sadat amended Article 2 of the 1971 Constitution – the Islamic supremacy clause – so as to move sharia from "a" source of legislation to "the" source of legislation in Egypt.[198]

Article 2 was amended to once again enhance the regime's legitimacy through Islamization, particularly to shift focus from Sadat's waning popularity and ineffective economic and foreign policies. While bolstering Sadat's legitimacy was certainly part of the reason for amending Article 2, coalitional bargaining was the more proximate cause. By the end of the 1970s, Sadat's "controlled liberalization" measures, as Beattie labels them, had significantly opened up the political scene in Egypt and greatly empowered the opposition, which included the Islamic opposition. This amendment then became necessary as an exchange for something Sadat wanted beyond simple legitimacy, that is, another term in office. And this seems to be what happened. As Clark Lombardi writes, "By the late 1970s, the government could no longer afford to ignore these calls to give Sharia a more important role. As a result, the government was finally forced in 1980 to respond to the concerns of its growing Muslim opposition by amending its constitution to give Islamic law

---

[194] Beattie, *Egypt During the Sadat Years* 253.
[195] Baker, *Sadat and After* 249 (detailing the growing differences between Sadat and the Muslim Brothers, particularly in the areas of foreign policy and student militancy, after their initial joint successes in attacking Nasser's legacy and fostering Islamic student groups).
[196] Dekmejian, *Islam in Revolution* 81.
[197] Perry, *History of Egypt* 125–27 (describing Sadat's growing authoritarianism characterized by his mass arrests of the opposition and his legal manipulations).
[198] Perry, *History of Egypt* 125–27; Clark Lombardi, "Constitutional Provisions" 733, 757.

a vital role in Egyptian society."[99] Lombardi and Brown also suggest that "dismayed by the secularization of Egyptian law, Islamist organizations eventually succeeded in pressuring the Egyptian government to adopt [Article 2]."[200] Article 2 was certainly not simply granted as a goodwill concession from Sadat; rather, it was part of a bargain. Sadat wished to stay in power, and Article 77 of the 1971 Constitution presented a stumbling block since it limited the president to two six-year terms. To do this, he needed the support of ordinary Egyptians and also the Islamists. Thus, the amendment to Article 2 was proposed alongside the amendment to Article 77. Article 2, as proposed, would now read, "the principles of the Islamic Sharia are the primary source of legislation." Article 77 would now add the phrase "the President may be re-elected for other successive terms."[201] Mohammed Abdelaal comments that by "using Article 2, [Sadat thus cunningly] played to the religious tendency of ordinary Egyptians, as well as the Islamists, in order to pass Article 77, as any opposition to Article 77 would have struck down Article 2 at the same time."[202] Thus, while Sadat's earlier Article 2 declaring Islamic law to be "a" source of law was indeed primarily motivated by a desire to boost legitimacy and mark a break from his predecessor's past – that is, as a goodwill gesture seeking to appeal to Egyptians and appease the Islamic constituency in particular – by 1980, the Egyptian political scene had changed dramatically. Therefore, the amendment of Article 2 reflected, or was at least partially, the "extracted" outcome of a bargain between the regime and increasingly open and vocal Islamic opposition, rather than a concession "granted" by Sadat unilaterally to enhance his legitimacy, as was the case in 1971.

The Egyptian example demonstrates how Islamic supremacy clauses serve varying functions depending on the level of political openness in a country. It shows not only how the motivations for adding or amending an Islamic supremacy clause in the constitution at any given time may be multiple and overlapping, but also shows how these motivations can alter and evolve over time based on the domestic political situation in which the constitution is being written or amended. Initially, the insertion of an Islamic supremacy clause in the 1971 Constitution had more to do with enhancing the legitimacy

---

[199] Clark B. Lombardi, "Islamic Law as a Source of Constitutional Law in Egypt: The Constitutionalization of the Sharia in a Modern Arab State" (1998) 37(1) Columbia Journal of Transnational Law 81, 86.

[200] Clark B. Lombardi and Nathan J. Brown, "Do Constitutions Requiring Adherence to Shari'a Threaten Human Rights? How Egypt's Constitution Reconciles Islamic Law with the Liberal Rule of Law" (2006) 21(1) American University International Law Review 379, 386.

[201] Abdelaal, "Religious Constitutionalism in Egypt" 35, 36.

[202] Abdelaal, "Religious Constitutionalism in Egypt" 35, 36.

of Sadat's one-man rule by signaling its Islamic credentials for domestic audiences and particularly the Islamist groups. As Egyptian society became politically more transparent and oppositional in the coming decade, the amendment to strengthen the Islamic supremacy clause in 1980 had more to do with facilitating negotiated exchange with increasingly vocal and agitating oppositional groups, rather than enhancing once again the legitimacy of Sadat's regime at a time of waning popularity.

That is, while Egypt was relatively less democratic and politically liberal in 1971, the motivations for inserting an Islamic supremacy clause were to legitimate the concentration of presidential power in Sadat and appeal to certain constituencies. As Egyptian society became more politically open, the motivations still remained largely the same: to legitimate Sadat's rule and extend his political power. Yet the amendment to Article 2 also came to represent a negotiated grand compromise between opposing factions rather than a clause merely "granted" by Sadat.

It is interesting that the Islamic supremacy clause has become a central part of the Egyptian constitutional order, even after the fall of the regime of Anwar Sadat's successor, Hosni Mubarak. Article 2 was retained in the constitution and hurriedly pushed through by Muslim Brotherhood–backed President Mohamed Morsi in late 2012.[203] Morsi's government was deposed by a military coup in the summer of 2013, and the new military-backed government drafted a new constitutional text that was approved by a national referendum in January 2014. The 2014 Constitution, however, kept Article 2 intact.[204]

4.4 IRAQ

Iraq's first constitution was enacted in 1925 to establish a constitutional monarchy when the country was still under British occupation. An amendment in 1943 increased the powers of the monarchy vis-à-vis the parliament.[205] After the monarch was overthrown in a coup that came to be known as the July 14 Revolution, this constitution was replaced with a new provisional constitution in 1958. The leaders of the revolution created a body with absolute authority – the Revolutionary Command Council.[206] This new constitution emphasized the Kurd and Arab identity of the country, created

---

[203] Constitution of the Arab Republic of Egypt 2012, art. 2.
[204] Constitution of the Arab Republic of Egypt 2014, art. 2.
[205] Adeed Dawisha, *Iraq: A Political History from Independence to Occupation* (Princeton University Press 2009) 161.
[206] Brown, *Constitutions in a Nonconstitutional World* 86; Kanan Makiya, *Republic of Fear* (University of California Press 1998) 6.

a republic, emphasized the sovereignty of the people, and granted certain rights, including, inter alia, freedom of the press and equality before the law.[207] Interim constitutions followed in 1963, 1964, 1968, and 1970. The 1970 Constitution, although deemed to be interim, stayed in force until Saddam Hussein's Baath regime was toppled in 2003. It proclaimed Iraq as a "sovereign people's democratic republic," recognized the Arab character of the state, and granted some economic and political rights.[208] All of these constitutions provided that Islam was to be the religion of the state, but none contained an Islamic supremacy clause. Ironically, the first time an Iraqi constitution would contain an Islamic supremacy clause was when it was drafted during foreign occupation.

4.4.1 *Foreign Invasion and Democracy Bring Iraq's First Islamic Supremacy Clause*

On March 19, 2003, the United States launched an invasion of Iraq – Operation Iraqi Freedom – the stated intention of which, in the words of President George W. Bush, was "to free its people and to defend the world from grave danger."[209] Soon after the invasion, as Saddam Hussein's regime crumbled, the Coalition Provisional Authority (CPA) was established as a transitional government with executive, legislative, and judicial authority. As reports circulated that the CPA was to appoint a body comprised of Iraqis to write a new constitution for Iraq, the leading Shi'ite cleric in Iraq, Grand Ayatollah Sistani, issued a fatwa, or religious opinion, on June 26, 2003, declaring that "those [occupation] forces have no jurisdiction whatsoever to appoint members of the Constitution preparation assembly" and demanded that Iraq's constitution drafters should be elected, not appointed.[210] Nevertheless, on July 22, 2003, the CPA formed the Iraqi Governing Council (IGC) and appointed its members. Twenty-five members representing various factions and ethnic groups comprised the IGC. These individuals were largely Iraqi dissidents who had fled the country during Saddam

---

[207] Juan Romero, *The Iraqi Revolution of 1958: A Revolutionary Quest for Unity and Security* (University Press of America 2010) 139.

[208] Leon M. Jeffries (ed), *Iraq: Issues, Historical Background, Bibliography* (Nova Biomedical 2002) 177–78.

[209] Oval Office, "President Bush Addresses the Nation" (The White House, October 19, 2003) <http://georgewbush-whitehouse.archives.gov/news/releases/2003/03/20030319-17.html> accessed January 15, 2022.

[210] Noah R. Feldman, "The Democratic Fatwa: Islam and Democracy in the Realm of Constitutional Politics" (2005) 58(1) Oklahoma Law Review 1, 6.

Hussein's regime. The influence of the fatwa was immense, since Sistani remained an extremely popular and influential figure in Iraq.[211] Soon after the fatwa, twenty-four of the IGC's twenty-five members traveled to meet Sistani and were certain that his argument could not be challenged.[212] By insisting on using a democratic process for constitution writing, Sistani greatly undermined the legitimacy of constitution making by an appointed body, as planned by the CPA. Andrew Arato wrote that "Sistani was obviously aware of the rhetorical power of advocating a democratic alternative against the American imposed model."[213] Soon, understanding its precarious position, the CPA agreed to adopt an arguably more "democratic direction."[214] As per an alternative proposal released on November 15, 2003, a two-stage constitution-writing process was envisaged: the constitution would eventually be written by an elected constituent assembly. In the interim though, beginning June 30, 2004, the country would be governed by a transitional national assembly to be selected by caucuses, rather than direct elections.[215] Also, a temporary "fundamental law" – known as the Transitional Administrative Law (TAL) – would be drafted by the IGC and be the governing document until a permanent constitution was promulgated. On November 26, 2004, Sistani denounced this plan and renewed his call for free and direct elections.[216] He also insisted that even the interim constitution being drafted by the IGC must be approved only by directly elected representatives of the people.[217] When the CPA did not entertain this idea, the interim constitution also

---

[211] Larry Diamond, *Squandered Victory: The American Occupation and the Bungled Effort to Bring Democracy to Iraq* (Holt Paperbacks 2006) 127 (relating stories of Sistani's power and general fear of disobeying him).

[212] Feldman, "The Democratic Fatwa" 1, 7.

[213] Andrew Arato, *Constitution Making Under Occupation: The Politics of Imposed Revolution in Iraq* (Columbia University Press 2009) 104.

[214] Arato, *Constitution Making Under Occupation* 102 (recounting the CPA's characteristic attempts to establish democratic legitimacy while initially operating under much confusion about the direction of the constitutional project).

[215] Feldman, "The Democratic Fatwa" 1, 7; Arato, *Constitution Making Under Occupation* 110 (describing the development of the November 15 Agreement on Political Process and citing the "Fundamental Law" and its various elements).

[216] Arato, *Constitution Making Under Occupation* 115 (quoting Sistani's rejection of the November 15 Agreement and analyzing the inherent contradictions and ambiguities in the agreement that led to Sistani's interpretation).

[217] Edward Wong, "Shiite Cleric Won't Back Down on Direct Elections" *Sun Sentinel* (January 12, 2004) <http://articles.sun-sentinel.com/2004-01-12/news/0401120065_1_al-sistani-grand-ayatollah-ali-influential-shiite-cleric> accessed January 15, 2022.

became unacceptable to Sistani.[218] Although the TAL was eventually written, by not acceding to Sistani's democratic request for approval of the interim constitution, the Americans "gained a determined enemy."[219] Over the next few months, Sistani would continually object that the TAL was not legitimate as "an unelected body could not bind an elected one."[220]

4.4.2 *Islam in the Interim Constitution*

Article 7 of the TAL, for the first time in any constitution of Iraq, incorporated two different types of Islamic supremacy clauses – a "source" and a "repugnancy" clause, which stated that "Islam ... is to be considered a source of legislation [and] no law that contradicts the universally agreed tenets of Islam, the principles of democracy, or the rights cited in Chapter 2 of this Law may be enacted during the transitional period."[221]

There was sufficient pressure on the CPA to avoid the inclusion of Islam in the TAL and later also in the permanent constitution; yet Islamic supremacy clauses were incorporated. Evangelical Christian groups in the United States strongly insisted on complete separation of religion and state in Iraq, with no role for Islam whatsoever. Noah Feldman argues that these groups had special access to President George W. Bush, who himself called on Paul Bremer, head of the CPA, to insist that that the religious liberty clauses in the International Declaration of Human Rights must be included in the TAL.[222] On another occasion, President Bush also asked Bremer whether "the ayatollahs [were] going to take over."[223] Further, these groups also made a concerted effort to advance this position through the Office of International Religious Freedom. Republican Senators Santorum and Brownback also "made public statements as well as back-channel telephone calls to U.S. personnel emphasizing the importance not only of establishing strong guarantees of religious freedom but also insisting on the marginalization of official

---

[218] Arato, *Constitution Making Under Occupation* 120 (presenting Sistani's desire for a freely elected transitional assembly to give the constitution validity, which conflicted with the United States' goals and rendered the interim constitution unacceptable).

[219] Arato, *Constitution Making Under Occupation* 128 (arguing that Sistani's opposition to the TAL was due to the changing negotiations with the United States over free elections and was therefore more reasonable than Bremer believes).

[220] Diamond, *Squandered Victory* 177.

[221] Law of Administration for the State of Iraq for the Transitional Period 2004, art. 2.

[222] Noah Feldman, "Imposed Constitutionalism" (2005) 37(1) *Connecticut Law Review* 857, 875–77.

[223] L Paul Bremer, *My Year in Iraq: The Struggle to Build a Future of Hope* (Threshold Editions 2006) 175.

Islam."[224] At one point, even Colin Powell asked Paul Bremer whether Iraq would now have shari'a law.[225]

Nevertheless, those advocating against the inclusion of Islam were to learn how futile it would be to take such a position. The opening up of the political arena to democratic forces in Iraq meant that it became inevitable that Islamic supremacy clauses would be a hallmark of any new constitution. Bremer writes that up to a few weeks before the deadline of March 1, 2004 set by the November 15 agreement, the issue of the role of Islam in the constitution – that is, Article 7 – remained unresolved. The Shi'i Islamist parties – Supreme Council for the Islamic Revolution in Iraq (SCIRI) – and Dawa, as per his account, were proposing that the TAL declare that Islam was "the" basis of all law.[226] They also referred back to Sistani before deciding on the issue of Islam.[227] Although the final draft referred to Islam only as "a" source, Bremer credits this to his back-channel communications with Sistani who was allegedly "softening" on the role of Islam.[228] However, in a later draft that referred to Islam as "*a* principal source," the Shia Islamists were keen that "a" be replaced with "the." Other members of the drafting committee resisted this replacement and the formula eventually agreed upon was that Islam would be "a" source of legislation, as long as a repugnancy clause would also be inserted in the TAL.[229]

Later on, during this process, the debate principally centered on the framing of these clauses. Although the Kurds agreed to this language, the Sunni Arabs in the committee demanded that a reference to "democratic values" be added to the repugnancy part of Article 7. Another Shi'a member of the committee, Dr. Rubaie, eventually made a counterproposal that Article 7 be drafted to forbid laws that "contradict the universally agreed tenets of Islam, the principles of democracy or the rights cited in Chapter 2 of the Law."[230] Feldman notes that this multifaceted repugnancy clause was "a core part of the political compromise on the role of Islam in the TAL."[231] That is "the Shi'i Islamist parties, led by SCIRI, began pressing hard for a series of demands that would enhance the TAL's commitment to Islam and strengthen

---

[224] Feldman, "Imposed Constitutionalism" 857, 876.
[225] Bremer, *My Year in Iraq* 73.
[226] Bremer, *My Year in Iraq* 292.
[227] Bremer, *My Year in Iraq* 293.
[228] Bremer, *My Year in Iraq* 294.
[229] Bremer, *My Year in Iraq* 296.
[230] Bremer, *My Year in Iraq* 299.
[231] Noah Feldman and Roman Martinez, "Constitutional Politics and Text in the New Iraq: An Experiment in Islamic Democracy" (2006) 75 Fordham Law Review 883, 904.

its majoritarian bent."[232] Similarly, Nathan Brown seems to corroborate this account of the final language as a compromise as he observes, "the final version of the Law represents a compromise between those who wished to have Islam serve as 'a source' and those who wished it to be 'the primary source' of legislation."[233]

4.4.3 *Islam in the 2005 Permanent Constitution*

An Islamic supremacy clause also found its way into Iraq's permanent Constitution of 2005, though it was formulated in different terms. Article 2 of the 2005 Constitution, inter alia, strengthened the clause previously contained in the TAL and declared Islam "a fundamental source of legislation" and that "no law that contradicts the established provisions of Islam may be established."[234] The clause also provides that "no law that contradicts the principles of democracy may be established [and] no law that contradicts the rights and basic freedoms stipulated in this constitution may be established" either. In this sense, this is also a multifaceted repugnancy clause.

What factors influenced the adoption of a stronger Islamic supremacy clause in the permanent constitution and in particular, what prompted the modified language strengthening the Islamic supremacy clause? Probably not a failure to learn or a lack of experience since Article 2 had no meaningful impact on lawmaking during the period.[235] Deeks and Burton comment that "if Iraq's brief democratic experience is any guide, we only once saw or heard legislators refer to Islam as a source of law during the year in which the TNA [Transitional National Assembly] produced legislation."[236] The answer lies in the fact that free elections for the National Constitutional Assembly had taken place in Iraq in January 2005, as scheduled. Sistani managed to organize the Shi'ites into a single electoral list as the United Iraqi Alliance (UIA), which brought together several smaller groups under a banner widely associated with Sistani. They won about 48 percent of the vote and secured 140 seats in the assembly. The Kurds acting through the Democratic Patriotic Alliance of Kurdistan/Kurdistan Coalition List came second with about 25 percent of

---

[232] Feldman and Martinez, "Constitutional Politics and Text" 896.

[233] Nathan J Brown, "Transitional Administrative Law" (George Washington University, March 8, 2004) <http://home.gwu.edu/~nbrown/interimiraqiconstitution.html> accessed January 15, 2022 (providing access to the draft of the Interim Iraqi Constitution).

[234] Iraq Constitution 2005, art. 2.

[235] Ashley S Deeks and Matthew D Burton, "Iraq's Constitution: A Drafting History" (2007) 40(1) Cornell International Law Journal 1, 12.

[236] Deeks and Burton, "Iraq's Constitution" 10.

the vote and 75 seats.[237] Thus, an outcome that Bremer had tried to resist was finally realized: a major Shi'ite victory in elections, making them the most significant political force in Iraq.[238] The secular group, the Iraqi List, which was openly and materially supported by the Americans, came in at a distant third, with only about 13 percent of the vote and 40 seats.[239] This meant that no government could be formed without the Shi'ite UIA.[240] Further, the Sunni boycott had ensured that the Sunnis were now significantly under-represented and that they would be left without much influence in drafting the constitution.[241]

In terms of compromises for making the permanent constitution, the Kurds, otherwise quite secular, were willing to make concessions on religious issues, as long as their main demand of federalism and regional autonomy was heeded.[242] On the other hand, Shi'ite Islamists wanted to entrench Islam's role in Iraq.[243] Feldman argues that "the Shi'i-Kurd understanding on federalism allowed a larger role for Islam at the national level than might otherwise have been possible."[244] This is a similar type of bargaining dynamic that we have observed in other cases of constitutional Islamization. In particular, the discussions on provisions relating to the role of Islam pitted Shi'ite Islamist politicians against a loose coalition of the Kurdish parties and more secular Arabs. Feldman argues that the Americans generally supported this latter group but ultimately only played a facilitative role and that the final settlement reflected the considerable strength of the Islamists who led the constitutional

---

[237] Arato, *Constitution Making Under Occupation* 208 (summarizing the results of the 2005 Iraqi legislative election, including names of parties and leaders, numbers of votes and seats, and total percentages of the votes).

[238] Arato, *Constitution Making Under Occupation* 207 (explaining the organization of the Shi'ite groupings under the UIA and the eventual legitimation process).

[239] Arato, *Constitution Making Under Occupation* 208 (summarizing, in a table, the results of the 2005 Iraqi legislative election, including names of parties and leaders, numbers of votes and seats, and total percentages of the votes).

[240] Arato, *Constitution Making Under Occupation* 211 (explaining the demographics of the election, such that the combined smaller parties would still not have enough of the seats necessary to elect a Presidential Council and form a government).

[241] Jonathan Morrow, "Special Report No. 155 Iraq's Constitutional Process II: An Opportunity Lost" (*U.S. Institute of Peace*, November 2005) 6 <www.usip.org/sites/default/files/sr155.pdf> accessed January 15, 2022.

[242] Arato, *Constitution Making Under Occupation* 211 (describing the political position and priorities of each coalition, including the Kurds, the Allawi, and the Shi'ites). See also Feisal Amin Rasoul Al-Istrabadi, "Islam and the State of Iraq: Post-2003 Constitutions" in Rainer Grote and Tilmann J Roder (eds), *Constitutionalism in Islamic Countries: Between Upheaval and Continuity* (Oxford University Press 2012) 607 (discussing the Kurdish coalition with Shi'ite religious parties in service to Kurdish regional rights).

[243] Feldman and Martinez, "Constitutional Politics and Text" 883, 898.

[244] Feldman and Martinez, "Constitutional Politics and Text" 883, 915.

drafting effort following their election victory.[245] While the Kurds were principally opposed to the Shi'ite inclination toward enhancing the role of Islam in the constitution any further,[246] the language of the constitution was ultimately bent toward the majority Shii'te position.

4.4.4 The Journey of Article 2: Islamic Supremacy

From one account of the constitutional deliberation, we know that the draft that emerged from the National Assembly's Constitutional Committee on July 22 was different from the final version. It stated that "Islam is the basic source of legislation. No law may be enacted that contradicts its tenets and provisions [its tenets that are universally agreed upon]."[247] Shi'ite Islamists apparently desired to make Islam "the" basic or fundamental source of legislation. However, others, including the Kurds, felt that Islam should be only "a" source of legislation. Deeks and Burton state the following.

> By August 6, a number of competing phrasings had appeared: "the fundamental source," "the first source," "the basic source," "a main source," "a source among sources," and "a fundamental source." The Kurds continued to prefer the TAL language, which used "a source," and they ultimately prevailed ... as by August 10, the drafts reflect the use of the indefinite article – "*a* principal source."[248]

Apart from "a" or "the," there was also debate around whether the word "principal" or "fundamental" would be used. Seculars wanted the word "principal" to be used so that Islam would not be the first or primary source. The Shi'ite Islamists in SCIRI were, however, still pushing for "*the principal source of law.*" In the following days, there was much going back and forth between "fundamental" and "principal," and "fundamental" seemed to have been what was decided. However, drafters eventually changed the wording from the adjectival "fundamental" to a noun that is best translated as "foundation," and thus "foundation" is what made it into the constitution.[249]

The TAL, like the permanent constitution, also contained a repugnancy clause. It seems that the influence of constitution making in other Muslim

---

[245] Feldman and Martinez, "Constitutional Politics and Text" 901.

[246] Arato, *Constitution Making Under Occupation* 236 (analyzing the debate between the Kurds, the Shi'ites, and Ambassador Khalilzad over the role of Islam in the state and, in particular, the inclusion of shari'a experts on the Supreme Federal Court). See also Haider Ala Hamoudi, "Ornamental Repugnancy: Identitarian Islam and the Iraqi Constitution" (2010) 7(3) St. Thomas University Law Journal 101, 108.

[247] Deeks and Burton, "Iraq's Constitution" 1, 7.

[248] Deeks and Burton, "Iraq's Constitution" 9.

[249] Deeks and Burton, "Iraq's Constitution" 10.

countries was clearly on the minds of various groups here.[250] Feldman argues that they may have been encouraged by US acquiescence to adopt similar language in the Afghan constitution. He notes that the Shi'as initially agreed to not having a repugnancy clause in the TAL but later changed their mind, after learning that the Afghan constitution would include one.[251] Secular and nationalist forces resisted this clause.[252] As such, even though the insertion of a repugnancy clause was almost certain, there were debates concerning its precise language. While Article 7 of the TAL referred to Islam's "universally agreed principles" along with democracy and rights, the proposals for the permanent constitution initially sought to replace that language with "Islam's confirmed rulings." Simultaneously, others wanted to retain the addition of the TAL formulation "or the principles of democracy" and "the fundamental rights and freedoms in the constitution."[253] While there was not much controversy in including these provisions in the permanent constitution, Shi'ite Islamists did try to cut back on the breadth of freedoms that were contained in the TAL.[254] Ultimately, certain Shi'ite negotiators wanted to use "constant rulings," "confirmed rulings," or "the tenets of its provisions" and to exclude concepts of democracy and rights from the repugnancy clause completely. On the other hand, the Kurds believed that the Shi'a-proposed language was too fundamentalist. Eventually, "established provisions" were agreed upon as a compromise.[255] This account is corroborated by another commentator (although he translates the constitution to use the word "settled" rather than "established") who states that "in the end, a compromise could only be reached as to Article 2 where the constitution made clear that law could not be enacted that violated the 'settled rulings of Islam' rather than, as the Shi'i Islamists wished, the 'rulings of *sharia*.'"[256]

---

[250] Haider Ala Hamoudi, "Repugnancy in the Arab World" (2012) 48(427) Williamette Law Review 427, 439 (arguing that "Iraqi constitutional drafters were aware during their negotiations that Egypt had been operating under a principle of repugnancy for nearly two decades. They were aware that repugnancy provisions had appeared in the constitution of Afghanistan, and as a result, Islamists within Iraq of both the Shiite and Sunni variety wanted to ensure that a similar provision appeared in the Iraqi constitution").

[251] Feldman and Martinez, "Constitutional Politics and Text" 883, 903.

[252] Hamoudi, "Repugnancy in the Arab World" 427, 439.

[253] Deeks and Burton, "Iraq's Constitution" 1, 13.

[254] Feldman and Martinez, "Constitutional Politics and Text" 883, 907.

[255] Deeks and Burton, "Iraq's Constitution" 1, 13.

[256] Hamoudi, "Ornamental Repugnancy" 101, 108 (putting forth the idea that an emphasis on shari'a as compared to Islam may have entrenched Islamic law interpretations of Shi'a Islam further).

It was also relevant for the purposes of the repugnancy clause, not just what the clause would say but who would reconcile its potential contradictions and interpret it. The Kurds were, in principle, willing to accept the Islamic nature of the repugnancy clause, but along with the secular Sunnis, they accordingly did not wish to see any jurists on the court,[257] despite the insistence of the Shi'as that there be at least four shari'a experts on the court.[258] The Kurds and Arabs were concerned that the presence of jurists meant that the court would be "Shi'i dominated and result in a particularly strong Shi'i version of Islam."[259] In fact, the Kurds were the strongest domestic force opposing the Article 2 formulations proposed by the Shi'a Islamists.[260] Nevertheless, the Shi'ites secured a further victory by entrenching in the constitution that the Federal Supreme Court would comprise of judges and experts in Islamic law.[261] Considering that, as per Article 2, laws also could not be repugnant to democracy *and* rights, and resolving potential contradictions would be left to the judiciary, this was significant.[262]

4.4.5 Why Constitutionalize Islam?

Iraq's experience of Islamic constitutionalism is particularly instructive to understand the raison d'état of constitutional Islamization. The accounts from the drafting process of both the 2004 TAL and the 2005 permanent constitution clearly depict that, despite the contrary wishes of the Americans, expansive room for democratic input in Iraq after the invasion resulted in the inclusion of the Islamic supremacy clauses. In this democratic space, the influence of the Shi'a groups, representing a majority of Iraqis, during the drafting of the TAL, within the IGC, and more strongly, after the elections, translated into more robustly entrenched Islamic supremacy clauses in the constitution.

This begs the question: Why did the Shi'as want a strong Islamic supremacy clause? Our study of constitutional negotiations in Iran reflects that the clerics

---

[257] Deeks and Burton, "Iraq's Constitution" 1, 13.

[258] Feldman and Martinez, "Constitutional Politics and Text" 883, 917.

[259] Hamoudi, "Ornamental Repugnancy" 101, 108.

[260] Hamoudi, "Ornamental Repugnancy" 121.

[261] Arato, *Constitution Making Under Occupation* 237 (detailing the compromise in the constitutional draft to include both judges and shari'a experts on the courts but delay the decision on their appointment and number until the next National Assembly due to lack of consensus over the role of Islam).

[262] Hamoudi, "Ornamental Repugnancy" 101, 109.

and conservatives lobbied for the insertion of a repugnancy clause and the formation of a clerical council that would review laws for compliance with this clause. It thus served as insurance or a safeguard to prevent the future enactment of "un-Islamic" laws and the extension of constitutionally guaranteed rights by the majlis in the context of a constitution that already contained many innovative rights. Such a constitution was, from one perspective, already usurping God's sovereignty and law. Fear of the unknown possibilities of lawmaking, in a sense, was a major part of the reason for entrenching the Islamic supremacy clause in Iran. In Afghanistan, King Amanullah brought in rapid modernization, centralized power, and codified the previously unwritten religious laws through promulgation of Afghanistan's first constitution. These changes deeply offended religious sensibilities and cast doubt on his efforts as an attack on Islam and Afghan values. Dampening opposition to such modernization required the insertion of progressively stronger Islamic supremacy clauses. Egypt reflects a different dynamic of constitutional negotiations for Islamic supremacy clauses. President Anwar Sadat wanted to legitimize his rule through an Islamic supremacy clause to win the political support of Islamic opposition in religious society. Therefore, he first inserted and then strengthened the Islamic supremacy clause.

In Iraq, the well-documented constitution drafting history illustrates that all parties recognized Islam's pivotal role in the constitutional framework. The accounts of the constitutional drafting indicate that all parties acknowledged that some role for Islam will be reserved in the constitution. There was "nearly unanimous resistance to placing rights above the Sharia."[263] Disagreements largely centered on the strength of the language to be used in defining that role. Further, those disagreements polarized the society along ethno-religious lines. It was the Shi'a parties who wished to entrench the strongest language possible for Islam in the constitution, while some of the more secularist Arabs, Kurds, and certainly the Americans wished it would have a limited role. The fact that all parties agreed to secure some role for Islam, even about rights, would imply that there was some consensus that laws and rights must not be contrary to Islamic values and the Islamic character of Iraqi society, at least at an abstract level. This is not surprising, as Professor Feldman writes: "Where the country is majority Muslim, many citizens will often want Islam to have some official role in state governance, beyond mere symbolism"[264] and that

---

[263] Yash Ghai, "A Journey around Constitutions: Reflections on Contemporary Constitutions" (2005) 122(4) South African Law Journal 804, 831.
[264] Feldman, "Imposed Constitutionalism" 857, 860.

Islamic democrats believe that "a majority of Muslim citizens would choose government with an Islamic cast if they were free to do so."[265]

That the Islamic supremacy clauses served for all an identitarian function is clear. For decades, Saddam Hussein operated a brutal, secular dictatorship in a Muslim-majority country with a religious population. With the fall of his regime, a democratic opportunity arose to establish a legal order and constitution that would loudly proclaim a break from the past – Islam stepped into the breach. In this context, the Islamic supremacy clauses served two functions: first, they asserted the Islamic identity of the Iraqi state; second, they took the form of the reaction to the dictatorial oppression of the past. As such, asserting the Islamic character of the Iraqi state through Islamic supremacy clauses, both as a prospective means of asserting identity and as a reaction to what had gone on in the past, perhaps had something to do with an assertion of identity. In fact, the constitution may not have been legitimized otherwise.[266] Hamoudi argues that the clause was clearly intended "to establish Iraq as a state that does not permit law to violate Islam's 'settled rulings'"[267] – and since settled rulings implies those rulings on which there is consensus, the motivations for the Islamic supremacy clause are therefore largely symbolic.[268] Such re-imagination of the Iraqi identity through constitution and symbolic reference to Islam was, however, not surprising, since it was more of a political statement against its past. Mere assertion of identity only through an Islamic clause is not a tenable explanation for the purpose of this clause since the disagreement over language of the clause and extreme polarization along ethno-religious lines arose during this process. This stance also fails to explain the need for inclusion of such a clause despite the presence of Article 2, which already functions as the identarian compass of Iraq's polity.[269] Professor Feldman notes that "there are numerous other constitutional provisions reaffirming the important role of religion in Iraqi society,"[270] which already asserted the Islamic religious identity of Iraq.

---

[265] Feldman, "Imposed Constitutionalism" 864.

[266] Feldman, "Imposed Constitutionalism" 878. "In the Iraqi case, Ambassador Bremer unwittingly strengthened the Islamists' position when, apparently in response to pressure from Senators Santorum and Brownback, he publicly stated in comments to reporters in the Iraqi town of Hillah that the Iraqi constitution would not be Islamic. This unfortunate statement had the effect of strengthening the hand of the Islamists precisely because it reeked of imposed constitutionalism." See also Hamoudi, "Ornamental Repugnancy" 101, 104.

[267] Hamoudi, "Ornamental Repugnancy" 101, 121.

[268] Hamoudi, "Ornamental Repugnancy" 101, 121.

[269] Constitution of Iraq 2005, art. 2.

[270] Feldman and Martinez, "Constitutional Politics and Text" 883, 906.

This is not to say that the Islamic supremacy clause does not have symbolic value or that there would have been no bargaining if it were just symbolic, but only that there is a possibility that something more than symbolism may have motivated the constitutional negotiators. To be clear, "settled rulings" was the end result, not the beginning; there was much acrimony before that result was achieved. As Hamoudi himself notes, the Kurds along with the Sunnis strongly opposed the Shi'a formulation of the clause.[271] Thus, while an assertion of identity is no doubt a major factor in the insertion of the clause, there must have been more at stake than symbolism in the minds of the negotiators. Rather, our view is that the language of the clause encompassed debates, not simply of symbolism, but of conflicts over whose vision of Islam would dominate. Essentially, our argument is that Shi'a negotiators wished to entrench Islam more deeply in the constitution since, based on Iraq's Shi'a majority and the significant influence of the clerics in Najaf – such as Ayatollah Sistani – it would be *their* interpretation of Islam that would become the correct interpretation. Furthermore, since Islam was of such constitutional significance, it was strategically important to have control over its interpretations. If, in Iraq, Islam were to be "the" source of law or repugnancy would be only defined in terms of Islam's "constant rulings" rather than "universally agreed tenets" of Islam, then there is less room for maneuver in terms of what is allowed or disallowed. On the other hand, if Islam were to be "a" rather than "the" source of law, it is certain that Islam would be the supreme source of law and the party that expects to be the majority in Iraq – in terms of demography, political representation in the legislature, and religious influence – would be in the best position to argue that Islam requires a particular legal outcome. Similarly, with the repugnancy clause, using language such as "constant rulings" provides narrower space for debate than if language such as "universally agreed tenets" is adopted. Not only are "rulings" more precise, providing less room for legislative deliberation, but the language also provides significantly less room for the opposition, since there is little need to debate what is or is not universally agreed upon. In fact, there are few tenets of Islam that are universally agreed upon. The language of "universal agreement" means that all the sects and groups under Islam have only one opinion as to whether a certain matter is agreed upon or contested.

In fact, Feldman's translation of Article 2 in the TAL explicitly refers to the language in TAL as meaning laws cannot be repugnant to "provisions of Islam on which *there is consensus*."[272] Similarly, the permanent constitution also

---

[271] Hamoudi, "Ornamental Repugnancy" 101, 121.
[272] Feldman and Martinez, "Constitutional Politics and Text" 883, 903.

required compliance with "settled rulings" rather than mere rulings regardless of their acceptance or legitimacy. In the absence of qualifications such as "settled" or "agreed" with "rulings," the majority in Iraq would have immense discretion to sift through diverse rulings and adopt any of them. Therefore, this precise language adopted in the Iraq constitution limits this majoritarian power and turns the legislative deliberations across the party/sectarian lines static with this strict criterion for a ruling to be a "settled" one to be adopted in legislative domain. Considering the possibility of "imposed" majoritarian law making by the Shi'a, it is probably not surprising that Kurdish and Sunni negotiators vigorously bargained for arguably counter-majoritarian checks. A provision that Islam be only one source of law among others provides leverage to argue that while *majoritarian* Shi'a Islam may require one outcome when legislating laws, the constitution requires reliance on other sources of law, and, therefore, debate and consensus becomes necessary.[273] Similarly, a repugnancy clause, which forbids the enactment of laws that contradict democracy and rights in *addition* to "settled rulings," provides room for dissenting voices to argue that a law, while compliant with the rulings of certain sects, is not yet settled since it has not met the required degree of acceptance as per other schools of thought.

Alternatively, it could be argued that a certain law, perhaps with a majoritarian bent, that is not necessarily repugnant to Islam but is offensive to certain rights contained in the constitution, could not be validly enacted. Even if such a law gets enacted, it could possibly be invalidated by the courts. Thus, unlike Afghanistan and Iran, where the Islamic supremacy clauses provided a safeguard against "imposed" notions of democracy or rights with an alien pedigree, the reverse seemed to be happening in Iraq; language moderating Islam and an insistence on democracy and rights provided a safeguard against "imposed" Islam, which may impinge on the position of the minority Sunnis, Kurds, and more secular groups. That is, as Feldman writes, "these clauses raise the possibility that future interpretations of the Islamic non-contradiction clause would be influenced by the principles of democracy, whatever these may be defined to constitute."[274]

Ultimately, since the wording in the constitution remains vague, the final determination – once it has moved beyond legislative debates between opposing factions – of what "settled rulings" or "democracy" of rights are, rests with the judiciary. And all parties realized this. Therefore, the Supreme Court

---

[273] Hamoudi argues that the parties wanted an entrenchment or protection for Shi'a Islam to protect from persecution. Hamoudi, "Ornamental Repugnancy" 101, 119.

[274] Feldman and Martinez, "Constitutional Politics and Text" 883, 904.

becomes the final arbiter to settle what these indeterminate words mean and how to reconcile the multifaceted repugnancy clause or assess how other sources of law sit beside the "foundational" source. Hence, it would make perfect sense for the Shi'a negotiators, to ensure entrenchment of their majoritarian interpretations of Islam by insisting on the inclusion of jurists on the Supreme Court. Similarly, it was a reasonable course of action for the Sunnis and Kurds to declare that they had no appetite for religious judges to sit on the Supreme Court. This is understandable: in a country with a majority Shi'a population, securing seats for jurists on the court means that laws reflecting the majoritarian, or Shi'a, interpretations of Islam would have a greater likelihood of not being declared void. On the other hand, judges, as compared to jurists, might be inclined to give greater weight to counter-majoritarian aspirations contained in the repugnancy clause or, at the very least, provide liberal, pluralist interpretations to religion.[275]

It then seems that, in Iraq, an overwhelmingly Muslim-majority country, occupation brought in a degree of democratization. Democratization meant that Islam would certainly play a far greater role in the constitutional order than it had in the past. That is, "as the constitutional process became increasingly participatory and democratic ... the constitution itself became increasingly Islamic in orientation and detail" and "more democracy meant more Islam."[276] Indeed, as Feldman adds, "most Iraqi politicians agreed that their new regime would embrace Islam, democracy, and human rights simultaneously. The only serious differences on these issues concerned precisely how to balance these commitments within the constitutional text."[277] That is, while democratization meant that all parties were in agreement that on an abstract or symbolic level, Islam would play some role, there were significant disagreements between sects as to how much Islam was appropriate for the constitution to include and whose version of Islam this would be. For the Kurds and Sunnis, entrenching Islam strongly in the constitution meant that there was a risk that their political interests might have, in the future, been subjugated to Shi'a, majoritarian interpretations that might have come out of Najaf or an increasingly Shi'a dominated legislature, where they might have been sitting in opposition. This required not only bargaining for a diluted role for Islam in the constitution but as a second-best solution, moderating the language of the Islamic supremacy clause and bargaining for counter-

---

[275] Ran Hirschl, *Constitutional Theocracy* (Harvard University Press 2010) 30 (arguing that judges bring theocratic governance in check as courts act as a bulwark against the threat of radical religion).

[276] Feldman and Martinez, "Constitutional Politics and Text" 883, 884.

[277] Feldman and Martinez, "Constitutional Politics and Text" 885.

majoritarian checks in the repugnancy clause – such as protections for democracy and rights. The different ethnic-religious groups were therefore, through the Islamic supremacy clause, vying to entrench competing constitutional and legal order which would protect their interests in an uncertain post-Saddam Iraq. Thus, Article 2 of the permanent Constitution and Article 7 of the TAL are not mere assertions of identity, as Hamoudi asserts, but also reflected and were indeed symptomatic of competing strategic political visions.

In this chapter, we argued that the phenomenon of constitutional Islamization, or the constitutional incorporation of Islamic supremacy clauses, are best understood not as impositions of theocracy, but as carefully negotiated provisions. In this sense, their incidence is consistent with democracy and should not be thought of as in inexorable tension with it. Constitutional Islamization is subject to a distinct political logic which, in every instance, involves coalitional politics. For this reason, we observe that essentially every instance of Islamization is accompanied by an *expansion* in the rights content of the constitutional order.

We also examined the historical origin and spread of constitutional Islamization. Our analysis of the data showed that Islamic repugnancy clauses likely emerged as a borrowed legal technique influenced by colonial repugnancy and, in fact, Islamic supremacy clauses are most likely to occur in countries that have in the past been associated with a British colonial legacy. Also, Islamic supremacy clauses generally, from their innovation in Iran in 1906, have become more popular as time has gone on, now being found in the constitutions of almost half of Muslim-majority states. This reflects the democratic demand for such clauses and gives the regimes that adopt them some resilience.

Our argument about coalitional politics was confirmed in the case studies. In Afghanistan, the first constitution was drafted by a popular, religious ruler, and it contained innovative rights and freedoms but no Islamic supremacy clauses. This provoked a strong conservative reaction and the constitution and the regime that promulgated it ultimately collapsed. Its successor constitution of 1931, which lasted over three decades, contained rights but also contained robust Islamic supremacy clauses. The new monarch, having witnessed the revolt that toppled his predecessor, would certainly have been cognizant of the adverse reactions a constitution could provoke if it contained rights and freedoms which could be seen as controversial. Considering his reputation as a "modernizer," his decision then to include Islamic supremacy clauses in the constitution would then have been partly motivated by the desire to co-opt clerics and conservatives to his reform programs. In Afghanistan, unlike Iran, the constitution-writing process had not been opened to those outside of the monarchic circle; thus, there was no element of coalitional compromise, yet Nadir Shah's choice in adopting Islamic supremacy clauses could be seen as a preemptive attempt to stave off prospective opposition to the constitution.

Similarly, in the case of Iran in 1906, the promulgation of a first constitution that contained rights provoked strong reactions. In response, the inclusion of Islamic supremacy clauses in the supplementary constitution could be seen as the "price" of including a bill of rights. In contrast with the Afghan case, in which the monarch simply promulgated a constitution in 1931 that contained Islamic supremacy clauses, constitution makers in Iran were constantly negotiating and debating the specific Islamic supremacy clauses and rights in the constitution. Although the motivations for including Islamic supremacy clauses in Iran and Afghanistan may have been similar in terms of pacifying opposition, the former case featured more extensive bargaining and negotiation, but the Afghan monarch was more interested in preempting any opposition to constitutionalism and rights, since the negative experience of his predecessor was still fresh. Bargaining was greater in Iran than in Afghanistan.

Iraq and Egypt present a similar contrast in the Arab world. Whereas the Islamic supremacy clauses were a key demand of Iraq's largest group, the Shi'a, in Egypt, the clauses were introduced by President Sadat – along with new constitutional rights – to preempt opposition and legitimate his presidency. The Iraqi negotiations in contrast reflected the familiar dynamic of a negotiated balance between rights and Islam, in which both sets of promises were incorporated as a form of mutual insurance against downstream lawmaking.

Our finding of the co-occurrence of rights and Islamization has several implications. At the broadest level, it is consistent with the work of scholars who have suggested the basic compatibility of Islam and constitutional democracy.[278] In this sense, it suggests that those outsiders monitoring constitutions in Muslim-majority countries – who argue for the exclusion of Islamic clauses – are focused on a straw man. Not only are these clauses popular, but they are accompanied by a set of provisions that advance basic values of liberal democracy. Like rights provisions, Islamic clauses certainly do not resolve all downstream disputes over their precise meaning. However, this in turn suggests that constitutional advisors should focus more attention on the basic political structures of the constitution, including the design of constitutional courts and other bodies that will engage in interpretation. The project of balancing rights and Islam cannot but be resolved in each country through its own political and judicial processes, and it is these that should be the main focus in constitutional design.

---

[278] Feldman and Martinez, "Constitutional Politics and Text" 884 (stating that in Iraq, "more democracy meant more Islam").

Part III

5

Islamic Supremacy Clauses and Rights

Islamic Review in Practice

Thus far, this book has elaborated on the origins, doctrine, history and empirical landscape of constitutional Islamization, alongside the political dynamics of Islam in constitution making and the relationship between constitutional Islamization and human rights. To deepen our understanding of constitutional Islamization, this book has generally focused on exploring in-depth studies of the incidence of Islamic supremacy clauses and rights. That is, this book is primarily concerned with the analysis of the design of constitutions rather than actual implementation and enforcement in courts of constitutional provisions. Yet we acknowledge that while the empirical analysis of constitutional Islam and rights provides us with a snapshot of the world of Muslim countries' constitutions in terms of design, it does not provide us with an analysis of what decision makers – most importantly courts – actually do in adjudicating cases that concern both Islam and rights.

Although the emphasis of this book is not on the application of Islam in courts, we feel that this book may be incomplete if it does not explore the application of Islamic supremacy clauses by the judiciary in cases that involve the determination of rights. That is, how do courts reconcile strong-form Islamic clauses – in particular, the Islamic repugnancy clause – with a constitutional commitment to rights? Do courts, as is sometimes presumed, allow Islamic supremacy clauses to subjugate rights, since Islam is often declared as the highest principle of the constitution? What do judges do with Islamic provisions? If not to Islamize the legal system and curtail rights, how do they balance these two potentially opposing strands of the constitution? This chapter deals with these questions by drawing on case studies of Pakistan and Egypt. These countries have been chosen because both are partially democratic with a relatively strong judiciary, and sufficient literature exists to assess the repercussions of having both Islamic supremacy clauses and a catalog of rights in the constitution. To be sure, the objective of this chapter is neither to predict how constitutional Islamization will pan out in every Muslim-majority country nor to exhaustively set out every single possibility of reconciling Islamic supremacy clauses with the liberal and progressive rule of law. The former is a momentous task to document, and the latter has been done by leading scholars in the field already.[1] This chapter concludes that the realization of popular demands for both Islam and rights does not necessarily lead down a tortuous path, even in practice; rather, there are pragmatic possibilities for the reconciliation of constitutional Islamization and liberal rights in courts.

5.1 PAKISTAN

5.1.1 *Constitutional Islamization in Pakistan*

Since Pakistan and its Islamic constitution have not been discussed in previous sections, it is important to briefly elaborate on the creation of Pakistan and summarily describe its constitutional history with regards to Islamic clauses. Pakistan, founded in 1947, was the world's first state based on explicit Islamic nationalism and the first in the world – before Israel – to be founded based on religion.[2] It was created as the British partitioned colonial India to create the two states of India and Pakistan (comprised as present-day Bangladesh and Pakistan – then known as East and West Pakistan, respectively). The idea of dividing India into two nation-states had been floated in the early twentieth century and the idea grew in strength as the Muslim League lent its support to it in the Lahore Resolution of 1940 in which the founder of Pakistan, Muhammad Ali Jinnah, emphasized the distinction between Islam and Hinduism as two separate civilizations that could not coexist in a Hindu-majority-dominated India.[3] And this distinction was not merely theoretical: tensions between the Hindu and Muslim communities in India had often resulted in immense violence. Muslims also feared their fate in a Hindu-

---

[1] For example see, Clark Lombardi, *State Law as Islamic Law in Modern Egypt: The Incorporation of the Sharia into Egyptian Constitutional Law* (Brill 2006); Clark Lombardi, "Can Islamizing a Legal System Ever Help Promote Liberal Democracy?: A View from Pakistan" (2010) 7(3) University of St. Thomas Law Journal 649; Martin Lau, *The Role of Islam in the Legal System of Pakistan* (Martinus Nijhoff 2006); NJ Brown and AO Sherif, "Inscribing the Islamic Shari'a in Arab Constitutional Law" in Yvonne Yazbeck Haddad and Barbara Freyer Stowasser (eds), *Islamic Law and the Challenges of Modernity* (Altamira Press 2004).

[2] Faisal Devji, *Muslim Zion: Pakistan as a Political Idea* (Harvard University Press 2013) 4.

[3] Address by Quaid-i-Azam Mohammad Ali Jinnah at Lahore Session of Muslim League, March 1940 (Islamabad: Directorate of Films and Publishing, Ministry of Information and Broadcasting, Government of Pakistan, Islamabad, 1983) 5–23.

dominated India when the British departed. Eventually, the movement led by Jinnah succeeded in gaining a separate independent state with a Muslim-majority population.

Many debates about the relationship of religion and state preceded the creation of the new state of Pakistan. Jinnah had repeatedly referenced Islamic nationalism to legitimize the foundations of the new state. Pakistan emerged in 1947, partly as a result of the Hindu-Muslim divide but also as a political experiment to provide a homeland to a religious minority in a politically unstable India. Interestingly, the Islamic party in India, the Jamaat-e-Islami under Mawdudi, had vehemently opposed the movement for the creation of Pakistan.[4] Mawdudi argued that Pakistan would be a state for Muslims rather than an Islamic theocratic state and therefore unacceptable. The opposition of the Jamaat-e-Islami to the creation of Pakistan was so clear and ideologically significant that even Mahatma Gandhi, an ardent opponent of the two-state solution, helped "hardliner Muslim Mullahs . . . to setup a political organization which implacably opposed"[5] Jinnah and his secular Muslim League. However, once it was clear that Pakistan would be formed despite the religious lobby's opposition and that staying in India might not be the most rational strategy, the Jamaat-e-Islami changed its position and began to deploy a theory of Islamic nationalism.

Jinnah rallied for a separate Muslim state, founded on pluralistic and socialist foundations.[6] Almost immediately after partition, Jinnah, in an address to the Pakistani parliament on August 11, 1947 declared that the "problem of religious differences has been the greatest hindrance in the progress of India. Therefore, we must learn a lesson from this. You are free; you are free to go to your temples, you are free to go to your mosques or to any other places of worship in this State of Pakistan. You may belong to any religion or caste or creed – that has nothing to do with the business of the State."[7] In other addresses, however, he invoked something distinct. For example, at a speech in Karachi, he declared "I cannot understand the logic of those who have been deliberately and mischievously propagating that the Constitution of Pakistan will not be based on Islamic Sharia. Islamic

---

[4] Aziz Ahmad, "Mawdudi and Orthodox Fundamentalism in Pakistan" (1967) 21(3) Middle East Journal 369.

[5] Hamza Alavi, "Social Forces and the Making of Pakistan" (2002) 37(51) Economic and Political Weekly 5,119, 5,122.

[6] Iftikhar H Malik, *Islam, Nationalism and the West: Issues of Identity in Pakistan* (Palgrave Macmillan 1999) 110.

[7] Address by Quaid-i-Azam Mohammad Ali Jinnah at Karachi Club on August 11, 1947. Jinnah was also the first governor-general (presidential equivalent) of Pakistan.

principles today are as much applicable to life as they were 1300 years ago."[8] In yet another statement, Jinnah stated that "Islam gives us a complete code. It is not only religion, but it contains laws, philosophy and politics. In fact, it contains everything that matters to a man from morning to night. When we talk of Islam, we take it as all-embracing word. We do not mean any ill. The foundation of our Islamic code is that we stand for liberty, equality and fraternity."[9]

Whatever Jinnah's intentions, debates continue to rage about whether Jinnah intended to create a secular state – only using Islam as a symbol of cultural identity or whether he intended a doctrinal Islamic state that would impose Islamic law.[10] Indeed, Pakistan, since its founding in 1947, has been a "configuration of competing political and social ideologies."[11] One can see how Jinnah's multiple statements and the appeal of Muslim nationalism that justified the state of Pakistan could be interpreted by secularists and Islamists as pulling in completely different directions. And this confusion has not helped with strengthening the state as it has served to deepen this divide. It is pertinent to note that many of those involved in the formation of Pakistan were "secular" Anglophone members of British India's Muslim elite. Having prospered under the British, they feared that a Hindu-majority state would discriminate against Muslims and deny them access to the power and prestige they had previously enjoyed. These figures had a democratic and liberal vision for their new state. "They imagined Pakistan as a country where a Muslim majority would use representative political mechanisms to determine the types of law that would be applied, with a judiciary ensuring that majoritarian laws did not violate the natural rights of citizens in the minority."[12] However, the creation of a separate nation-state for the Muslims of India gave considerable space to the argument that Pakistan was meant to be a theocratic state.[13]

---

[8]   Mohammad Ali Jinnah, *Jinnah: Speeches and Statements 1947–48* (Oxford University Press 2000) 97–98.

[9]   Address by Quaid-i-Azam Mohammad Ali Jinnah at the Gaya Muslim League Conference in January 1938.

[10] Christophe Jaffrelot, "Secularity without Secularism in Pakistan: The Politics of Islam from Sir Syed to Zia" in Mirjam Künkler, John Madeley, and Shylashri Shanker (eds), *A Secular Age beyond the West: Religion, Law and the State in Asia, the Middle East and North Africa* (Cambridge University Press 2018) 152–84.

[11] Kamran Asdar Ali, "Pakistan Islamists Gamble on the General" (2004) 231 Middle East Research and Information Project <https://merip.org/2004/06/pakistani-islamists-gamble-on-the-general/> accessed January 12, 2022.

[12] Lombardi, "Can Islamizing a Legal System Ever Help Promote Liberal Democracy?" 649, 654.

[13] Moeen H Cheema, "Beyond Beliefs: Deconstructing the Dominant Narratives of the Islamization of Pakistan's Law" (2012) 60(4) The American Journal of Comparative Law 875, 878.

Pakistan's constitution has also been subject to this constant and confusing tension between the secular and Islamic identity of the state. The first Constituent Assembly of Pakistan was set up by the Indian Independence Act 1947. It was to draft a new constitution and act as a legislature. Drafting the new constitution meant grappling with the issue of the role of Islam in the new state. On March 12, 1949, the Constituent Assembly passed the Objectives Resolution, which provided guidance on the substance of the new constitution and proclaimed that the future constitution of Pakistan would be modeled on the ideology and faith of Islam. It is an important document that has formed the preamble of all of Pakistan's constitutions until Zia-ul-Haq made it an operative part of the constitution in 1985.[14] Indeed, it has been declared as the *"grundnorm"* of the Pakistani constitution. It stated, inter alia, that sovereignty over the universe belonged to Allah and that Muslims would be able to lead their life in accordance with Islam. Yet it also provided for several rights and declared that the state would observe the principles of democracy, tolerance, freedom, and equality. Liaquat Ali Khan, Pakistan's first prime minister, emphasized that Pakistan would not be a theocratic state, while some non-Muslim members asserted that if sovereignty rested in God, Pakistan could not be a democratic state.[15]

In design, the 1956 constitution included several rights and Islamic clauses. Pakistan formally became the "Islamic Republic of Pakistan," where only a Muslim could become the head of the state – the president. The constitution, however, did not bar non-Muslims from becoming the prime minister, or the head of government. The constitution protected the right of all citizens to profess, propagate, and practice their own faith. Under the chapter of Islamic provisions, the repugnancy clause declared that no law should be "repugnant" to the injunctions of Islam as laid down in the Holy Quran and Sunnah.[16] There were several other Islamic provisions included in the principles of policy, such as to promote Islamic teachings, but the constitution did not declare Islam to be the state religion.

Subsequently, the 1962 constitution tempered down some of the Islamic provisions. Ayub Khan, Pakistan's military dictator, considered religious scholars (ulama) responsible for Pakistan's rising sectarian problem, and he moved to limit their power. Yet he did not fully eliminate the Islamic provisions as stated in the previous constitution, as he understood the need to

---

[14] Presidential Order No. XIV of 1985, Article 2 and Schedule (item 2).
[15] Hamid Khan, *Constitutional and Political History of Pakistan* (3rd ed, Oxford University Press 2017) 59.
[16] Constitution of Islamic Republic of Pakistan 1956, Article 198(1).

provide a common and shared heritage for Pakistan. He used Islam for this because of the lack of national cohesion between the two far-flung wings of Pakistan, which were different in culture, language, and habits. Therefore, national ideology had to permeate with Islamic ideals to achieve political integration.[17] Ayub Khan modified the Islamic clauses to suit his modernist interpretation of Islam. The repugnancy clause was simply stated as "no law shall be repugnant to Islam" and this article was not enforceable by the courts.[18] Even the Objectives Resolution, though retained as the preamble to the 1962 constitution, was slightly changed in order to remove any reference to a limitation of the legislative powers of parliament on the basis of Islam.[19] The 1962 constitution also renamed "Islamic Republic of Pakistan" as "Republic of Pakistan," removing "Islamic." Yet this was not sustainable. This is evident from the fact that in Pakistan – as in many other Muslim-majority countries – the insertion of Islam in the political vocabulary of the constitution is and remains popular. According to one poll undertaken by the Constitution Commission, which was tasked with drafting the 1962 consti-tution, "the preponderance of opinion (95.64%) is in favour of adopting this [Islamic] Preamble and a minority opinion did not consider it necessary to adopt this Preamble."[20] Therefore, it is unsurprising that political pressure resulted in the First Constitutional Amendment of 1963 that renamed the country the "Islamic Republic of Pakistan" and extended the powers of the Advisory Council of Islamic Ideology, which was to advise regarding the application of the repugnancy clause by examining "whether a proposed law is or is not repugnant to the teachings and requirements of Islam as set by the Holy Quran and Sunnah."[21] Simultaneously, the constitutional amendment made fundamental rights enforceable through courts. The original consti-tution enshrined fundamental rights but did not make them justiciable.[22] In this way, the 1962 constitution illustrates that Islam and fundamental rights are

---

[17] Manzooruddin Ahmed and SM Sharif, "Islamic Aspects of the New Constitution of Pakistan" (1963) 2(2) Islamic Studies 249.

[18] The Constitution of Republic of Pakistan 1962, Articles 6 and 204.

[19] "Whereas sovereignty over the entire universe belongs to God Almighty alone and the authority which He has delegated to the State of Pakistan through its people for being exercised within the limits prescribed by Him is a sacred trust." The underlined words were omitted. Lau, *Role of Islam* 7.

[20] Ahmed and Sharif, "Islamic Aspects of the New Constitution" 249, 252.

[21] Constitution (First Amendment) Act 1963, Article 204 (1) (b).

[22] The Supreme Court did not wait long to enforce fundamental rights. In 1964, the court declared a law that banned the activities of the Islamist political party, Jamaat-e-Islami, as unconstitutional on the basis of the violation of the fundamental right to "freedom of association." *Abul Ala Maudoodi v Government of West Pakistan* PLD 1964 SC 673.

closely and indivisibly connected. Initially, the marginalization of the role of Islam in the constitution coincided with a weaker position of fundamental rights, and when the role of Islam was increased through constitutional amendment, it coincided with stronger human rights protections.

A similar relationship between human rights and Islam is evident with in Pakistan's third constitution, adopted in 1973, and in its subsequent amendments.[23] The 1973 constitution undertook deeper constitutional Islamization: for the first time, the constitution declared Islam as the state religion (Article 2), and only Muslims were eligible to run for the offices of president and prime minister. The 1973 constitution even defined who was "Muslim." Despite the heavily Islamized nature of the 1973 constitution, it is also arguably the most democratic of Pakistan's three constitutions (1956, 1962, and 1973), both as a matter of process and substance.[24] This constitutional balance of democratic and religious principles (some of which would curtail the freedom of minorities) once again illustrates the curious ideological mix of modernity and tradition/religion that has been a parallel and prevalent part of the constitutional order in Pakistan since the country's founding as an independent state. In fact, even as the 1973 constitution was heavily Islamized, it also contained more rights than any of the preceding two constitutions – 41 versus 29 (almost 35% more rights) as compared to the 1962 Constitution, written only a decade earlier.[25]

According to the Islamic Constitutions Index (ICI), the 1973 constitution is the third-most Islamized constitution in the world.[26] Among other statements regarding Islam, it declares Pakistan as an "Islamic Republic" (Article 1); its preamble states that "sovereignty over the entire Universe belongs to Almighty Allah alone"; it makes Islam the state religion (Article 2); and it requires the candidates for president and prime minister to be Muslim and to swear an oath referencing Islamic idiom (Article 41). Further, the oath declares that the president, prime minister, and other ministers "will strive to preserve the Islamic Ideology which is the basis for the creation of Pakistan" (Articles 42, 91, and 92). The constitution also declares that "no law shall be enacted which is repugnant to Islamic Injunctions" (Article 227). Few other countries in the

---

[23] Pakistan also had an interim constitution that was adopted in April 1972. It was primarily based on the previous two constitutions of 1956 and 1962.

[24] Jeffrey A Redding, "Constitutionalizing Islam: Theory and Pakistan" (2004) 44 Virginia Journal of International Law 759, 764.

[25] Dawood Ahmed and Tom Ginsburg, "Constitutional Islamization and Human Rights: The Surprising Origin and Spread of Islamic Supremacy Clauses" (2014) (54(3) Virginia Journal of International Law 615.

[26] Dawood Ahmed and Moamen Gouda, "Measuring Constitutional Islamization: The Islamic Constitutions Index" (2014) 38 Hastings International and Comparative Law Review 1, 50.

Muslim world have such a strong form of Islamic supremacy clause.[27] Further, in clauses that are unique only to the Pakistani constitution, the constitution declares that: (a) "steps shall be taken to enable the Muslims of Pakistan, individually and collectively, to order their lives in accordance with the fundamental principles and basic concepts of Islam" (Article 31); (b) "the state shall eliminate *riba* (usury) as early as possible" (Article 38); (c) members of parliament must have "adequate knowledge of Islamic teachings" and not be "commonly known as one who violates Islamic Injunctions" (Article 62); (d) a Federal Shariat Court shall be established to monitor the Islamicity of laws (Article 203C); and (e) "all existing laws shall be brought in conformity with the Injunctions of Islam as laid down in the Holy Quran and Sunnah" (Article 227). Unlike any other constitution in the Muslim world, the constitution even defines who is a Muslim (Article 260) and explicitly excludes some unortho-dox Muslim minority groups – such as the Ahmadiyya – who declare them-selves to be Muslims. It describes "non-Muslim" as a person who is not a Muslim and includes people belonging to the Christian, Hindu, Sikh, Buddhist, and Parsi communities; people of the Qadiani Group or the Lahori Group who call themselves "Ahmadis" or by any other name; Bahai; and people belonging to any of the Scheduled Castes.

During the martial law rule of Zia-ul-Haq, the 1973 constitution was suspended along with the fundamental rights enshrined in it. The Zia-ul-Haq regime justified the suppression of fundamental rights by enhancing the legal role of Islam through Islamic judicial review by establishing the Federal Shariat Court and the Shariat Appellate Bench of the Supreme Court. General Zia-ul-Haq was desperate to find some basis for popular support and legitimacy. Therefore, he relied upon constitutional Islamization.[28] To his dismay, and perhaps surprisingly, the judges of the Shariat Courts exer-cised the powers of Islamic judicial review to endorse fundamental rights and basic freedoms of citizens by supplanting these rights and freedoms with Islamic legal principles derived from the Quran and Sunnah.[29] Through the

---

[27] Ahmed and Gouda, "Measuring Constitutional Islamization" 1, 50.

[28] Pakistan's involvement in the Afghan war also provided a new impetus to state-sponsored Islamization in the context of the Iranian Revolution of 1979. Cheema, "Beyond Beliefs" 875, 879.

[29] The FSC held that certain provisions of the Pakistan Army Act (section 133), the Pakistan Air Force Act 1953 (section 162), and the Pakistan Navy Ordinance 1961 (section 138) are repugnant to the injunctions of Islam because they barred the right of appeal. *Pakistan through Secretary Defense v Public at Large* PLD 1985 FSC 365. The FSC held that equality before the law and equal protection of the law are inherent principles of Islamic law and policy. Therefore, the law that allowed the government to dismiss civil servants before the age of retirement without

endorsement of fundamental rights with reference to Islamic legal principles, the judges of the Shariat Courts realized the potential of constitutional Islamization to constrain executive authority and empower the judicial branch. It is this potential of using Islamic constitutional provisions to push a judicial agenda that inspired the judges of the Shariat Courts to enthusiastically embrace Islamic judicial review even as the military regime of Zia-ul-Haq conversely intended to maintain the status quo through the judicial Islamization of laws.[30]

This section particularly focuses on the Islamic supremacy clause in Pakistani constitutions. From the first constitution in 1956 to the third constitution in 1973, Pakistan has contained an Islamic supremacy clause in its strongest form – a repugnancy clause that declared that no law violative of Islamic injunctions would be enacted and that all existing laws would be brought in conformity with Islam. Alongside such robust Islamic supremacy clauses, the constitutions also contain several modern-day human rights, including freedom of speech, religion, and expression; indeed, Pakistan is an evolving democracy and its constitution ranks highly in its rights provisions.[31] Having this mix of clauses, the cases from Pakistan present a useful understanding of the judicial attitude toward interpretation of such constitutional provisions.

5.1.2 *Islamic Supremacy Clauses in Pakistani Courts*

The judicial attitude in Pakistani courts presents an interesting case study of how courts operate to reconcile the Islamic provisions of the constitution with other constitutional rights largely considered as Western. Indeed, Pakistan's experience of incorporating Islam in its constitutional setup illustrates the flexibility and dynamism of constitutional Islamization. While the repugnancy clause and the clause requiring all laws to be in conformity with Islam have been a feature of successive Pakistani constitutions, it was only in 1980 that Pakistani courts were explicitly empowered to engage in judicial review of

---

giving a show cause notice is invalid. *Muhammad Ramzan Qureshi v Federal Government* PLD 1986 FSC 200.

[30] Daniel P Collins, "Islamization of Pakistani Law: A Historical Perspective" (1987–88) 24 Stanford Journal of International Law 511. (Based on the analysis of the FSC judgment from 1980 to 1988, the author argues that the FSC avoided deciding controversial issues by using its jurisdictional limits and when it chose to decide, it adopted a flexible approach to Islamic law that was in line with the practice of secular common law courts rather than with classical Islamic legal theory.)

[31] See Table 3.1 in chapter 3.

legislation to ensure compliance with the repugnancy clause.[32] Until 1979, the Islamic repugnancy clause had remained nonjusticiable and the Council of Islamic Ideology could only advise the parliament on the conformity of state laws with Islam. However, the dictatorial military regime of General Zia-ul-Haq established the Shariat Benches at the four provincial high courts to Islamize laws in 1979. A year later, the Federal Shariat Court (FSC) replaced the Shariat Benches to centralize the process of the Islamization of laws. Despite relying upon the Islamization of laws for legitimacy, the Zia-ul-Haq regime carefully crafted the jurisdiction of the FSC to exclude the review of constitutional provisions for their conformity with the injunctions of Islam as laid down in the Quran and Sunnah. Judges of the superior courts of Pakistan rationalized this limitation on FSC's jurisdiction on the basis that since the FSC was created by the constitution, it cannot declare invalid the constitution itself.[33] Relying upon this argument, judges refused to assign themselves a supra-constitutional role, as exercised by the Iranian Guardian Council.[34]

Yet, likely not foreseen by Zia-ul-Haq, the judicial review power of the FSC evolved to become so significant that it was thought to have no parallel in the judicial history of Pakistan. Although initially the creation of the FSC raised the haunting specter of an orthodox and antidemocratic Islamist judiciary,[35] since its inception in 1979, Islamic judicial review through the FSC was, in practice, unlikely to cause major constitutional and legal changes because of its inherent design to maintain the status quo. This can be explained by a number of factors. First, the FSC did not have jurisdiction over the provisions of the constitution. In its early years, the judges of the FSC cautiously exercised their review powers and even refused to examine laws that were indirectly linked to the constitution.[36] Second, the controversial areas of laws such as Muslim personal law, procedural laws of courts, and fiscal laws were

---

[32]   Haider Ala Hamoudi, "Repugnancy in the Arab World" (2012) 48(427) Williamette Law Review 427, 429.

[33]   *BZ Kaikaus v President of Pakistan* PLD 1980 SC 160.

[34]   It is true that the Council of Islamic Ideology, comprised of ulama, has the authority to review the provisions of the constitution for their conformity with Islamic injunctions, but the recommendations of the Council are nonbinding upon the legislature, unlike the judgments of the FSC.

[35]   Cheema, "Beyond Beliefs" 875, 880.

[36]   The FSC held that it did not have the jurisdiction to review the Political Parties Act 1962 and the Representative of the People Act 1976 because they relate to various articles of the constitution. *Habib-ur-Rehman v Government of Pakistan*, PLD 1981 FSC 131.

also excluded from the jurisdiction of the FSC.[37] Third, the judges of the FSC did not have security of tenure as they served at the discretion of the president and could be removed at any time.[38] Fourth, the FSC did not include any ulama judges initially, and when the constitution provided for the appointment of ulama judges, they were a minority: three out of the eight judges at the FSC. Finally, FSC judgments were appealable before the Shariat Appellate Bench of the Supreme Court (SAB), which included two ulama judges and three regular judges of the Supreme Court; FSC judgments did not become effective until the appeal was decided, and in a number of politically sensitive legal issues, the SAB did not adjudicate appeal cases for decades.[39]

Due to these structural and jurisdictional limitations, the expected specter of an antidemocratic Islamist judiciary never materialized. Instead, what has happened in Pakistan is that the higher courts – the Supreme Court and indeed the FSC have, rather than using Islamic clauses to subjugate human rights, in fact handed down decisions that endorse and propagate rights. Indeed, the FSC endorsed rights on the basis of Islamic legal principles and developed a parallel catalog of "Islamic human rights jurisprudence" through its judgments.[40]

For instance, the FSC upheld the right to nondiscrimination and gender equality by declaring the provisions of the Citizenship Act 1951 as repugnant for denying the husband of a Pakistani woman the right to citizenship of Pakistan.[41] In another judgment, the FSC rejected petitions that challenged the appointment of female judges and endorsed the principle of general

---

[37] The FSC could not review any fiscal law or any law relating to the levy of taxes, fees, banking, or insurance practice and procedures for three years. This period was extended to ten years starting from 1980. The Constitution (Amendment) Order of 1980.

[38] The Chief Justice of the FSC, Aftab Hussain, was removed from his office in 1984 when the Zia-ul-Haq regime expected unfavorable judgment from him in a case relating to the Ahmadiyya community. Sadia Saeed, "Politics of Exclusion: Muslim Nationalism, State Formation and Legal Representations of the Ahmadiyya Community in Pakistan" (PhD thesis, University of Michigan, 2010) 329–33. This power was removed in 2010, and a judge could only be removed under the process that applied to a judge of the Supreme Court, as per Act No. 10 of 2010.

[39] Currently, around thirty appeals against FSC judgments have been pending before the SAB. The oldest appeal has been pending since 1989. In *Begum Rashida Patel v Government of Pakistan* PLD 1989 FSC 95, the FSC had declared certain sections of the Offence of Zina (Enforcement of Hudood) Ordinance 1979 as repugnant to the injunctions of Islam.

[40] Lau, *Role of Islam* 210.

[41] *In re Suo Motu Case No. 1/K of 2006 (Gender Equality)* PLD 2008 FSC 1.

equality as enshrined in verse 2:228 of the Quran.[42] The FSC also endorsed the right to due process of the law and declared the laws related to the armed forces, administrative law, and civil service regulations as repugnant to the injunctions of Islam because they did not provide the right to a hearing, fair trial, and appeal.[43] Further, judges of the FSC and the SAB have softened the rigors of "Islamized" state-enforced laws. In doing so, they frequently relied upon Islamic legal principles.[44] Thus, rather than pitting Islam against secularist Western human rights, the judges of the Shariat Courts mitigated political manipulation of Islam by invoking the humanitarian and liberal principles of Islam.[45]

---

[42] *Mian Hammad Murtaza v Federation of Pakistan* PLD 2011 FSC 117; *Ansar Burney v Federation of Pakistan* PLD 1983 FSC 73. Not all judgments of the FSC, however, have been pro-women. In 2016, the FSC refused to declare a colonial law as un-Islamic that allowed husbands to get a decree of restitution of conjugal rights against their wives. *Nadeem Siddiqui v Islamic Republic of Pakistan* PLD 2016 FSC 1. Similarly, the FSC recommended the criminalization of surrogacy without providing adequate safeguards for the protection of surrogate mothers. *Farooq Siddiqui v Mst. Farzana Naheed* PLD 2017 FSC 78.

[43] The FSC held that equality before the law and equal protection of the law are inherent principles of Islamic law and policy. Therefore, the law that allowed the government to dismiss civil servants before the age of retirement without giving a show cause notice is invalid. *Muhammad Ramzan Qureshi v Federal Government* PLD 1986 FSC 200. The FSC held that certain provisions of the Pakistan Army Act (section 133), the Pakistan Air Force Act 1953 (section 162), and the Pakistan Navy Ordinance 1961 (section 138) are repugnant to the injunctions of Islam because they barred the right of appeal. *Pakistan through Secretary Defense v Public at Large* PLD 1985 FSC 365.

[44] In 1981, the FSC declared the punishment of stoning (*rajm*) for adultery (*zina*) as un-Islamic. *Hazoor Bakhsh v Federation of Pakistan* PLD 1981 FSC 145. The Zia regime reconstituted the bench of the FSC to reverse this judgment. *Federation of Pakistan v Hazoor Bakhsh* PLD 1983 FSC 255. The FSC clarified that blasphemy is not a wrong of strict liability, in which neither wrongful intent (mens rea) nor culpable negligence is required for liability even when it proposed that the death sentence is the only punishment for blasphemy and the alternative punishment of life imprisonment is un-Islamic. *Muhammad Ismail Qureshi v Pakistan* PLD 1991 FSC 10. The Shariat Courts established the principles that a woman can never be guilty of consensual sex (*zina*) if she complains of rape at any stage, no matter how belatedly; and that mere pregnancy is not sufficient to convict a woman for consensual sex, especially if she claims that the pregnancy was a result of rape. Moeen H Cheema, "Cases and Controversies: Pregnancy as Proof of Guilt under Pakistan's Hudood Laws" (2006) 32(1) Brooklyn Journal of International Law 121. In several judgments, the FSC held that pregnancy alone is not sufficient proof of rape or consensual sex. *Mst. Zafran Bibi v The State* PLD 2002 FSC 1; *Juma Gul v The State* 1997 PCrLJ 1,291; *Noor Zaman v The State* 1998 PCrLJ 476; *Mst. Sakina v The State* PLD 1981 FSC 320; *Iqbal Hussain v The State* PLD 1981 FSC 329.

[45] An evaluation of case law shows that in most cases judges have invoked Islamic legal principles either to reinforce fundamental rights or to expand them. In very few cases, judges referred to Islam to limit fundamental rights. One such case relates to the disqualification of the ousted prime minister Nawaz Sharif to head his political party. *Zulfiqar Ahmed Bhutta v Federation of Pakistan* PLD 2018 SC 370.

The FSC has in fact employed principles of Islam to limit state authority by declaring various laws repugnant to the injunctions of Islam. In particular, the impact of the judgments of the FSC has been significant upon criminal laws and land reform laws. For example, as a result of the FSC judgment, the Islamic laws of retribution and compensation (*qisas* and *diyat*)[46] have been incorporated into the Pakistan Penal Code 1860 (PPC).[47] The relevant provisions in the Code of Criminal Procedure 1898 have also been amended to remove executive discretion to compound offenses of murder and bodily injury.[48] Similarly, several land reform laws were declared as repugnant because they violated the sanctity of private property enshrined under Islamic law by seizing land above certain limitations and imposing restrictions on the ownership rights of landlords.[49] The FSC judgments also impacted civil services regulations as the FSC declared various regulations repugnant to secure the rights and entitlements of civil servants.[50] While the incorporation of the Islamic laws of *qisas* and *diyat* into the statutory law and invalidation of land reform laws have been widely criticized for adversely affecting vulnerable and marginalized groups, scholars have commended the rights-based jurisprudence of the FSC and the SAB.[51] On balance, the achievements of Islamic judicial review have been significant in terms of promoting human rights, especially during the 1980s when fundamental rights enshrined in the 1973 constitution were suspended during the martial law regime of Zia-ul-Haq from 1977 to 1985. During the dictatorial regime of Zia-ul-Haq, the superior judiciary was unable to adjudicate on the constitutionality of the legislative and administrative actions of the military regime. In this context, the FSC and the SAB relied upon the principles of Islamic law to derive

---

[46] Muslim jurists classify offenses into three categories: *hudud* (fixed penalties), *qisas* (retribution) and *diyat* (compensation), and *ta'zir* (dependent upon the discretion of the ruler/state). *Hudud* penalties are fixed in the Quran and Sunnah for offenses that include illicit sexual intercourse (*zina*), false accusation of *zina* (*qadhf*), theft (*sariqa*), and consumption of intoxicants (*shurb al-khamr*). Offenses of *qisas* (retaliation) and *diyat* (compensation) relate to homicide and bodily injuries. *Ta'zir* offenses depend upon the discretion of the ruler and include offenses other than the *hudud* and *qisas* offenses.

[47] *Muhammad Riaz v The Federal Government* PLD 1980 FSC 1.

[48] *Federation of Pakistan v Gul Hassan Khan* PLD 1989 SC 633. For details see Tahir Wasti, *The Application of Islamic Criminal Law in Pakistan: Sharia in Practice* (Brill 2009).

[49] *Sajwara v Federal Government of Pakistan* PLD 1989 FSC 80; *Muhammad Ismail Qureshi v Government of Punjab* PLD 1991 FSC 80; *Qazalbash Waqf v Chief Land Commissioner* PLD 1990 SC 99.

[50] *In re Civil Servants Act 1973* PLD 1984 FSC 34; *I. A. Sharwani v Government of Pakistan* MLD 1991 FSC 2,613.

[51] Charles Kennedy, "Islamization and Legal Reform in Pakistan, 1979–1989" (1990) 63(1) *Pacific Affairs* 62; Lau, *Role of Islam*.

various principles of natural justice and human liberties from the Quran and Sunnah. While declaring a number of state laws repugnant to the injunctions of Islam to protect fundamental rights and liberties, the judges of the SAB formulated legal rules based on Islamic principles of *adl* (justice), *qist* (fairness), and *ihsan* (equity) to support the right to due process: namely, the right to be heard and the right to defense.[52]

More particularly, with regards to the Hudood Ordinances (laws designed to implement Islamic criminal law for offenses such as adultery, theft, and highway robbery), the courts also heavily moderated the supposed "Islamicity" of these laws. These laws incorporated statutory provisions that discriminated against women and religious minorities and often involved the abuse of Hudood Ordinances to prosecute women and men who had dared to defy conservative norms of gender interaction. Under these laws, floggings, stoning, and amputations were possible punishments. The expectation was that a robust Islamic supremacy clause in the form of a repugnancy clause complemented with judicial powers to review all the legislation was expected to materially repress and regress human rights. However, this did not happen in practice. The FSC consistently overturned the questionable decisions of the trial courts and minimized the chances of successful prosecution of the offenses related to extramarital sex (*zina*). The FSC stipulated that a woman had the right to choose her own husband even if her parents disapproved.[53] Ultimately, the result of Zia's creation of an "Islamic law" basis to challenge legislation was that various courts gradually began to use a wide range of Islamic law arguments for purposes including human rights. Islamic law principles began to appear in their decisions even in matters not usually considered core Islamic concerns and hence seemed to have bolstered judicial creativity. Much of the appellate courts' decisions employing Islamic principles can be characterized as liberal or even progressive, thus enhancing the protection of rights. And only in a minority of instances was there a curtailment of rights.[54] Even outside the Hudood Ordinance, appellate courts generally used Islamic legal principles to expand judicial review power in the 1990s and legitimize progressive activism in public interest litigation cases,

---

[52] *Pakistan v Public at Large* PLD 1987 SC 304 (rights of civil servants were given protection); *Province of Sindh v Public at Large* PLD 1988 SC 138 (right to show cause notice is provided); *Pakistan v Public at Large* PLD 1989 SC 6 (right to appeal against the orders passed by the Court Martials is provided).

[53] *Muhammad Imtiaz v State* PLD 1981 FSC 308 and *Muhammad Yaqoob v The State* 1985 PCrLJ 1,064.

[54] Cheema, "Beyond Beliefs" 875, 900.

human rights petitions challenging legislative enactments, and writ petitions challenging executive overreach.[55]

Interestingly, the FSC (the very court designed to imbue the constitutional-political sphere with constitutional Islam) also started to advance it's own jurisprudence of Islamic rights. In doing so, these courts endorsed the right to make the government and public officials accountable, the right of access to justice, the right to equality, and right to due process.[56] For example, the SAB held Section 13 of the Civil Servants Act 1973 to be "repugnant to the injunctions of Islam" on the grounds that it did not meet certain due process requirements. Based on this case, Cheema argues that "the Federal Shariat Court had granted the status of Islamic law to the 'principles of natural justice' including the right to a fair hearing and the rule against bias."[57] In one case, the SAB decided that the chair of a public authority could not be removed without first being granted a hearing.[58] In another judgment, it was reaffirmed that the limitation on the government's power to confiscate passports required that a right to a hearing must be provided to the affected citizens prior to confiscation. Justice Nasim Hasan Shah held that according to the injunctions of Islam, a person must be given an opportunity of showing cause before any action is taken that may adversely affect his or her rights.[59] In a different case, as successive elected governments attempted to further reduce the independence of the bureaucracy and administrative bodies, the Supreme Court held that a new concept has developed that has introduced not only the principles of natural justice but also such principles of justice and equity which are enshrined in the injunctions of Islam: the orders, acts, and actions of government functionaries, corporate authorities, and statutory bodies can be examined on the basis of well-recognized principles of Islamic common law and injunctions of Islam.[60] In this way, the Shariat Courts have laid down "the groundwork for the most recent Rule of Law advancements in Pakistan by articulating strong principles of accountability of the executive."[61]

The use of constitutional Islamization has not been limited to promoting rights in a few isolated issues. Rather, its deployment has been strategic and systematic: Cheema argues that it has also been used to bolster the independence of the judiciary and control governmental overreach impinging on

---

[55] Cheema, "Beyond Beliefs" 903–4.
[56] Cheema, "Beyond Beliefs" 906.
[57] Cheema, "Beyond Beliefs" 907.
[58] *Pakistan v Public at Large* 1989 SCMR 1,690.
[59] *Federal Government of Pakistan v Government of Punjab* PLD 1991 SC 505.
[60] *Pakistan Broadcasting Corporation v Nasir Ahmad* 1995 SCMR 1,593.
[61] Cheema, "Beyond Beliefs" 875, 909.

rights. In one case, the Supreme Court declared that limitations imposed on human rights were themselves "subordinated to the most fundamental of all human rights in Islam, the one which cannot at all be abridged by any limitation ... namely, [the] right to justice."[62] It also declared that it was the "duty of an Islamic state to administer justice to its citizens irrespective of caste, creed or colour free of any charge."[63] The Shariat Courts ruled that martial law regulations were subject to review for repugnancy to the injunctions of Islam and did not enjoy any special status or protection.[64] The Shariat Courts also held that the exemption granted to members of parliament from appearing before courts while parliament is in session could effectively result in immunity from prosecution and, therefore, was repugnant to the injunctions of Islam. In support of its decision, the Shariat Courts referred to Muslim history to demonstrate that rulers are subject to the law and answerable before the courts.[65] Over time, Shariat Courts deployed Islamic legal principles to reinforce a range of rights including socioeconomic entitlements during public interest litigation. For example, in one case, the FSC referred to the freedom of movement as a fundamental right recognized in Islam.[66] In another case, the right to shelter, food, clothing, education, and health were recognized as "necessities" in Islam.[67]

In addition to Cheema, Lau has also documented how judges have used constitutional Islam to bolster certain rights.[68] For example, in the case of *National I.C.C. Corporation Ltd. v Province of Punjab*,[69] constitutional Islam was deployed to allow a cooperative society to move the Lahore High Court for the enforcement of a fundamental right since the court held that the principle of equality in Islam had been extended to corporations. In another case, *Darshan Masih v State*,[70] concerning the rights of bonded laborers, even though bonded laborer contracts were not illegal under Pakistani law, the court held that prospectively these contracts may be declared void on the ground of being against public policy as enunciated in Islam. Other human rights–related cases were also partly justified on rights grounds, including cases

---

[62] *Federation of Pakistan v General Public* PLD 1988 SC 645, 655.
[63] *Mahmood-ur-Rahman Faisal v Secretary, Ministry of Law* PLD 1992 FSC 195.
[64] *Nusrat Baig Mirza v Government of Pakistan* PLD 1991 SC 509.
[65] *In re Members of the National Assembly (Exemption from Preventive Detention and Personal Appearance) Ordinance IX of 1963* PLD 1989 FSC 3.
[66] *In re Passports Act, 1974* PLD 1989 FSC 39.
[67] *In re Islamization of Laws* PLD 1985 FSC 193.
[68] Lau, *Role of Islam* 96.
[69] PLD 1992 Lah 462.
[70] PLD 1990 SC 513.

regarding injuries of people in stove blasts, access to justice, corruption, and the accountability of high-ranking officials. Lau adds that "the advent of public interest litigation in Pakistan was closely linked to the Islamization of the legal and judicial discourse: since the early 1990s it has become common-place for judges to make references to Islamic law and to apply fundamental rights in an indigenized manner, namely by interpreting them in the light of Islam."[71]

Judges of both, the lay and Shariat Courts, have deployed constitutional Islam strategically to bolster rights protections, including due process and socioeconomic rights. This would support the argument that constitutional Islam (which was and is perhaps expected to remain in popular demand in many Muslim countries, perhaps more so where there is democratization) can and does sit comfortably, in some cases, with the rule of law and the promotion of fundamental rights, and therefore can be accommodated in constitutional frameworks that seek to promote rights.

However, it is pertinent to mention that in some cases, as might be expected, the courts' application of Islamic law has validated discriminatory and culturally harmful practices. For example, in *Zaheeruddin v State*,[72] the Supreme Court legitimated discrimination against and persecution of the Ahmadi community in Pakistan (although even in this decision, it was careful to use arguments grounded in utilitarian "public order" and "trademark" principles, rather than Orthodox Islamic doctrine, to bolster its argument). This case stands starkly in contrast to the development of public interest litigation in Pakistan that was deployed on the argument that Islamic law could add, rather than limit constitutional rights. In short, by harmoniously construing the various provisions of the constitution,[73] the judges of superior courts have relied upon Islam and human rights to promote public interest litigation,[74] ensure the independence of the judiciary,[75] restrain executive

---

[71] Lau, *Role of Islam* 98.

[72] 1993 SCMR 1,718.

[73] In *Hakim Khan v Government of Pakistan* PLD 1992 SC 595. (The Supreme Court ruled that Islamic provisions of the constitution do not supersede other constitutional provisions, but in *Zaheeruddin v State* 1993 SCMR 1,718, the court held that the injunctions of Islam may supersede fundamental rights. However, in a subsequent judgment in *Qazi Hussain Ahmed v General Pervez Musharraf* PLD 2002 SC 853, the court held that all constitutional provisions "should be read together and harmonious construction should be placed on such provisions so that no provision is rendered nugatory.")

[74] *Darshan Masih v The State* PLD 1990 SC 513. (The Supreme Court enforced the rights of laborers by outlawing bonded labor.)

[75] *Govt of Sindh v Sharaf Faridi* PLD 1994 SC 105. (The Supreme Court ordered the government to separate the judiciary from the executive based on Article 2A [Objectives Resolution] of the

authority to prosecute alleged offenders of terrorism through speedy trials,[76] protect rape victims from character assassination,[77] promote the rights of disabled persons,[78] and save the environment by protecting endangered migratory birds.[79]

These examples from Pakistan illustrate that the reconciliation of constitutional Islam and rights is not only possible, but in some cases, "Islamic" review could help with the advancement of progressive rights, in particular where the constitutional catalog of rights contains gaps. In Pakistan, this constitutional model has checked the potentially regressive tendencies resulting from the substantial role of Islam in the legal system through a curious synthesis of Islamic constitutionalism and liberal constitutionalism. This has been helped by the fact that instead of assigning the interpretative authority of Islamic legal texts to a particular state institution, as is the case in the Islamic Republic of Iran and the Kingdom of Saudi Arabia, the Pakistani constitution distributes this authority among the legislature as the representative of the people, the judges of the FSC and the SAB as impartial arbiters, and the Council of Islamic Ideology (representing ulama belonging to various sects) as an advisory body. This distribution forecloses the possibility of the monopoly of one institution on the interpretation of Islam and functions as a system of checks and balances to safeguard the constitutional model, without compromising its Islamic identity. This idea, however, does not suggest that, in the absence of constitutional Islam, judges would not have found some other constitutional or normative grounds to promote justice, that constitutional Islam has caused a promotion of rights, that it does not lead to judicial

---

Constitution, which requires full independence of the judiciary to ensure access to the fundamental right to justice.)

[76] *Mehram Ali v Federation of Pakistan* PLD 1998 SC 1,445. (The Supreme Court held that the admissibility of a confession made before a police officer violates fundamental rights as well as Islamic law.)

[77] The law of evidence under Article 151(4) of the Qanun-e-shahadat Order 1984 provided the right of a male defendant in cases of rape to impeach the character of the alleged victim. The Federal Shariat Court declared this law void on the basis that it violates the principle of gender equality as enshrined in Article 25(2) of the constitution and provided in the Quran. *Capt. (retd.) Mukhtar Ahmad Shaikh v Government of Pakistan* PLD 2009 FSC 65.

[78] *Muhammad Yousaf v Chairman, Federal Public Service Commission* PLD 2017 Lahore 406. (The Court declared the Rules of Competitive Examination 2014 as unconstitutional because they did not accommodate persons with disabilities in foreign and public administration services.)

[79] *Province of Sindh v Lal Khan Chandio* 2016 SCMR 48. (The Court referred to the "environmental teachings of Islam" and the "fundamental right to life and to live with dignity ... in a world that has an abundance of all species not only for the duration of our lives but available for our progeny too.")

uncertainty, or that it is a panacea for multiple legal problems. This study only finds that constitutional Islam can coexist with, and in fact, legitimize and reinforce the realization of rights, provided, inter alia, the judiciary is able and willing to balance the two.

5.2 EGYPT

Egypt faced dire economic problems during the mid-nineteenth century. Khedive Ismail, who ruled from 1863 to 1879, ceded power to the landowners to make up for economic default by giving them membership in the National Assembly to influence the agricultural and financial policy of the government.[80] Subsequent to the declaration of bankruptcy in 1876, British and French financial advisors acquired management of the Egyptian treasury. As part of foreign imposed reforms, the French and British required Ismail to govern through a cabinet that had immense autonomy; for example, it could block legislation and appoint or dismiss civil servants in the ministries.[81] In this way, the concepts of accountability and constraints on the executive took their roots in Egyptian constitutional history as a direct result of economic friction. This eventually led to the promulgation of the constitution in 1882, creating a parliament- and cabinet-centric form of government. Although external pressures precipitated constitutional reform, the reforms essentially paved the way for cementing British and the French control of Egypt and rationalizing their presence and influence. But the Western-inspired model of liberal constitutionalism could not last long and resulted in counter movements seeking protection of rights and putting constraints on British and French administrative models with reference to Islamic principles of constitutionalism.

The Salafi movement reacted to the late nineteenth century Western European–inspired reforms in Egypt that advocated limited government, constraints on the executive, independent judiciary, and public participation in the political processes. Consequently, Islamic intellectuals searched to find justifications for these reforms in Islamic thought. They recognized the impetus for the reforms, accepting the need for such changes, but rejected the Western premise upon which the rulers introduced such changes. Mohammad Abduh and Rashid Rida were the most prominent thinkers of this movement; they called for a society based on moderation, consultative

---

[80] Bruce K Rutherford, "The Struggle for Constitutionalism in Egypt: Understanding the Obstacles to Democratic Transition in the Arab World" (PhD thesis, Yale University 1999) 114.
[81] Rutherford, "The Struggle for Constitutionalism in Egypt" 15–16.

rule, equality before the law, and the ruler's accountability.[82] The work of both these scholars shaped the landscape of Islamic constitutionalism in Egypt. Rashid Rida advocated for the need to ensure that executive authority was based on the principles of rule of law and consultation.[83] He also supported the establishment of a legislature with the right to apply Islamic principles for the public interest.[84] With the work of these Islamic thinkers providing the intellectual support for struggles against the British, the 1923 constitution took effect essentially as a consensus document borne out of pragmatism and compromise. It transformed Egypt into a constitutional monarchy and proclaimed Islam as the religion of the state while also guaranteeing freedom of religion. The 1923 constitution continued in force (with two suspensions) until 1952, when a group of officers overthrew the monarchy, canceled the constitution, replaced it with a series of constitutional declarations, and set the stage for Gamal Abdel Nasser to become president.[85]

Gamal Abdel Nasser governed for almost a decade through temporary laws that did not contain an Islamic supremacy clause. After the death of President Abdel Nasser in 1970, his successor, Anwar Sadat, decided to draft a new constitution to reach out to a wide variety of constituencies, including the Islamists.[86] For this purpose, a Constitutional Drafting Committee was set up with members from across the ideological spectrum in Egypt. This exercise to find a support base within society gave way to Islamists as well. At that juncture, expanding the role of Islam in society was clearly an important issue for the Egyptian public. Therefore, the government held several open public meetings to discuss the constitutional proposals. In these meetings, ordinary citizens unsurprisingly called for an increased role for Islam in public life as well as in the constitution.

The 1971 constitution thus oriented toward a parallel scheme of rights provision and rule of law. For this purpose, the constitution consolidated the former Supreme Court, created through a presidential decree, into the Supreme Constitutional Court (SCC). The SCC was entrusted to evaluate the constitutionality of legislative enactments. Article 2 of the 1971 constitution also declared the "principles of Islamic law" to be a source of legislation.[87]

---

[82] Malcolm H Kerr, *Islamic Reform: The Political and Legal Theories of Muhammad Abduh and Rashid Rida* (University of California Press, 1966) 172–73.

[83] Kerr, *Islamic Reform* 177.

[84] Kerr, *Islamic Reform* 188.

[85] Clark B Lombardi, *State Law as Islamic Law in Modern Egypt: The Incorporation of the Sharia into Egyptian Constitutional Law* (Brill 2006) 111.

[86] Lombardi, *State Law as Islamic Law* 119.

[87] The Constitution of the Arab Republic of Egypt 1971, Article 2.

This recognition of Islamic law coupled with the judicial review powers of the SCC set the ground for the courts to be arbiters in matters impacting Islamic law. The SCC exercised its powers of judicial review on Article 2 for the first time in 1976. Although it ruled that the law challenged was in conformity with the principles of Islamic law, the reasoning in the judgment suggested that the door was left ajar to entertain challenges to laws on the basis of Islamic principles.[88] However, since it was unclear which principles of Islamic law were to be "a" source of legislation, the judicial review powers of the courts were not aligned with the popular narrative, but with the regime. In the 1980s, the revival of Islamist sentiments in the public and potential political challenge to the regime resulted in amendment to Article 2 of the 1971 constitution to make the "principles of Islamic law" "*the* principal source of legislation" instead of merely *a* chief source of law. The Report of the Drafting Committee, which proposed this amendment, suggests that this amendment required that existing laws must be reviewed and amended "in such a manner to make them conform to the principles of Islamic law."[89]

The amendment, however, neither specified a particular institution (legislature, judiciary, or al-Azhar) nor laid down the time period for bringing existing laws in conformity with Islamic law. Despite such ambiguities, "the change in the wording of Article 2 transformed the formerly innocuous clause into a highly controversial and potentially powerful clause . . . it implied that Islamic sharia was henceforth to have a more important role in Egyptian society."[90] Unsurprisingly, this amendment ushered in a period of judicial activism in "Islamic review" as various legislative measures were challenged for their lack of conformity with Islamic principles under this clause. The amended Article 2 in fact became a touchstone for challenging the legislative amendments before the SCC.

In 2011, the Egyptian army abrogated the 1971 constitution with a promise to ensure democracy through free and fair elections and accountability. As a harbinger of legitimacy, the 2012 constitution was drafted and enacted. The role of Islam and its justiciability through courts once again became a topic of contestation. Eventually, all stakeholders agreed to restore Article 2 of the 1971 constitution, which was amended in 1980. Therefore, "the Principles of the Islamic Sharia" continued to be "*the* principal source of Egyptian legislation"

---

[88] Rudolph Peters, "Divine Law or Man-Made Law? Egypt and the Application of the Shari'a" (1988) 3 Arab Law Quarterly 231, 241.

[89] Lombardi, *State Law as Islamic* 133.

[90] Clark B Lombardi, "Islamic Law as a Source of Constitutional Law in Egypt: The Constitutionalization of the Sharia in a Modern Arab State" (1998) 37(1) Columbia Journal of Transnational Law 81, 86.

and served as the touchstone for challenging legislative enactments before the SCC. This time, the debate on the role of Islam became more focused on a particular question: which version or interpretation of Islam should be embraced? To deal with this, the compromise between the Salafi, traditional, and modernist groups resulted in the inclusion of two new provisions: Article 219 and Article 4. Article 219 provided that "the principles of the Islamic Shari'ah include its general principles (*adillāt kullīyah*), methodological principles (*al-qawā'id uṣūlīyah*), jurisprudential principles (*al-qawā'id al-fiqhīyah*), and the sources considered by the Sunni schools (*madhāhib*)." Article 4 deals with the question of authority: who can be entrusted to interpret the principles of shari'a as defined in Article 219. Article 4 provided that al-Azhar is "an independent Islamic institution of higher learning. It handles all its affairs without outside interference. It leads the call into Islam and assumes responsibility for religious studies and the Arabic language in Egypt and the world." Thus, Article 4 required consultation with the body of senior scholars of al-Azhar in relation to matters regarding the shari'a. Article 4, however, did not clarify whether such consultation was legally binding upon the legislature and the executive.

While Articles 4 and 219 of the 2012 constitution assigned al-Azhar a key role in the legislative process, Article 175 vested the authority of judicial review in the SCC.[91] In this way, in Rachel Scott's words,

> The Supreme Constitutional Court had been established as the ultimate arbiter on the constitutionality of legislation according to Article 175 of the 1971 Constitution. Yet, in stating that the Supreme Constitutional Court "alone" decides on the constitutionality of laws and statutes, Article 175 of the 2012 Constitution further established that it was the Supreme Constitutional Court and not the ulama of al-Azhar that would decide on Article 2 cases. Thus, while Articles 4 and 219 established more authority for al-Azhar, this authority was restricted by Article 175.[92]

Articles 2, 4, 175, and 219 of the 2012 constitution, however, raised several constitutional questions regarding the relationship between the shari'a and state law. For instance, who has the final authority to decide the validity of laws on the basis of the shari'a? If al-Azhar was to be consulted regarding shari'a-related issues, was such consultation advisory or binding? If al-Azhar

---

[91] Article 175 of the 2012 Constitution reads, "The Supreme Constitutional Court is an independent judicial entity, which is based in Cairo, and which alone decides on the constitutionality of laws and statutes."

[92] Rachel M Scott, *Recasting Islamic Law: Religion and the Nation State in Egyptian Constitution Making* (Cornell University Press 2021) 96.

declared that a certain statute was not in compliance with shari'a, could the legislature or the SCC overrule such a determination?[93] As could be imagined, subsequent to these substantial changes, the SCC and al-Azhar became the site for political contestation on questions of constitutionality of the laws and the interpretation of the principles of Islamic law.

Following the military coup led by General Abdel Fattah el-Sisi on July 3, 2013, a new constitution was promulgated in 2014. With the promulgation of the new constitution in 2014, al-Azhar lost the consultative authority in legislative matters that it had under Article 4 and Article 219. In the 2014 constitution, the whole of Article 219 and part of Article 4 were removed, and the remainder of Article 4 was moved to Article 7. Article 7 removed the 2012 requirement that al-Azhar was to be consulted regarding shari'a-related issues. The 2014 constitution clarified the role of the SCC by removing the ambiguity concerning its role over shari'a. While the 2014 constitution does not provide that al-Azhar should be consulted on matters of legislation, al-Azhar continues to firmly claim its right as constitutionally enshrined in Article 7 regarding matters pertaining to the shari'a. Yet, as Rachel Scott observes, "while reinforcing al-Azhar's role as the representative of Islam, the Constitution of 2014 did not resolve the question of the extent and nature of this authority. Nor did it resolve how the line between the Islamic and the non-Islamic would be drawn."[94]

Given the material impact of the constitutional provisions, the following questions need to be answered: did the Islamic supremacy clause lead, as could be popularly assumed, to the implementation of conservative shari'a rules? Did it lead to the curtailment of rights, or was the result somewhat moderated and even enhanced rights, as was the case in Pakistan? Clark Lombardi, Nathan Brown, and Tamir Moustafa, among others, have explored answers to these questions through the case study of Egypt. This section largely relies on the work of these authors to examine the questions of judicial reconciliation of Islam, rule of law, and rights.

5.2.1 *Islamic Supremacy Clauses in Egyptian Courts*

The justiciability of Article 2 in the Egyptian constitution remained under contestation until 1985 when the SCC issued a "politically savvy opinion" that helped it establish its legal authority as an arbiter of Islamic law while simultaneously avoiding a clash with other political (parliament) and religious

---

[93] Scott, *Recasting Islamic Law* 97.
[94] Scott, *Recasting Islamic Law* 114.

institutions (al-Azhar and other ulama).[95] The SCC held that while it did not
have jurisdiction to hear challenges to legislation that was in force on the date
that Article 2 was amended, it *did* have jurisdiction to hear challenges to
legislation enacted thereafter.[96] Besides the question of applicability of Article
2, this was a landmark ruling on the constitutionality of interest (usury,
sometimes interpreted as interest, is generally thought to be un-Islamic).
The Shaikh of al-Azhar University – a significant center of religious learning
in Egypt and throughout much of the Muslim world – had initiated this case.
In this case, a seller demanded al-Azhar University to pay a certain sum as
interest in addition to the payment for the purchase of some medical equip-
ment. Article 226 of the Civil Code of 1948 (which required the charging of
4% interest on delayed payment) was in violation of the prohibition of *riba*
(usury) and was therefore un-Islamic. The lower court referred this case to the
SCC. This was a difficult case for the SCC, which was vested with the
authority of judicial review only a few years ago in 1979. Yet, the judges of
the SCC came up with ingenious legal arguments that helped establish its
authority as a constitutional court but without destabilizing the existing legal
order. The SCC affirmed that Article 2 imposes on the legislature an obliga-
tion to ensure that Egyptian laws must conform to the principles of shari'a.
However, when it comes to the judicial review of laws for conformity with the
principles of shari'a, the SCC has the authority to do so regarding the laws that
are enacted after the amendment of Article 2 in 1980. It held that the legislature retained for itself the power to Islamize the existing laws and the retention
of this power imposes responsibility upon the legislature to Islamize the
existing law. The SCC observed:

> And [w]hereas, nevertheless, the restriction introduced by this limitation on
> future legislation does not mean that the Legislator is freed from all responsi-
> bility concerning past legislative enactments, despite their being contrary to
> the principles of Islamic law. On the contrary, it imposes on the Legislator,
> from a political point view, the duty of purifying the texts of such past
> legislation and clearing them any trespass against the said principles.[97]

The SCC cautioned that, if citizens were allowed to challenge laws that were
issued before the 1980 amendment to the constitution, it would "lead to

---

[95] Clark B Lombardi and Nathan J Brown, "Do Constitutions Requiring Adherence to Shari'a
Threaten Human Rights? How Egypt's Constitution Reconciles Islamic Law with the Liberal
Rule of Law" (2006) 21(1) American University International Law Review 379, 392.

[96] Saba Habachy, "Supreme Constitutional Court (Egypt): Shari'a and Riba: Decision in Case
no. 20 of Judicial Year no. 1" (1985) 1(1) Arab Law Quarterly 100.

[97] Habachy, "Supreme Constitutional Court (Egypt)" 106.

contradictions and confusion in the judicial process in a manner which would threaten stability"[98] and lead to significant economic uncertainty and instability. In effect, the SCC held that Article 2 of the constitution would not have retroactive effect and would only be applied to laws that were issued after the 1980 amendment.[99] With this ruling, the SCC largely dismissed several cases challenging existing laws that were pending on its docket. While not strictly a human rights case, Islamic law could have justified a different decision that would, at least if the contract was void because it involved payment of *riba* (usury), have affected economic and political stability and impinged upon freedom of contract and property rights and potentially conferred a windfall on certain parties. The SCC averted such a risk despite the presence of Article 2, the supremacy clause.

Although the SCC began to deploy Article 2 during the mid-1980s, it was only during the early 1990s that a number of Article 2 cases were referred to the SCC, as the 1985 judgment paved the way for the courts to review legislation. In these judgments, the SCC

> interpreted Islamic law *de novo* using its own distinctive, somewhat idiosyncratic, version of modernist reasoning. According to the court [SCC], state law would be measured against two different types of Islamic principles: First, it would be measured for conformity with a subset of *al-adillāt al-kullīyah* [general principles]. That is, laws would be checked to ensure that they were consistent with all principles clearly and explicitly announced in the Qur'an and with the principles revealed clearly in *aḥādīth* whose authenticity was entirely beyond doubt. Second, the law would have to be consistent with the "goals of law," the *maqāṣid al-sharī'ah*, as the court [SCC] understood them.[100]

With the increased influence of Islamists in the political and social sphere as a result of President Anwar Sadat's policy to win the support of Islamists for legitimacy, the space for avoiding challenges to laws on "retroactivity basis," as held in the 1985 *riba* judgment, became constrained. Consequently, by the early 1990s, new challenges to legislation and even executive action emerged.[101] Through this change in the sociopolitical sphere with the

---

[98] Habachy, "Supreme Constitutional Court (Egypt)" 106.

[99] Habachy, "Supreme Constitutional Court (Egypt)" 106.

[100] Nathan J Brown and Clark Lombardi, "Contesting Islamic Constitutionalism After the Arab Spring: Islam in Egypt's Post-Mubarak Constitutions" in Rainer Grote, Tilmann J Röder and Ali M El-Haj (eds), *Constitutionalism, Human Rights, and Islam After the Arab Spring* (Oxford University Press 2016) 245, 254.

[101] Tamir Moustafa, "The Islamist Trend in Egyptian Law" (2010) 3(1) *Politics and Religion* 610, 622.

participation of Islamist groups, the SCC's role became more prominent as the arbiter in matters concerning interpretations of Islamic law. These challenges did not necessarily bring more Islam to the public space or legal framework, but they certainly led to some repressive outcomes.

The blasphemy case against Dr. Nasr Hamid Abu Zayd, a professor of Islamic and Arabic Studies at Cairo University, is instructive of this repressive phenomenon, which found its way through a challenge under Article 2. The lawyers from Islamist groups accused Dr. Nasr Hamid Abu Zayd of blasphemy and apostasy and sought court orders for the annulment of Dr. Abu Zayd's marriage. The Court of First Instance of Giza dismissed this case for lack of standing of the petitioner in the matter. However, in appeal, the Court of Appeal invoked the Islamic concept of *hisba* that allows individuals to bring claims before the court so as to assert "rights of God" for the common good, despite not having a direct interest in the matter. Through this doctrine, the Court of Appeal found the matter to be covered under the purview of *hisba* and ruled:

> What [Abu Zayd] had written contravenes not only religion, but also the Constitution of the Arab Republic of Egypt. Its Article 2 states that Islam is the religion of the State ... Thus, an attack on the [foundation of Islam] is an attack against the State which is founded upon it. He also contravenes Article 9 of the constitution that states that the family is the basis of society, and its basis is religion ...[102]

The court further stretched the doctrine of *hisba* and opined that:

> *Hisba*, according to the Court and the Islamic scholars, is for God, and is for the regulations of Good and the prevention of evil and is therefore a necessary practice for all Muslims. It is the duty of all, and all Muslims should practice it by going to the court to file suits, or to provide testimony.[103]

With these observations, the Court of Appeal of Cairo declared Dr. Abu Zayd an apostate, which was later upheld by the Court of Cassation, the highest court of appeal in civil and criminal cases. This radical shift in Egyptian jurisprudence under Article 2 followed a series of challenges against film directors, actors, and a Nobel Prize–winning author, turning the courts into a public spectacle. This alerted the government, which

---

[102] Moustafa, "Islamist Trend in Egyptian Law" 624.
[103] Moustafa, "Islamist Trend in Egyptian Law."

promulgated a law in 1998 to prevent individuals from initiating *hisba* petitions in courts.[104]

Despite the abovementioned cases, it is pertinent to note that Article 2 did not necessarily result in increased Islamization; rather, the courts attempted to exercise their agency within the limited political space accorded to them to avoid interference in executive decisions by not overreaching. For instance, in one case, the father of two schoolgirls challenged a ministerial decree that restricted students from wearing the *niqab* (full veil) while attending public schools until they got parental permission. The father argued that the executive decree violated Article 2 of the constitution for being violative of the principles of the shari'a, restricting the freedom of religion and the freedom of individuality. The SCC held in favor of the ministerial decree and ruled that the decree did not interfere with any fundamental requirement of Islam. The SCC further held that the decree did not violate the freedom of religion as guaranteed under Article 46 of the Constitution, which the SCC interpreted as guaranteeing religious freedom.[105] To reach this conclusion, the SCC began with a two-prong test: first, the impugned decree shall not "violate any indubitably authentic and unambiguous scriptural command"; second, the decree "must also not work counter to the goals of the law, which include a general goal of maximizing social benefit."[106] Applying this test, the SCC explored the commandment under the Quran and Sunnah regarding the requirement of *niqab* for women. The SCC observed that Islamic doctrines did not categorically require women to wear a veil over their hair or face; rather, the Quran and Sunnah required that women must cover some parts of their body – that is, general modesty. In this regard, the SCC ruled:

> There is no indicator in the Qur'anic texts or in our honorable *sunna* that legally conforming women's clothing, to be approved by the shari'a, must veil totally; [that it must] include a *niqab* draped over her so that nothing appears except her eyes and two eye sockets; and [that it] must require the covering of her face, palms, (and, according to some, feet). This is not an acceptable interpretation, nor is it known by necessity of religion.[107]

---

[104] Moustafa, "Islamist Trend in Egyptian Law" 625; Maurits S Berger, "Apostasy and Public Policy in Contemporary Egypt: An Evaluation of Recent Cases from Egypt's Highest Courts" (2003) 25(3) Human Rights Quarterly 720.

[105] Moustafa, "Islamist Trend in Egyptian Law" 625; Berger, "Apostasy and Public Policy in Contemporary Egypt" 623.

[106] Lombardi and Brown, "Do Constitutions Requiring Adherence to Shari'a Threaten Human Rights?" 379, 427.

[107] Moustafa, "Islamist Trend in Egyptian Law" 610, 623

Based on this reading of the Quran and Sunnah, the SCC reasoned that, in the absence of a clear requirement and scholarly debate on the topic, *niqab* (full veil) could not be concluded to be a definite part of Islam.[108] After this conclusion, the SCC found that the purpose of veiling, as reflected in the Quran, is the promotion of modesty and ruled the executive decree to be not in violation of the goals of shari'a by banning the veil for women. This case is particularly instructive on how the SCC extricated itself from indulgence in the matter and refrained from intervening in and perhaps challenging executive power.

It is interesting to note that in cases where the courts inclined toward liberal modernist interpretations or approaches in the matters under adjudication, they have emphasized the *absence of clear commandments* in the Quran and Sunnah. For example, in one case concerning grandparental visitation rights under the Egypt's personal status law, the SCC declared the law to be against Article 2 for being inconsistent with the principles of Islamic law. The SCC, without giving substantive evaluation to hadith and *fiqh* literature, concluded that the there was no clear textual provision on this matter. Therefore, the court concluded that the "*maqāṣid* of the Sharī'ah required an approach more generous to the grandparents than the text of the law suggested."[109]

Further, all the challenges brought before the SCC were not aimed at establishing Islamic supremacy in Egypt; certain petitions were brought only to strengthen individual property rights or determine personal status issues of divorce, alimony, and child custody.[110] For such challenges, Article 2 provided a touchstone to contest family law regulations. It is pertinent to note though that the challenges brought under family law or property law did not all stem from Islamist tendencies; rather, the individual concerns found their way through Islamic constitutional provision.

Interestingly, the challenges brought before the SCC are substantially similar to ones that were brought before the FSC in Pakistan. However, curiously, in Egypt, these challenges are materially ineffective. In one petition, the petitioner challenged the laws that regulated the alcohol and gambling industry in Egypt as being against Article 2 of the constitution. The petitioner also invoked Article 12, which states that "society shall be committed to safeguarding and protecting morals, promoting the genuine Egyptian traditions, and abiding by the high standards of religious education, moral and national values ... and public manners within the limits of the law. The State is committed to abiding by these principles and promoting

---

[108] Lombardi, "Islamic Law as a Source of Constitutional Law" 81, 109.
[109] Brown and Lombardi, "Contesting Islamic Constitutionalism" 245, 258.
[110] Moustafa, "Islamist Trend in Egyptian Law" 610, 620.

them."[111] In addition to the constitutionality of the impugned laws, the petitioner also sought the complete abolition of extant places for alcohol and gambling and the replacement of such places by mosques. The civil court referred this constitutional challenge to the SCC, which dismissed the petition on the grounds that the petitioner had no vested interest in the matter.

It appears that the views of lower court judges are more conservative in Egypt. For example, in a criminal case, the lower court judge opined that the law on the consumption of alcohol (63/1976) is against Islamic law because the law provided the punishment of imprisonment rather than the punishment of lashing as required under Islamic law. Similarly, another lower court judge argued that Islamic law requires stoning as punishment for adultery and lashings for fornication; therefore, the law (10/1961) punishing prostitution with imprisonment should be declared against Islamic law.[112] Allowing such challenges by the judges of the lower courts unveiled an ideological schism in Egypt's judiciary. The "lower court judges were sympathetic to Islamist challenges, but Islamist litigation made little headway once constitutional petitions reached the SCC."[113] As Moustafa concludes, eventually "the SCC proved to be remarkably adept at circumventing a number of thorny questions related to religion and public policy through the non-retroactivity principle. In other cases that were addressed directly, the SCC used its power to interpret Article 2 of the Constitution in a fashion that granted virtually no concessions to Islamist activists."[114]

Similar to Pakistan, constitutional Islam did not necessarily subjugate human rights in the Egyptian context. Rather, the SCC has on several occasions protected negative liberties, particularly in the areas of economic regulation and human rights. Indeed, the SCC interpreted the constitution's rule of law provisions to incorporate into the Egyptian constitution a requirement that the government respect international human rights norms.[115]

The SCC's decisions in the past, however, do not guarantee that the judicial interpretation of Islamic precepts in relation to law will be progressive in the future or that constitutional Islam will not override human rights claims in the future. Although it claims to be a bulwark against the doctrinaire interpretation of Islamic law, according to Lombardi, it could easily be co-opted by Islamists

---

[111] Moustafa, "Islamist Trend in Egyptian Law" 610, 620.

[112] The lower court judges referred the cases to the SCC which rejected them because the relevant laws were passed before 1980. Moustafa, "Islamist Trend in Egyptian Law" 621.

[113] Moustafa, "Islamist Trend in Egyptian Law" 622.

[114] Moustafa, "Islamist Trend in Egyptian Law" 627.

[115] Lombardi and Brown, "Do Constitutions Requiring Adherence to Shari'a Threaten Human Rights?" 379, 417.

who wish to impose reactionary laws. Yet, to date, it has injected conceptions of "justice" and social utility into case law that implicated religious arguments, propounding general moral principles that must be interpreted anew in accordance with public welfare.[116] Lombardi and Brown observe that

> looking at the SCC's cases as a whole, it seems that the Court [has] established commitments to liberal economic philosophy and to the protection of certain civil and political rights — particularly women's rights ... The SCC's Article 2 opinions consistently suggest that "justice" requires people to respect each other's human rights ... for example, the SCC has upheld as "Islamic" legislation that requires husbands to pay alimony, legislation that provides women with a right to retroactive child support and legislation that provides Egyptian women with the right to dissolve their marriage for "harm" if their husband takes a second wife.[117]

The example of Egyptian jurisprudence illustrates that the SCC has been able to balance progressive ideas with constitutional Islam. Even the Muslim Brotherhood, the leading Islamist party in Egypt, which won Egypt's first ever presidential elections, embraced the SCC's interpretation of Article 2 and its liberal methodology so that Article 2 would remain untouchable, even if the court's interpretation was inconsistent with their religious ideology.[118]

On balance, Egypt's experiment with constitutionalizing Islam has rocked to-and-fro due to political upheavals that resulted in amendments to its constitutions and the promulgation of new constitutions. What has remained consistent for the past four decades, however, is the SCC, and especially its exercise of the powers of judicial review under Article 2 of the constitution. Initially, the SCC was reluctant to exercise its authority, although it eventually did, albeit restrictively. The SCC in the 1990s was influenced by the political and social currents toward Islamization, but the sort of Islamization that it pronounced and the jurisprudence it developed did not trample upon constitutional democratic rights. The SCC balanced the demands of Islam with liberal constitutional values and freedoms. That is, the SCC, with authority under Article 2 and Article 219 of the constitution, adopted a rationalist and utilitarian approach toward the Islamic supremacy clause in the constitution.[119] This allowed the SCC to reinforce liberal values from within the

---

[116] Lombardi and Brown, "Do Constitutions Requiring Adherence to Shari'a Threaten Human Rights?" 423.

[117] Lombardi and Brown, "Do Constitutions Requiring Adherence to Shari'a Threaten Human Rights?" 423–25.

[118] Mohamed Abdelaal, "Religious Constitutionalism in Egypt: A Case Study" (2013) 37 Fletcher Forum of World Affairs 35, 41.

[119] Lombardi, *State Law as Islamic Law* 271.

principles of shari'a. The SCC could do this due to the nature of its jurisdiction, since it is not bound to follow the views of conservative ulama; rather, it relied upon modernist interpretations of Islamic law. It has a unique position as the sole authority to give an authoritative pronouncement on the constitutionality statutes. Its judges, who are trained in civil and constitutional law and not *fiqh*, have applied Article 2 in light of the settled principles and goals of shari'a. These judges have not deferred the interpretation of Islamic law to the leading ulama (such as those of al-Azhar). In doing so, the judges of the SCC have relied upon the wealth of scholarship on Islamic law to chart out broad principles that lead to a harmonious reading of Islam and modern liberal constitutional values.[120]

5.3 COMPARING PAKISTAN AND EGYPT

The judicial application of Islamic supremacy clauses in the constitutions of Pakistan and Egypt bears some close resemblances. The judges of the FSC in Pakistan and the SCC in Egypt reconciled Article 2A (Objectives Resolution) and Article 2 (shari'a as the source of legislation) with other clauses of their respective constitutions. This enabled them to endorse such liberal rights as the right to private property, due process of law, and nondiscrimination and equality, including gender equality. Indeed, judges of both higher courts developed Islamic human rights jurisprudence by reinforcing various principles of human rights law from within the Islamic legal tradition. Both courts simultaneously applied the principles of Islamic law as well as human rights norms while determining the constitutionality of impugned laws. Indeed, in one judgment, the SCC equated the violation of human rights with the violation of the spirit and tenets of the shari'a.[121] Similarly, the FSC frequently referred to the constitutionally guaranteed fundamental human rights while adjudicating cases in which the validity of laws was challenged on the basis of

---

[120] However, it is in curbing the excessive executive authority of the state in protection of its citizens' rights through independent judiciary that the limitations of international human rights laws and shari'a norms are tested and exposed. Constitutionally protected human rights remain suspended during the proclamations of emergency that remained operative during the major parts of the last hundred years of Egyptian constitutional history. Sadiq Reza, "Endless Emergency: The Case of Egypt" (2007) 10(4) New Criminal Law Review 532. The 2019 amendment in the 2014 constitution not only extended the term of the president to rule for another decade but it also vested in him enormous powers over the judiciary. Gianluca P Parolin, "Drifting Power Relations in the Egyptian Constitution: The 2019 Amendments" (2020) 44(3) DPCE Online.

[121] Supreme Constitutional Court Case no. 7, Judicial Year 8. Abdelaal, "Religious Constitutionalism in Egypt" 35, 44.

their repugnancy to the injunctions of Islam.[122] In one judgment, the FSC declared that the last sermon of the Prophet Muhammad was the "first Charter of Human Rights."[123]

The harmonious construction of Islam and human rights by judges of superior courts in Pakistan and Egypt does not necessarily mean that constitutional Islamization did not cause tension between Islam and rights. In fact, the frequent leveling of blasphemy charges against non-Muslim minorities and liberal scholars in Pakistan and Egypt draws much media attention. It may be argued that the presence of Islamic supremacy clauses exacerbates if not causes recourse to blasphemy charges by the Islamists in both of these countries. In Egypt, in the infamous trial of Professor Dr. Nasr Hamid Abu Zayd, the court referred to Article 2 of the constitution for the prosecution on the basis of blasphemy charges.[124] Similarly, the FSC endorsed the blasphemy law as provided under section 295-C of the Pakistan Penal Code 1860 as a *hadd* offense punishable by death.[125] The court, however, also clarified that criminal intention (mens rea) is a prerequisite to prove this offense and that repentance serves as waiver of blasphemy charges.[126] Therefore, no one has ever been executed by the state under this law, but numerous extrajudicial killings of both Muslims and non-Muslims, who were charged under this law, have occurred.[127]

---

[122] For instance, in cases involving women's rights, the judges of the Federal Shariat Court referred to Article 25, which enshrines principles of equality, including gender equality, of the Constitution of Islamic Republic of Pakistan 1973 along with the verses of the Quran and Sunnah. In two judgments – *Ansar Burney v Federation of Pakistan* PLD 1983 FSC 73 and *Mian Hammad Murtaza v Federation of Pakistan* PLD 2011 FSC 117 – the FSC rejected petitions that challenged the appointment of female judges on the basis of the principles of Islamic law. In *Mukhtar Ahmad Shaikh v Government of Pakistan* PLD 2009 FSC 65, the FSC declared Article 151(4) of the Qanun-e-Shahadat Order 1984 as invalid on the basis of Islamic legal principles as well as Article 25 of the constitution because the law permitted impeachment of the character of a female victim in rape trials.

[123] *In re Suo Motu Case No. 1/K of 2006 (Gender Equality)* PLD 2008 FSC 1.

[124] Court of Cassation, Nos. 475, 478, 481, Year 65, 5 August 1996. Berger, "Apostasy and Public Policy" 720, 728.

[125] *Muhammad Ismail Qureshi v Pakistan* PLD 1991 FSC 10.

[126] Lau, *Role of Islam* 194. Commentators have pointed out that the judgment does not reflect the principles of Islamic law and it also fails to propose procedural safeguards against false allegations of blasphemy. See Muhammad Mushtaq Ahmad, "Pakistani Blasphemy Law between Ḥadd and Siyāsah: A Plea for Reappraisal of the Ismail Qureshi Case" (2018) 57(1–2) Islamic Studies 9.

[127] Osama Siddique and Zahra Hayat, "Unholy Speech and Holy Laws: Blasphemy Laws in Pakistan: Controversial Origins, Design Defects, and Free Speech Implications" (2008) 17(2) Minnesota Journal of International Law 305, 380. Farhat Haq, *Sharia and the State in Pakistan* (Routledge 2019) 3–4.

Conclusion

In much of the Muslim world, the idea of incorporating Islam into a constitution seems to be very popular and, in some cases, understood as a panacea for political ills including, but not limited to, corruption and autocracy. It is sometimes assumed that adopting Islam in political life will resolve a range of social, political, and economic problems and therefore democratic demand for the incorporation of Islam during constitution-making moments often appears strong. This is not new: constitution making in the Muslim world since almost a century and a half earlier has sought to grapple with this tension where the adoption of "modern" constitutions must be blended and synchronized with Islamic concepts to remain legitimate and acceptable to the masses – so that the resulting outcome is an "Islamic" constitution.

In stark contrast, there seems to be some anxiety among Western policy makers when the issue of incorporating Islam in a constitution arises – this has been observed in multiple contexts over the last decade as some foreign observers may assume that secular democracy is the best model of constitution making for every country – religious or otherwise. The perception tends to be that constitutions that incorporate Islam may necessarily be antithetical to human rights and democracy. Conversely, in many postcolonial Muslim nations, secularized democracy and secularism in constitution making is frowned upon as a "godless" and elitist endeavor that will rid them of human rights – as a means to rid public space of a cherished religious identity. Islam and "God," or "Allah" in contrast, seems to be invoked to provide a language of rights; the removal of Islam from political discourse or any effort to achieve such an outcome is thus viewed with suspicion and erodes political legitimacy.

This book has sought to deconstruct some of these narratives and relate them to an analysis of the role of Islam in constitution making in the Muslim world empirically and its historical genesis. While popular perceptions about constitutional Islamization have persisted on both sides, despite its rich potential, to date, there had been little empirical measurement and investigation of the universe of constitutional Islamization. This book attempts to fill this gap. It has explained the historical and colonial origins of constitutional Islamization and elaborated on the theory of Islamic constitutionalism. In doing so, it undertook an analysis of constitutional Islamization, or the constitutional incorporation of Islamic clauses. Accordingly, it included the world's first ranking of constitutions based on Islamicity – the "Islamic Constitutions Index."[1]

It showed how constitutional Islamization was prevalent in almost half of all constitutions of Muslim-majority countries, save for countries in Central Asia and some in Africa – this reflects the democratic demand for such clauses in these regions, in part a function of colonial history, and gives the regimes that adopt them some resilience. It also showed that colonial origins, geography, and Muslim population seemed to impact how Islamic the constitution is. In particular, it reasoned that the identity of the colonizer was an influential factor in determining the extent of Islam in a colonized Muslim country's constitution; in particular, it argued that British colonialism was more tolerant and accommodating of Islam and this allowed Islamic political structures to take birth in and largely survive colonization in countries colonized by the British; this was not the case in Muslim countries colonized by the Soviets or French, due to their hostile and intolerant attitude towards Islam. It then undertook a deeper study of Islamic supremacy clauses – clauses incorporating Islam as a preferred source of law and/or declaring that no law can be passed that is repugnant to Islam. It argued that these are best understood not as impositions of theocracy, but as carefully negotiated provisions. In this sense, their incidence is consistent with democracy and should not be thought of as in inexorable tension with it. The insertion of Islamic supremacy clauses is subject to a distinct political logic which, in every instance, involves coalitional politics and bargained outcomes. For this reason, it is observed that essentially every instance of the insertion of this particular clause is accompanied by an expansion in the rights content of the constitutional order. The analysis of the data showed that Islamic repugnancy clauses emerged as a borrowed legal technique influenced by colonial repugnancy, which also has its roots in British

---

[1]   Dawood Ahmed, Moamen Gouda, and Tom Ginsburg, "Islamic Constitutionalism Project" (SHARIAsource, Harvard Law School, 2018) <https://beta.shariasource.com/projects/islamic-constitutionalism> accessed May 1, 2021.

colonialism and, in fact unsurprisingly, Islamic supremacy clauses are most likely to occur in countries that have in the past been associated with a British colonial legacy. Also, Islamic supremacy clauses generally, from their innovation in Iran in 1906, have become more popular as time has gone on, now being found in the constitutions of almost half of Muslim-majority states. The argument about coalitional politics was confirmed in the case studies. In Afghanistan, the first constitution was drafted by a modernist ruler, Amanullah Khan, and it contained innovative rights and freedoms but no Islamic supremacy clauses. This provoked a strong conservative reaction and the constitution and regime that promulgated it ultimately collapsed. Its successor constitution of 1931, which lasted over three decades, contained rights but also contained robust Islamic supremacy clauses. The new monarch, Nadir Shah, having witnessed the revolt that toppled his predecessor, Amanullah Khan, would certainly have been cognizant of the adverse reactions a constitution could provoke if it contained rights and freedoms that could be seen as controversial. Considering his reputation as a "modernizer," his decision then to include Islamic supremacy clauses in the constitution would have been partly motivated by the desire to co-opt clerics and conservatives to his reform programs. In Afghanistan, unlike Iran, the constitution-writing process had not been opened up to those outside of the monarchic circle, thus there was no element of coalitional compromise, yet Nadir Shah's choice in adopting Islamic supremacy clauses could be seen as a preemptive attempt to stave off prospective opposition to the constitution.

Similarly, in the case of Iran in 1906, the promulgation of the first constitution that contained rights provoked strong reactions. In response, the inclusion of Islamic supremacy clauses in the supplementary constitution could be seen as the "price" of including a bill of rights. In contrast with the Afghan case, in which the monarch simply promulgated a new constitution in 1931 that contained Islamic supremacy clauses, constitution makers in Iran were constantly negotiating and debating the specific Islamic supremacy clauses and rights in the constitution. Although the motivations for including Islamic supremacy clauses in Iran and Afghanistan may have been similar in terms of pacifying opposition, the former case featured more extensive bargaining and negotiation, but the Afghan monarch was more interested in preempting any opposition to constitutionalism and rights, since the negative experience of his predecessor was still fresh. Bargaining was greater in Iran than in Afghanistan.

Iraq and Egypt present a similar contrast in the Arab world. Whereas the Islamic supremacy clauses were a key demand of Iraq's largest group, the Shi'a, in Egypt, the clauses were introduced by Anwar Sadat – along with new constitutional rights – to preempt opposition and legitimate his presidency. Whereas Gamal Abdel Nasser was in a strong position to dictate outcomes, Anwar Sadat was initially a weak ruler. The Iraqi negotiations in contrast reflected the familiar dynamic of a negotiated balance between rights and Islam, in which both sets of promises were incorporated as a form of mutual insurance against downstream lawmaking.

The book then briefly explored the effect of incorporating Islamic supremacy clauses when judges used "Islamic review" to examine legislation for Islamicity due to the constitutional privileging of Islam. This was done by surveying the literature on the experience of judicial decision-making in two populous Muslim-majority countries – Pakistan and Egypt. In both cases, it demonstrated that while constitutional Islamization can lead to some cases where individual rights may suffer, on the whole, in both countries, higher courts had either balanced the progressive rule of law and rights adequately with Islam or in some cases, particularly in Pakistan, even used constitutional Islamization to bolster rights, hold the government accountable, challenge corruption, and facilitate access to justice. This shows that the effect of incorporating Islam into the constitution does not necessarily have to be detrimental to the project of democracy and rights and in fact can even help legitimate and promote it. Of course, the example of these two countries may or may not be replicated in other Muslim countries and there may certainly be adverse side effects of balancing these two constitutional features. To put it simply, caution is in order. Larry Backer has stated that "in the case of Pakistan, one may well have a case of sham or partial theocratic constitutionalism ... Pakistani elites are currently struggling for control of the character of Pakistani constitutionalism as grounded in secular or religious principles. The institutional centre of that struggle is the judiciary" and then analogized Egypt to be a variation to Pakistan, as a state "that occupies a space between the secular and the religious forms of transnational constitutionalism. It is a compromise state, a state that seeks a reconciliation of the irreconcilable and one that in reality may even be impossible in the long term."[2] This may be true or unique in constitutional settings and this may be inevitable for Muslim countries, but so is the hybrid constitutional solution of rights and Islam that Muslim countries aspire to achieve.

The basic thesis of this book has been to argue that colonization may explain a large part of the variance in Islamic constitutionalism (and politics) and that the coexistence of constitutional Islam and rights is possible, albeit of

---

[2] Larry Backer, "Theocratic Constitutionalism: An Introduction to a New Global Legal Ordering" (2008) 16(1) Indiana Journal of Global Legal Studies 85, 165.

course not seamless or without some tension; constitutional design analysis and an observance of court decisions from Pakistan and Egypt seem to suggest that this is the case. At the broadest level, the argument of this book is consistent with the work of scholars who have suggested the basic compatibility of Islam and constitutional democracy or at least that the Muslim world will chart its own version of constitutional democracy that may not reflect the Western paradigm of secular democracy. In this sense, it suggests that those outsiders monitoring constitution making in Muslim-majority countries – who argue for the exclusion of Islamic clauses – are focused on a straw man. Not only is constitutional Islam popular, but it can be accompanied by a set of provisions and institutions that can advance basic values of liberal democracy. Like rights provisions, Islamic clauses certainly do not resolve all downstream disputes over their precise meaning. However, this in turn suggests that constitutional advisors should focus more attention on the basic political structures of the constitution, including the design of constitutional courts and other bodies that will engage in interpretation. The project of balancing rights and Islam can be resolved in each country through its own political and judicial processes. Accordingly, more attention should be focused on the design and architecture of courts and bodies that will be interpreting the rights and Islamic provisions, rather than the provisions themselves. These will include an analysis of design options concerning the mechanisms of judicial appointment, the role of jurists and religious scholars in legal decision-making, standing rules to challenge laws, qualifications of judges, and so forth.

Bibliography

CONSTITUTIONS

Constitution of Afghanistan 1923
Constitution of Afghanistan 1931
Constitution of the Arab Republic of Egypt 1971
Constitution of the Arab Republic of Egypt 2012
Constitution of the Arab Republic of Egypt 2014
Constitution of the Federal Islamic Republic of the Comoros 1996
Constitution of Iraq 2005
Constitution of Islamic Republic of Iran 1907
Constitution of Islamic Republic of Pakistan 1956
Constitution of Islamic Republic of Pakistan 1973
Constitution of Republic of Pakistan 1962
Danmarks Riges Grundlov 1953 (The Constitutional Act of the Kingdom of Denmark 1953)
Draft Constitution of the Arab Republic of Egypt 2013
Interim National Constitution of Republic of Sudan July 6, 2005
Law of Administration for the State of Iraq for the Transitional Period 2004
Provisional Constitution of the Arab Republic of Egypt 2011
Stjórnarskrá lýðveldisins Íslands 1944 (The Constitution of the Republic of Iceland 1944)

STATUTES

The Pakistan Air Force Act 1953
The Pakistan Army Act 1952
The Pakistan Navy Ordinance 1961
The Political Parties Act 1962
The Qanun-e-Shahadat Order 1984
The Representative of the People Act 1976

CASES

Abul Ala Maudoodi v Government of West Pakistan PLD 1964 SC 673

Ansar Burney v Federation of Pakistan PLD 1983 FSC 73

Begum Rashida Patel v Government of Pakistan PLD 1989 FSC 95

BZ Kaikaus v President of Pakistan PLD 1980 SC 16

Capt. (retd.) Mukhtar Ahmad Shaikh v Government of Pakistan PLD 2009 FSC 65

Darshan Masih v State PLD 1990 SC 513

Eshugbaye Eleko v Government of Nigeria 1931

Farooq Siddiqui v Mst. Farzana Naheed PLD 2017 FSC 78

Federal Government of Pakistan v Government of Punjab PLD 1991 SC 505

Federation of Pakistan v General Public PLD 1988 SC 645, 655

Federation of Pakistan v Gul Hassan Khan PLD 1989 SC 633

Federation of Pakistan v Hazoor Bakhsh PLD 1983 FSC 255

Govt of Sindh v Sharaf Faridi PLD 1994 SC 105

Habib-ur-Rehman v Government of Pakistan PLD 1981 FSC 131

Hakim Khan v Government of Pakistan PLD 1992 SC 595

Hazoor Bakhsh v Federation of Pakistan PLD 1981 FSC 145

I.A. Sharwani v Government of Pakistan MLD 1991 FSC 2613

In re Civil Servants Act 1973 PLD 1984 FSC 34

In re Islamization of Laws PLD 1985 FSC 193

In re Members of the National Assembly (Exemption from Preventive Detention and Personal Appearance) Ordinance IX of 1963 PLD 1989 FSC 3

In re Passports Act 1974 PLD 1989 FSC 39

In re Suo Motu Case No.1/K of 2006 (Gender Equality) PLD 2008 FSC 1

Iqbal Hussain v the State PLD 1981 FSC 329

Juma Gul v the State 1997 PCrLJ 1291

Mahmood-ur-Rahman Faisal v Secretary, Ministry of Law PLD 1992 FSC 195

Mehram Ali v Federation of Pakistan PLD 1998 SC 1445

Mian Hammad Murtaza v Federation of Pakistan PLD 2011 FSC 117

Mst. Sakina v the State PLD 1981 FSC 320

Mst. Zafran Bibi v the State PLD 2002 FSC 1

Muhammad Imtiaz v State PLD 1981 FSC 308

Muhammad Ismail Qureshi v Government of Punjab PLD 1991 FSC 80

Muhammad Ismail Qureshi v Pakistan PLD 1991 FSC 10

Muhammad Ramzan Qureshi v Federal Government PLD 1986 FSC 200

Muhammad Riaz v the Federal Government PLD 1980 FSC 1

Muhammad Yaqoob v the State 1985 PCrLJ 1064

Muhammad Yousaf v Chairman, Federal Public Service Commission PLD 2017 Lahore 406

Mukhtar Ahmad Shaikh v Government of Pakistan PLD 2009 FSC 65

Nadeem Siddiqui v Islamic Republic of Pakistan PLD 2016 FSC 1

National I.C.C. Corporation Ltd. v Province of Punjab PLD 1992 Lah 462

Noor Zaman v the State 1998 PCrLJ 476

Nusrat Baig Mirza v Government of Pakistan PLD 1991 SC 509

Pakistan Broadcasting Corporation v Nasir Ahmad 1995 SCMR 1593

Pakistan through Secretary Defense v Public at Large PLD 1985 FSC 365

Pakistan v Public at Large 1989 SCMR 1690
Pakistan v Public at Large PLD 1987 SC 304
Pakistan v Public at Large PLD 1989 SC 6
Province of Sindh v Lal Khan Chandio 2016 SCMR 48
Province of Sindh v Public at Large PLD 1988 SC 138
Qazalbash Waqf v Chief Land Commissioner PLD 1990 SC 99
Qazi Hussain Ahmed v General Pervez Musharraf PLD 2002 SC 853
Sajwara v Federal Government of Pakistan PLD 1989 FSC 80
Zaheeruddin v State 1993 SCMR 1718
Zulfiqar Ahmed Bhutta v Federation of Pakistan PLD 2018 SC 370

BOOKS

Abi al-Diyaf A, *Consult Them in the Matter: A Nineteenth-Century Islamic Argument for Constitutional Government* (L. Carl Brown tr University of Arkansas Press 2005).
Afary J, *The Iranian Constitutional Revolution, 1906–11: Grassroots Democracy, Social Democracy and the Origins of Feminism* (Columbian University Press 1996).
"Social Democracy and the Iranian Constitutional Revolution of 1906–11" in John Foran (ed), *A Century of Revolution: Social Movements in Iran* (University of Minnesota Press 1982).
Ajami F, *The Arab Predicament: Arab Political Thought and Practice Since 1967* (Cambridge University Press 1982).
Akhavi S, "Iran: Implementation of an Islamic State in Islam" in John L Esposito (ed), *Islam in Asia: Religion, Politics and Society* (Oxford University Press 1987).
Al-Istrabadi FAR, "Islam and the State of Iraq: Post-2003 Constitutions" in Rainer Grote and Tilmann J Roder (eds), *Constitutionalism in Islamic Countries: Between Upheaval and Continuity* (Oxford University Press 2012).
An-Na'im AA, *Islam and the Secular State: Negotiating the Future of Shari'a* (Harvard University Press 2008).
Arato A, *Constitution Making Under Occupation: The Politics of Imposed Revolution in Iraq* (Columbia University Press 2009).
Arjomand SA, *The Turban for the Crown: The Islamic Revolution in Iran* (Oxford University Press 1989).
Baker RW, *Sadat and After: Struggles for Egypt's Political Soul* (Harvard University Press 1990).
Beattie KJ, *Egypt During the Sadat Years* (Palgrave 2000).
Bennett C, *Muslims and Modernity: An Introduction to the Issues and Debates* (Bloomsbury 3PL 2005).
Berger M and Sonneveld N, "Sharia and National Law in Egypt" in Jan Michiel Otto (ed), *Sharia Incorporated: A Comparative Overview of the Legal Systems of Twelve Countries in Past and Present* (Leiden University Press 2011).
Berger P, *The Desecularization of the World: Resurgent Religion and World Politics* (Eerdmans 1999).
Bonakdarian M, *Britain and the Iranian Constitutional Revolution of 1906–1911: Foreign Policy, Imperialism, and Dissent* (Syracuse University Press 2006).

Boozari A, *Shi'i Jurisprudence and Constitution: Revolution in Iran* (Palgrave Macmillan 2011).

Bradley JR, *After the Arab Spring: How Islamists Hijacked the Middle East Revolts* (St. Martin's Press 2012).

Bremmer ALP, *My Year in Iraq: The Struggle to Build a Future of Hope* (Threshold Editions 2006).

Brown NJ and Sherif AO, "Inscribing the Islamic Shari'a in Arab Constitutional Law" in Yvonne Yazbeck Haddad and Barbara Freyer Stowasser (eds), *Islamic Law and the Challenges of Modernity* (Altamira Press 2004).

Brown NJ and Amit R, "Constitutionalism in Egypt" in Daniel P Frankling and Michael J Baun (eds), *Political Culture and Constitutionalism: A Comparative Approach* (Routledge 1995).

Brown NJ and Lombardi CB, "Contesting Islamic Constitutionalism After the Arab Spring: Islam in Egypt's Post-Mubarak Constitutions" in Rainer Grote, Tilmann J Röder, and Ali M El-Haj (eds), *Constitutionalism, Human Rights, and Islam After the Arab Spring* (Oxford University Press 2016).

Brown NJ, "Islam in Egypt's Cacophonous Constitutional Order" in Nathan J Brown and Said Amir Arjomand (eds), *The Rule of Law, Islam and Constitutional Politics in Egypt and Iran* (State University of New York Press 2013).

Constitutions in a Nonconstitutional World: Arab Basic Laws and the Prospects for Accountable Government (State University of New York Press 2001).

Burgess JW, *Political Science and Comparative Constitutional Law* (University of Michigan Library 1896).

Chishti NM, *Constitutional Development in Afghanistan* (Royal Book Co 1998).

Christelow A, *Muslim Courts and the French Colonial State in Algeria* (Princeton University Press 1985).

Cronin S, "The Constitutional Revolution, Popular Politics, and State-Building in Iran" in HE Chehabi and Vanessa Martin (eds), *Iran's Constitutional Revolution: Popular Politics, Cultural Transformations and Transnational Connections* (I. B. Tauris 2010).

Dawisha A, Iraq: *A Political History from Independence to Occupation* (Princeton University Press 2009).

Dekmejian RH, *Islam in Revolution: Fundamentalism in the Arab World* (Syracuse University Press 1995).

Devji F, *Muslim Zion: Pakistan as a Political Idea* (Harvard University Press 2013).

Diamond L, *Squandered Victory: The American Occupation and the Bungled Effort to Bring Democracy to Iraq* (Holt Paperbacks 2006).

Dupree L, *Afghanistan* (Princeton 1980).

Elias TO, *The Nature of African Customary Law* (Manchester University Press 1956).

Elkins Z, Ginsburg T, and Melton J, *The Endurance of National Constitutions* (Cambridge University Press 2009).

Esposito JL and Voll JO, *Islam and Democracy* (Oxford University Press 1996)

Esposito JL, Sonn T, and Voll JO, *Islam and Democracy after the Arab Spring* (Oxford University Press 2016).

Etling B, *Legal Authorities in the Afghan Legal System* (1964–1979), Afghan Legal History Project at Harvard Law School 11, (2013) <www.law.harvard.edu/pro grams/ilsp/research/etling.pdf> accessed September 3, 2013.

Fadl KA, "The Centrality of Shari'ah to Government and Constitutionalism in Islam" in Rainer Grote and Tilmann J Roder (eds), *Constitutionalism in Islamic Countries: Between Upheaval and Continuity* (Oxford University Press 2012).

Feldman N, *The Fall and Rise of the Islamic State* (Princeton University Press 2008).

Geissari A, "Constitutional Rights and the Development of Civil Law in Iran, 1907–41" in HE Chehabi and Vanessa Martin (eds), *Iran's Constitutional Revolution: Popular Politics, Cultural Transformations and Transnational Connections* (I. B. Tauris 2010).

Ghobashy M, "Unsettling the Authorities: Constitutional Reform in Egypt" in Jeannie Sowers and Toesnsing (eds), *The Journey to Tahrir: Revolution, Protest, and Social Change in Egypt* (Verso 2012).

Grassroots Democracy, *Social Democracy and the Origins of Feminism* (Columbian University Press 1996).

Groot J, "Whose Revolution? Stakeholders and Stories of the 'Constitutional Movement' in Iran, 1905-1911" in H. E. Chehabi and Vanessa Martin (eds), *Iran's Constitutional Revolution: Popular Politics, Cultural Transformations and Transnational Connections* (I. B. Tauris 2010).

Grote R and Roder TJ (eds), *Constitutionalism in Islamic Countries: Between Upheaval and Continuity* (Oxford University Press 2012).

Haddad YY and Stowasser BF, *Islamic Law and The Challenge of Modernity* (Almitra Press 2004).

Haq F, *Sharia and the State in Pakistan* (Routledge 2019).

Hardy P, *The Muslims of British India* (Cambridge University Press 1972).

Hashim A, "Coping with Conflicts: Colonial Policy Towards Muslim Personal Law in Kenya and Post-Colonial Court Practice" in Shamil Jeppie, Ebrahim Moosa, and Richard Roberts (eds), *Muslim Family Law in Colonial and Postcolonial Sub-Saharan Africa* (Amsterdam University Press 2010).

Henkin L and others, *Human Rights* (2nd ed, Foundation Press 2009) 369.

Hirschl R, *Constitutional Theocracy* (Harvard University Press 2010).

Towards Juristocracy: The Origins and Consequences of the New Constitutionalism (Harvard University Press 2007).

Hiskett M, *The Course of Islam in Africa* (Edinburgh University Press 1994).

Huntington SP, *The Clash of Civilizations and the Remaking of World Order* (Simon and Schuster 2011).

Ibhawoh B, *Imperialism and Human Rights: Colonial Discourses of Rights and Liberties in African History* (State University of New York Press 2007).

Jaffrelot C, "Secularity without Secularism in Pakistan: The Politics of Islam from Sir Syed to Zia" in Mirjam Künkler, John Madeley, and Shylashri Shanker (eds), *A Secular Age beyond the West: Religion, Law and the State in Asia, the Middle East and North Africa* (Cambridge University Press 2018).

Jain MP, *Indian Legal History* (5th ed, MM Tripathi Pvt Ltd 1990).

Otto Jan Michiel, "Sharia and Law in a Birds Eye View: Reform, Moderation and Ambiguity" in Jan Michiel Otto and Hannah Mason (eds), *Delicate Debates on Islam: Policymakers and Academics Speaking with Each Other (Islam and Society* (Leiden University Press 2012).

Jeffries LM (ed), *Iraq: Issues, Historical Background, Bibliography* (Nova Biomedical 2002).

Jinnah MA, *Jinnah: Speeches and Statements 1947–48* (Oxford University Press 2000).

Johnson R, *Oil, Islam and Conflict: Central Asia Since 1945* (University of Chicago Press, 2007).

Kamali M, *Revolutionary Iran: Civil Society and State in the Modernization Process* (Ashgate Pub Ltd 1998).

Kamali MH, *Law in Afghanistan: A Study of the Constitutions, Matrimonial Law and the Judiciary* (Brill Academic Pub 1985).

Makiya K, *Republic of Fear* (University of California Press 1998).

Kar M, "Shari'a Law in Iran" in Paul Marshall (ed), *Radical Islam's Rules: The Worldwide Spread of Extreme: Shari'a Law* (Rowman and Littlefield Publishers 2005).

Kassem M, *Egyptian Politics: The Dynamics of Authoritarian Rule* (Lynne Rienner Publishers 2004).

Keddie N and Amanat M, "Iran under the Late Qajars 1848–1922" in P Avery, GRG Hambly, and C Melviller (eds), *The Cambridge History*, vol 7 (Cambridge University Press 1991).

Keddie N, *Modern Iran: Roots and Results of Revolution* (Yale University Press 2006).

Keddie NR, *Iran and the Muslim World: Resistance and Revolution* (Palgrave Macmillan 1995).

Kedourie E, *Democracy and Arab Political Culture* (Routledge 1992).

Kembayev Z, *Regime Transition in Central Asia: Stateness, Nationalism and Political Change in Tajikistan and Uzbekistan* (Routledge 2013).

"The Rise of Presidentialism in Post-Soviet Central Asia" in Rainer Grote and Tilmann J. Roder (eds) *Constitutionalism in Islamic Countries: Between Upheaval and Continuity* (Oxford University Press 2012) 436.

Kepel G, *The Revenge of God: The Resurgence of Islam, Christianity, and Judaism in the Modern World* (Penn State University Press1993).

Kerr MH, *Islamic Reform: The Political and Legal Theories of Muhammad Abduh and Rashid Rida* (University of California Press 1966).

Khalid A, *Islam After Communism: Religion and Politics in Central Asia* (University of California Press, 2014).

Khan H, *Constitutional and Political History of Pakistan* (3rd ed, Oxford University Press 2017) 59.

Khatab S and Bouma GD, *Democracy in Islam* (Routledge 2007).

Esposito JL and Voll JO, *Islam and Democracy* (Oxford University Press 1996).

Lau M, *The Role of Islam in the Legal System of Pakistan* (Martinus Nijhoff 2005).

Loimeieir R, "The Secular State and Islam in Senegal: Islam in Africa under French Colonial Rule" in D Westerlund, CF Hallencreutz, and D Westerhund (eds) *Questioning the Secular State: The Worldwide Resurgence of Religion in Politics* (Hurst and Company 1996).

Muslim Societies in African: A Historical Anthropology (Indiana University Press 2013).

Lombardi CB, *State Law as Islamic Law in Modern Egypt: The Incorporation of the Sharia into Egyptian Constitutional Law* (Brill 2006).

Maghaoui AM, *Liberalism without Democracy: Nationhood and Citizenship in Egypt, 1922–1936* (Duke University Press 2006).

Martin V, *Islam and Modernism: The Iranian Revolution of 1906* (Syracuse University Press 1989).

Mayer AE, *Islam and Human Rights: Tradition and Politics* (Routledge 1991).

McGlinchey E, *Chaos, Violence, Dynasty: Politics and Islam in Central Asia* (University of Pittsburgh Press 2011).

Melvin N, *Uzbekistan: Transition to Authoritarianism on the Silk Road* (Harwood Academic Publishers 2000).

Menski W, *Hindu Law: Beyond Tradition and Modernity* (Oxford University Press 2009).

Minogue K, "The History of the Idea of Human Rights in W Laqueur and B Rubin (eds), *The Human Rights Reader* (Plume 1979).

Mogahed D, *Islam and Democracy* (Gallup 2006).

Moschtaghi R, *Max Planck Manual on Afghan Constitutional Law* (vol 1, Max Planck Institute for Comparative Public Law and International Law, Heidelberg 2009).

Moustafa T, *The Struggle for Constitutional Power: Law, Politics, and Economic Development in Egypt* (Cambridge University Press 2009).

Nasr SV, "European Colonialism and the Emergence of Modern Muslim States" in JL Esposito (ed) *The Oxford History of Islam* (Oxford Islamic Studies Online) www.oxfordislamicstudies.com/article/book/islam-9780195107999/islam-9780195107999-chapter-13 accessed April 6, 2021.

Nawid SK, *Religious Response to Social Change in Afghanistan, 1919–29: King Aman-Allah and the Afghan Ulama* (Mazda Pub 2000).

Na'im AA, *African Constitutionalism and the Role of Islam* (University of Pennsylvania Press 2006).

Newbury CW, *British Policy Towards West Africa: Select Documents 1875–1914; with Statistical Appendices, 1800–1914* (Clarendon Press 1971).

Malik IH, *Islam, Nationalism and the West: Issues of Identity in Pakistan* (Palgrave Macmillan 1999).

Mamdani M, *Citizen and Subject: Contemporary Africa and the Legacy of Late Colonialism* (Princeton University Press 1996).

Marshall P, *Radical Islam's Rules: The Worldwide Spread of Extreme Shari'a Law* (Rowman and Littlefield Publishers 2005).

Olcott MB, *Roots of Radical Islam in Central Asia* (Carnegie Endowment for International Peace 2007).

Olesen A, *Islam and Politics in Afghanistan* (Routledge 1995).

Otto JM, *Sharia and National Law in Muslim Countries* (Leiden University Press 2008).

"Sharia and Law in a Birds Eye View: Reform, Moderation and Ambiguity" in JM Otto and H Mason (eds), *Delicate Debates on Islam: Policymakers and Academics Speaking with Each Other* (Leiden University Press 2012).

Perry GE, *The History of Egypt* (Greenwood 2004).

Poullada B, *Reform and Rebellion in Afghanistan, 1919–1929; King Amanullah's Failure to Modernize a Tribal Society* (Cornell University Press 1973).

Ramadan T, *Islam and the Arab Awakening* (Oxford University Press 2012).

Reichman R, "Undignified Details: The Colonial Subject of Law" in H Bloom, *Bloom's Modern Critical Interpretations: Chinua Achebe's Things Fall Apart* (Chelsea House Publisher 2001).

Robinson D, *Paths of Accommodation: Muslim Societies and French Colonial Authorities in Senegal and Mauritania, 1880–1920* (Ohio University Press 2000).

Romero J, *The Iraqi Revolution of 1958: A Revolutionary Quest for Unity and Security* (University Press of America 2010).

Rutherford BK, *Egypt after Mubarak: Liberalism, Islam, and Democracy in the Arab World* (Princeton University Press 2013).

The Struggle for Constitutionalism in Egypt: Understanding the Obstacles to Democratic Transition in the Arab World (PhD thesis, Yale University 1999).

Saboory MH, "The Progress of Constitutionalism in Afghanistan" in N Yassari (ed), *The Sharia in the Constitutions of Afghanistan, Iran and Egypt* (Mohr Siebeck 2005).

Sachedina A, *Islam and the Challenge of Human Rights* (Oxford University Press 2014).

Schacht J, *An Introduction to Islamic Law* (Oxford University Press 1964).

Schirazi A, *The Constitution of Iran: Politics and the State in the Islamic Republic* (I. B. Tauris 1998).

Schulze R, "Citizens of Islam: The Institutionalization and Internationalization of Muslim Debate" in C Toll and J Skovgaard-Petersen, *Law and the Islamic World: Past and Present* (Munksgaard 1995).

Scott RM, *Recasting Islamic Law: Religion and the Nation State in Egyptian Constitution Making* (Cornell University Press 2019).

Sheleff L, *The Future of Tradition: Customary Law, Common Law and Legal Pluralism* (Routledge 2000).

Simmons BA, *Mobilizing for Human Rights: International Law in Domestic Politics* (Harvard University Press 2009).

Smith JC, "Islam and the French Empire in North Africa," in D Motadel (ed) *Islam and the European Empires* (Oxford University Press 2014).

Stilt KA, "Constitution in Authoritarian Regimes: The Case of Egypt" in Tom Ginsberg and A Simpser (eds), *Constitutions in Authoritarian Regimes* (Cambridge University Press 2013).

Stokes E, *The English Utilitarians and India* (Oxford University Press 1990).

Toprak B, *Islam and Political Development in Turkey* (Brill 1981).

Triand JL, "Islam in Africa under French Colonial Rule" in N Levtzion and RL Pouwels (eds) *The History of Islam in Africa* (Ohio University Press 2000).

Tūnisī K, *The Surest Path: The Political Treatise of a Nineteenth-Century Muslim Statesman* (Harvard University Press 1967).

Van Der Veer P, "Secrecy and Publicity in the South Asian Public Arena" in A Salvatore and DE Eickleman (eds), *Public Islam and the Common Good* (Brill 2004).

Wasti T, *The Application of Islamic Criminal Law in Pakistan: Sharia in Practice* (Brill 2009).

Zubaida S, *Law and Power in the Islamic World* (I. B. Tauris 2003).

(ed), *Constitutional Politics in the Middle East: With Special Reference to Turkey, Iraq, Iran and Afghanistan* (Hart Publishing 2008).

ARTICLES

Abdelaal M, "Religious Constitutionalism in Egypt: A Case Study" (2013) 37 *Fletcher Forum of World Affairs* 35.

Afary J, "Civil Liberties and the Making of Iran's First Constitution" (2005) 25(2) *Comparative Studies of South Asia, Africa and the Middle East* 341.

Ahmad A, "Mawdudi and Orthodox Fundamentalism in Pakistan" (1967) 21(3) *Middle East Journal* 369.

Ahmad MM, "Pakistani Blasphemy Law between Hadd and Siyasah: A Plea for Reappraisal of the Ismail Qureshi Case" (2018) 57(1–2) *Islamic Studies* 9.

Ahmed D and Ginsburg T, "Constitutional Islamization and Human Rights: The Surprising Origin and Spread of Islamic Supremacy Clauses" (2014) 54(3) *Virginia Journal of International Law* 615.

Ahmed D and Gouda M, "Measuring Constitutional Islamization: The Islamic Constitutions Index" (2014) 38 *Hastings International and Comparative Law Review* 1.

Ahmed M and Sharif SM, "Islamic Aspects of the New Constitution of Pakistan" (1963) 2(2) *Islamic Studies* 249.

Ala Hamoudi H, "Ornamental Repugnancy: Identitarian Islam and the Iraqi Constitution" (2010) 7(3) *St. Thomas University Law Journal* 101.

"Repugnancy in the Arab World" (2012) 48(427) *Williamette Law Review* 427.

Alavi H, "Social Forces and the Making of Pakistan" (2002) 37(51) *Economic and Political Weekly* 5119.

Ali KA, "Pakistan Islamists Gamble on the General" (2004) 231 *Middle East Research and Information Project* https://merip.org/2004/06/pakistani-islamists-gamble-on-the-general/ accessed January 12, 2022.

Alston P, "A Third Generation of Solidarity Rights: Progressive Development or Obfuscation of International Human Rights Law?" (1982) 29 *Netherlands International Law Review* 307.

Amos MS, "Constitutional History of Egypt for the Last Forty Years" (1928) 14 *Transactions Grotius Society* 131.

Arjomand SA, "Constitutional Developments in Afghanistan: A Comparative and Historical Perspective" (2005) 53 *Drake Law Review* 943, 950.

"The Ulama's Traditionalist Opposition to Parliamentarianism: 1907-1909" (1981) 17 (2) *Journal of Middle Eastern Studies* 174.

Ayubi NNM, "The Political Revival of Islam: The Case of Egypt" (1980) 12(4) *International Journal of Middle East Studies* 481.

Backer L, "Theocratic Constitutionalism: An Introduction to a New Global Legal Ordering" (2008) 16(1) *Indiana Journal of Global Legal Studies* 85.

Bakker P, "Indigenous Family Law in South Africa: From Colonial Repugnancy to Constitutional Repugnancy," paper delivered at Law and Society Association Annual Meetings, Denver, CO (May 25-29, 2009).

Berger MS, "Apostasy and Public Policy in Contemporary Egypt: An Evaluation of Recent Cases from Egypt's Highest Courts" (2003) 25(3) *Human Rights Quarterly* 720.

Biloslavo F, "The Afghanistan Constitution between Hope and Fear" (2004) 2(1) *CeMiSS Quarterly* 61.

Caplan GM, "The Making of 'Natural Justice' in British Africa: An Exercise in Comparative Law" (1964) 13(1) *Journal of Public Law* 120.

Cheema MH, "Beyond Beliefs: Deconstructing the Dominant Narratives of the Islamization of Pakistan's Law" (2012) 60(4) *The American Journal of Comparative Law* 875.

"Cases and Controversies: Pregnancy as Proof of Guilt under Pakistan's Hudood Laws" (2006) 32(1) *Brooklyn Journal of International Law* 121.

Cirakman A, "From Tyranny to Despotism: The Enlightenment's Unenlightened Image of the Turks" (2001) 33(1) *International Journal of Middle East Studies* 49.

Clark AF, "Imperialism, Independence, and Islam in Senegal and Mali" (1999) 46 *Africa Today* 149.

Collins DP, "Islamization of Pakistani Law: A Historical Perspective" (1987–88) 24 *Stanford Journal of International Law* 511.

Crowder M, "Indirect Rule: French and British Style" (1964) 34 *Africa: Journal of the International African Institute* 198.

Cruise O and Brian D, "Towards an "Islamic Policy" in French West Africa, 1854–1914" (1967) 8 *Journal of African History* 303.

Deeks AS and Burton MD, "Iraq's Constitution: A Drafting History" (2007) 40(1) *Cornell International Law Journal* 1.

Dixon R and Ginsburg T, "The South African Constitutional Court and Socio-Economic Rights as 'Insurance Swaps'" (2011) 4(1) *Constitutional Court Review* 1.

Elkins Z and others, "Getting to Rights: Treaty Ratification, Constitutional Convergence, and Human Rights Practice" (2013) 54 *Harvard International Law Journal* 61.

Elkins Z and Simmons B, "On Waves, Clusters, and Diffusion: A Conceptual Framework" (2005) 33 *The ANNALS of the American Academy of Political and Social Science* 598.

Feldman N and Martinez R, "Constitutional Politics and Text in the New Iraq: An Experiment in Islamic Democracy" (2006) 75 *Fordham Law Review* 883.

Feldman N, "Imposed Constitutionalism" (2005) 37(1) *Connecticut Law Review* 857.

Feldman NR, "The Democratic Fatwa: Islam and Democracy in the Realm of Constitutional Politics" (2005) 58(1) *Oklahoma Law Review* 1.

Feuille J, "Reforming Egypt's Constitution: Hope for Egyptian Democracy?" (2011) 47 (1) *Texas International Law Journal* 237.

Fischer MMJ, "Islam and the Revolt of the Petit Bourgeoisie" (1982) 111(1) *Daedalus* 101.

Floor WF, "The Revolutionary Character of the Iranian Ulama" (1980) 12(4) *International Journal of Middle East Studies* 501, 502.

Galanter M, "The Displacement of Traditional Law in Modern India" (1968) 24 *Journal of Social Issues* 65.

Ghai Y, "A Journey around Constitutions: Reflections on Contemporary Constitutions" (2005) 122(4) *South African Law Journal* 804.

Ginsburg T and others, "When to Overthrow your Government: The Right to Resist in the World's Constitutions" (2013) 60(1) *UCLA Law Review* 1184.

"An Economic Interpretation of the Pashtunwali" (2011) University of Chicago Legal Forum 89.

Giunchi E, "The Reinvention of Sharī'a under the British Raj: In Search of Authenticity and Certainty" (2010) 69 *The Journal of Asian Studies* 1119.

Glaeser E and Shleifer A, "Legal Origins" (2002) 117 (4) *Quarterly Journal of Economics* 1193.

Gouda M, "Islamic Constitutionalism and Rule of Law: A Constitutional Economics Perspective" (2013) 24(1) *Constitutional Political Economy* 57.

Gunn TJ, "Shaping an Islamic Identity: Religion, Islamism, and the State in Central Asia" (2003) 64 *Sociology of Religion* 389.

Guttman J and Voigt S, "The Rule of Law and Constitutionalism in Muslim Countries" (2015) 162 *Public Choice* 351.

Habachy S, "Supreme Constitutional Court (Egypt): Shari'a and Riba: Decision in Case no. 20 of Judicial Year no. 1" (1985) 1(1) *Arab Law Quarterly* 100.

Hirschl R, "The Theocratic Challenge to Constitution Drafting in Post-Conflict States" (2008) 49 *William and Mary Law Review* 1179.

Huntington S, "The Clash of Civilizations" (1993) 72(3) *Foreign Affairs* 22.

Karagiannis E, "Political Islam in Central Asia: The Challenge of Hizb Ut-Tahrir" (2007) 13 *Nationalism and Ethnic Politics* 297.

Keddie NR, "Iranian Revolutions in Comparative Perspective" (1983) 88(3) *The American Historical Review* 579.

Kennedy C, "Islamization and Legal Reform in Pakistan, 1979–1989" (1990) 63(1) *Pacific Affairs* 62.

Khalid A, "A Secular Islam: Nation, State, and Religion in Uzbekistan" (2003) 35 *International Journal of Middle East Studies* 573.

Klein M A, "Islam and Imperialism in Senegal: Sine-Saloum, 1847–1914" (1969) 74 *The American Historical Review* 285.

Klerman DM and others, "Legal Origin or Colonial History" (2011) 3(1) *Journal of Legal Analysis* 379.

Kugle SA, "Framed, Blamed and Renamed: The Recasting of Islamic Jurisprudence in Colonial South Asia" (2001) 35 *Modern Asian Studies* 257.

Law DS and Versteeg M, "The Evolution and Ideology of Global Constitutionalism" (2011) 99 *CLR* 1163.

Lombardi C, "Constitutional Provisions Making Sharia 'A' of 'The' Chief Source of Legislation: Where Did they Come From? What do they Mean? Do they Matter?" (2013) 28(1) *American University International Law Review* 733.

Lombardi CB and Brown NJ, "Do Constitutions Requiring Adherence to Shari'a Threaten Human Rights? How Egypt's Constitution Reconciles Islamic Law with the Liberal Rule of Law" (2006) 21(1) *American University International Law Review* 379.

Lombardi CB, "Can Islamizing a Legal System Ever Help Promote Liberal Democracy?: A View from Pakistan" (2010) 7(3) *University of St. Thomas Law Journal* 649.

"Designing Islamic Constitutions: Past Trends and Options for a Democratic Future" (2013) 11(3) *International Journal of Constitutional Law* 615.

"Islamic Law as a Source of Constitutional Law in Egypt: The Constitutionalization of the Sharia in a Modern Arab State" (1998) 37(1) *Columbia Journal of Transnational Law* 81.

Mann G and Lecocq B, "Between Empire, Umma and the Muslim Third World: The French Union and African Pilgrims to Mecca" (2007) 27(2) *Comparative Studies of South Asia, African and the Middle East* 167.

Masud MK, "The Construction and Deconstruction of Secularism as an Ideology in Contemporary Muslim Thought" (2005) 33(3) *Asian Journal of Social Science* 363.

Mayer T and Zignago S, "Notes on CEPIH's Distance Measures: The GeoDist Database" 8 (2011) <www.cepii.fr/PDF_PUB/wp/2011/wp2011-25.pdf> accessed on 15 January 2022.

Miles WFS, "Partitioned Royalty: The Evolution of Hausa Chiefs in Nigeria and Niger" (1987) 25 *Journal of Modern African Studies* 233.

Moaddel M, "The Shi'i Ulama and the State in Iran" (1986) 15(4) *Theory and Society* 519.

Motadel A, "Islam and the European Empires" (2012) 55 *The Historical Journal* 831.

Moustafa T, "The Islamist Trend in Egyptian Law" (2010) 3(1) *Politics and Religion* 610.

Natoli C, "Legal Independence in Australia" (2011) 7(1) *Bruce Hall Academy Journal* 65.

Nawid S, "The Khost Rebellion: The Reaction of Afghan Clerical and Tribal Forces to Social Change" (1996) 56 *Review of Department of Asian Studies and Department of Study and Research on African and Arab Countries* 311 <http://opar.unior.it/1317/1/Annali_1996_56_%28f3%29_S.Nawid.pdf> accessed January 15, 2022.

Parolin GP, "Drifting Power Relations in the Egyptian Constitution: The 2019 Amendments" (2020) 44(3) *DPCE Online*.

Pemstein D and others, "Democratic Compromise: A Latent Variable Analysis of Ten Measures of Regime Type" (2010) 18 *Political Analysis* 426.

Peters R, "Divine Law or Man-Made Law? Egypt and the Application of the Shari'a" (1988) 3 *Arab Law Quarterly* 231, 241.

Porta R, Lopez-De-Silanes F, and Shleifer A, "The Economic Consequences of Legal Origins" (2008) 46 *Journal of Economic Literature* 285.

Rabb I, "The Least Religious Branch: Judicial Review and the New Islamic Constitutionalism" (2013) 17 *UCLA Journal of International Law and Foreign Affairs* 75.

Redding JA, "Constitutionalizing Islam: Theory and Pakistan" (2004) 44 *Virginia Journal of International Law* 759.

Reynolds J, "Good and Bad Muslims: Islam and Indirect Rule in Northern Nigeria" (2001) 34 *The International Journal of African Historical Studies* 601.

Reza S, "Endless Emergency: The Case of Egypt" (2007) 10(4) *New Criminal Law Review* 532.

Robinson D, "French 'Islamic' Policy and Practice in Late Nineteenth-Century Senegal" (1988) 29 *Journal of African History* 415.

Robinson F, "The British Empire and Muslim Identity in South Asia" (1998) 8 *Transactions of the Royal Historical Society* 271.

Saeed S, "Politics of Exclusion: Muslim Nationalism, State Formation and Legal Representations of the Ahmadiyya Community in Pakistan" (PhD thesis, University of Michigan 2010).

Siddique O and Hayat Z, "Unholy Speech and Holy Laws: Blasphemy Laws in Pakistan: Controversial Origins, Design Defects, and Free Speech Implications" (2008) 17(2) *Minnesota Journal of International Law* 305.

Stilt K, "'Islam Is the Solution': Constitutional Visions of the Egyptian Muslim Brotherhood" (2010) 46(1) *Texas International Law Journal* 73.

Taiwo EA, "Repugnancy Clause and Its Impact on Customary Law: Comparing the South African and Nigerian Positions: Some Lessons for Nigeria" (2009) 34(1) *Journal for Juridical Science* 89.

Thier JA, "The Making of a Constitution in Afghanistan" (2006) 51(4) *New York Law School Law Review* 557.

Uweru BC, "Repugnancy Doctrine and Customary Law in Nigeria: A Positive Aspect of British Colonialism" (2008) 2 *African Research Review* 286.

Voll JO, "Islam and Democracy: Is Modernization a Barrier?" (2007) 1(1) *Religion Compass* 170.

Ward D, "Legislation, Repugnancy and the Disallowance of Colonial Laws: The Legal Structure of Empire and Lloyd's Case (1844)" (2010) 41(1) *Victoria University of Wellington Law Review* 381.

Weingast B, "The Political Foundations of Democracy and the Rule of Law" (1997) 91 (2) *American Political Science Review* 245.

Weiss H, "Variations in the Colonial Representation of Islam and Muslims in Northern Ghana, ca. 1900–1930, Working Papers on Ghana: Historical and Contemporary Studies 2" (January 2004) available at <chrome-extension://efaidnbmnnnibp-cajpcglclefindmkaj/viewer.html?pdfurl=https%3A%2F%2Fwww.muslimpopula-tion.com%2Fpdf%2FGhana%2520northern_studies1900-1930.pdfandclen=209668andchunk=true> accessed April 8, 2021.

Wiktor-Mach D, "On Secularization, Modernity and Islamic Revival in the Post-Soviet Context" (2011) 175 *Polish Sociological Review* 393.

Wong E, "Shiite Cleric Won't Back Down on Direct Elections" Sun Sentinel (12 January 2004) <http://articles.sun-sentinel.com/2004-01-12/news/0401120065_1_al-sistani-grand-ayatollah-ali-influential-shiite-cleric> accessed January 15, 2022.

Yadudu AH, "Colonialism and the Transformation of the Substance and Form of Islamic Law in the Northern States of Nigeria" (1991) Journal of Law and Religion 17.

Zakaria F, "Islam, Democracy and Constitutional Liberalism" (2004) 119 *Political Science Quarterly* 1.

NEWSPAPERS AND WEBSITES

"Beliefs About Sharia" (*Pew Research Center*, April 30, 2013) <www.pewforum.org/2013/04/30/the-worlds-muslims-religion-politics-society-beliefs-about-sharia/> accessed June 20, 2020.

"Number of Muslims in Western Europe" (*PEW Research Center*, December 2, 2014) <http://features.pewforum.org/muslim-population/> accessed on January 15, 2022.

"Oklahoma Sharia Law Blocked by Federal Judge" *Huffington Post* (May 25, 2011) <http://www.huffingtonpost.com/2010/11/08/oklahoma-sharia-law-struck-down-_n_780632.html> accessed June 20, 2020.

"The Uprisings: Islam and the Arab Revolutions" *The Economist* (March 31, 2011) <www.economist.com/node/18486005> accessed June 19, 2020.

Ahmed D, Gouda M, and Ginsburg T, "Islamic Constitutionalism Project" (SHARIAsource, Harvard Law School, 2018) <https://beta.shariasource.com/pro jects/islamic-constitutionalism> accessed May 1, 2021.

Azaab S, "In Conversation with Kamal El-Helbawy" (*Asharq Al Awsat*, 12 October 2013) <www.aawsat.net/2013/10/article55318241>accessed 1 July 2020.

Brooks D, "Huntington's Clash Revisited" *The New York Times* (March 3, 2011) <www .nytimes.com/2011/03/04/opinion/04brooks.html> accessed March 25, 2021.

Brown NJ, "Egypt's Daring Constitutional Gang of 50" (*Foreign Policy*, September 20, 2013)<https://carnegieendowment.org/2013/09/20/egypt-s-daring-constitutional-gang-of-50-pub-53079> accessed July 1, 2020.

"Transitional Administrative Law" (*George Washington University*, March 8, 2004) <http://home.gwu.edu/~nbrown/interimiraqiconstitution.html> accessed on January 15, 2022.

Dabash H, "Al-Azhar and Salafi scholars Prepare Islamic Constitution" *Egypt Independent* (July 7, 2011) <http://www.egyptindependent.com//news/al-azhar-and-salafi-scholars-prepare-islamic-constitution> accessed August 11, 2014.

Dorell O, "Syrian Rebels Said to Seek Islamic Democracy" *USA Today* (September 24, 2012) <http://usatoday30.usatoday.com/news/world/story/2012 /09/24/syrian-rebels-said-to-seek-islami c-democracy/57826584/1> accessed July 1, 2020.

El-Din GE, "Fierce Debates Over Preamble of Egypt's New Constitution" (*AhramOnline*, November 26, 2013) <http://english.ahram.org.eg/NewsContent/ 1/64/87562/Egypt/Politics-/Fierce-debates-over-preamble-of-Egypts-new-constit .aspx> accessed July 1, 2020.

El Akkad O, "Egypt's Draft Constitution Limits Role of Islam" (*The Globe and Mail*, August 30, 2013) <www.theglobeandmail.com/news/world/egypts-draft-constitu tion-limits-role-of-islam/article14060190/> accessed July 1, 2020.

Fishstein P, "Afghanistan's Arc of Modernization: 1880 to 1978" (*The Globalist*, September 1, 2010), <www.theglobalist.com/afghanistans-arc-of-modernization-1880-to-1978/> accessed January 15, 2022.

Hirsch A, "Sharia Law Incompatible with Human Rights Legislation, Lords Say" *Guardian* (October 23, 2008) <www.guardian.co.uk/world/2008/oct/23/religion-islam> accessed June 20, 2020.

"Sharia Law Incompatible with Human Rights Legislation, Lords say" *The Guardian* (October 23, 2008).

HuffPost, "Oklahoma Sharia Law Blocked by Federal Judge" (May 25, 2011) <www .huffpost.com/entry/oklahoma-sharia-law-struck-down-_n_780632> accessed July 1, 2020.

Human Rights Watch, "Kuwait: Court Victory for Women's Rights" (May 6, 2012) <www.hrw.org/news/2012/05/06/kuwait-court-victory-women-s-rights> accessed January 12, 2022.

Jilani J, "At Least 13 States Have Introduced Bills Guarding Against Non-Existent Threat of Sharia Law" *Think Progress* (February 8, 2011) <http://thinkprogress .org/politics/2011/02/08/142590/sharia-states/?mobile=nc>

Jilani Z, "Report: At Least 13 States Have Introduced Bills Guarding Against Non-Existent Threat of Sharia Law" (*ThinkProgress*, February 8, 2011) <https://archive

.thinkprogress.org/report-at-least-13-states-have-introduced-bills-guarding-against-non-existent-threat-of-sharia-law-49c0ab42be1f/> accessed July 1, 2020.

Joyce R, "Tunisia's Neglected Constitution" *Cairo Review of Global Affairs* (October 14, 2013) <www.aucegypt.edu/GAPP/CairoReview/Pages/articleDetails.aspx? aid=439> accessed July 1, 2020.

Kherigi I, "Tunisia: The Calm After the Storm" *Aljazeera* (November 28, 2011) <www.cfr.org/tunisia/al-jazeera-tunisia-calm-after-storm/p26744> accessed June 19, 2020.

Maher H, "Muslim Protests: Has Obama Helped Bring on an Anti-U.S. 'Islamist Spring'?" *The Atlantic* (September 23, 2012).

Melton J and others, "Democracy Scores" (*Unified Democracy Scores*, May 12, 2014) <www.unified-democracy-scores.org/uds.html> accessed January 15, 2022.

Morrow J, "Special Report No. 155 Iraq's Constitutional Process II: An Opportunity Lost" (*U.S Institute of Peace*, November 2005) 6 <www.usip.org/sites/default/files/sr155.pdf> accessed January 15, 2022.

Nasralla S, "Rows Over Egypt's Constitutional Decree Signal Hurdles Ahead" (*Reuters*, July 10, 2013) <www.reuters.com/article/us-egypt-protests-constitution/rows-over-egypts-con stitutional-decree-signal-hurdles-ahead-idUSBRE96815R20130709> accessed July 1, 2020.

Palmer R, "Egypt's New Constitution More Islamic Than the Last" (*The Trumpet*, July 13, 2013) <www.thetrumpet.com/10805-egypts-new-constitution-more-islamic-than-the-last> accessed July 1, 2020.

Penzev K, "When Will the Great Game End?" (*Oriental Review*, November 15, 2010) <http://orientalreview.org/2010/11/15/when-will-the-great-game-end/> accessed January 15, 2022.

Reuters, "Sudan Constitution to be '100 Percent Islamic': Bashir" (July 8, 2012) <https://uk.reuters.com/article/uk-sudan-constitution/sudan-constitution-to-be-100-percent-islamic-bashir-idUKBRE866oIB20120707> accessed July 1, 2020.

Rheault M and Mogahed D, "Many Turks, Iranians, Egyptians Link Sharia and Justice" (*Gallup*, July 25, 2008) <www.gallup.com/poll/109072/many-turks-iran ians-egyptians-link-sharia-justice.aspx> accessed January 12, 2022.

Richard Wike, "The Tahrir Square Legacy: Egyptians Want Democracy, a Better Economy, and a Major Role for Islam" (*Pew Research Center*, January 24, 2013).

Rohde D, "The Islamist Spring" *Reuters* (April 5, 2012).

Satloff R and Trager E, "Egypt's Theocratic Future: The Constitutional Crisis and U.S. Policy" (*The Washington Institute*, December 3, 2012) <www.washingtoninstitute .org/policy-analysis/view/egypts-theocratic-future-the-constitutional-crisis-and-u.s.-policy> accessed July 1, 2020.

The Economist, "An Endless Debate Over Religion's Role" (Cairo, October 6, 2012) <www.economist.com/middle-east-and-africa/2012/10/06/an-endless-debate-over-religions-role> accessed July 1, 2020.

Wormald B, "Beliefs About Sharia" (*Pew Research Center*, April 30, 2013) <www.pewforum.org/2013/04/30/the-worlds-muslims-religion-politics-society-beliefs-about-sharia/> accessed June 20, 2020.

Index

CPSIA information can be obtained
at www.ICGtesting.com
Printed in the USA
LVHW021938180323
741944LV00007B/257

9 781316 610572